Library of
Davidson College

SPECTRUM
ON
SOCIAL PROBLEMS

MERRILL SOCIOLOGY SERIES

Under the Editorship of
Richard L. Simpson
University of North Carolina at Chapel Hill
and
Paul E. Mott
University of Pennsylvania

SPECTRUM ON SOCIAL PROBLEMS

Society, Economy, and Man

Edited by

Jon M. Shepard

University of Kentucky

Charles E. Merrill Publishing Company
A Bell & Howell Company
Columbus, Ohio

Published by
Charles E. Merrill Publishing Company
A Bell & Howell Company
Columbus, Ohio 43216

Copyright © 1973, by Bell & Howell Company. All rights reserved. No part of this book may be reproduced in any form, electronic or mechanical, including photocopy, recording, or any information storage and retrieval system without permission in writing from the publisher.

ISBN: 0-675-09049-0

Library of Congress Catalog Card Number: 72-85876

1 2 3 4 5 6 7 8 — 77 76 75 74 73

Printed in the United States of America

To Angie and Dick

Contents

INTRODUCTION

I   Introduction   3

    C. WRIGHT MILLS, The Promise   6

SOCIETY AND ECONOMY

II   Who Has the Power in American Society?   19

    WILLIAM KORNHAUSER, "Power Elite" or "Veto Groups"?   21

    ARNOLD M. ROSE, The Power Structure: Introduction   28

    ARNOLD M. ROSE, The Power Structure: Conclusion   30

    G. WILLIAM DOMHOFF, How the Power Elite Set National Goals   40

III   Does Business Have a Responsibility to Society?   51

    ALBERT Z. CARR, Can an Executive Afford a Conscience?   53

    GEORGE CABOT LODGE, Top Priority: Renovating Our Ideology   65

    THEODORE LEVITT, The Dangers of Social Responsibility   87

| IV | The Poor: Who Are They and Are They Really Different? | 103 |

OSCAR LEWIS, The Culture of Poverty — 106
LEE RAINWATER, The Lessons of Pruitt-Igoe — 119
HYMAN RODMAN, The Lower-Class Value Stretch — 127
RICHARD A. BALL, The Analgesic Subculture — 134

| V | Minorities in the Labor Force: Gains in Equal Opportunity? | 147 |

MICHAEL HARRINGTON, If You're Black, Stay Back — 149
PETER M. BLAU and OTIS DUDLEY DUNCAN, Inequality of Opportunity — 158
MANPOWER REPORTS OF THE PRESIDENT, Toward Equal Employment Opportunity — 162

| VI | Working Women: Toward Occupational Parity? | 179 |

GUNNAR MYRDAL, Women: A Parallel to the Negro Problem — 181
MARIJEAN SUELZLE, Women in Labor — 188
DONALD J. McNULTY, Differences in Pay Between Men and Women Workers — 206
ROBERT D. MORAN, Reducing Discrimination Among Working Women — 214

SOCIAL CHANGE AND MAN

| VII | Technology, Leisure, and Work: Alienation or Freedom? | 223 |

FRANK LINDENFELD, Work, Automation and Alienation — 225
BEN S. SELIGMAN, The Work-Leisure Bond — 238
REGINALD CARTER, The Myth of Increasing Leisure Time — 245

Acknowledgments

Two people made the work involved in completing this collection of readings immeasurably easier. Mrs. Karen Conley never ceased to amaze me in her capacity for checking details and ferreting out inconsistencies and errors. She went far beyond the role of typist, for which I am grateful. My wife, Kay, encouraged me to take up the project and stuck with me even when the morning sun at Myrtle Beach, South Carolina got no closer to me than the roof of our vacation motel room where I began this reader.

I also wish to thank Thomas R. Panko, a friend and colleague, for his help in time of need and Roger Ratliff, sociology editor at Charles E. Merrill, for his original interest in the book and for his aid when called upon.

When we talk about intelligence, we do not mean the ability to get a good score on a certain kind of test, or even the ability to do well in school; these are at best only indicators of something larger, deeper, and far more important. By intelligence we mean a style of life, a way of behaving in various situations, and particularly in new, strange, and perplexing situations. The true test of intelligence is not how much we know how to do, but how we behave when we don't know what to do.

John Holt, *How Children Fail*, 1964

INTRODUCTION

1

Introduction

Students should assume a more personally active role in their institutional environment—this is the first premise of this reader. The "student activism" desired here is quite different from that associated with campus unrest of the past decade. Rather, it is increased involvement in and responsibility for the acquisition of an education which this book seeks to promote. From the pen of Emerson flows this wisdom: "Meek young men grow up in colleges and believe it is their duty to accept the views which books have given, and grow up slaves."

A primary aim of learning, in or out of the classroom, is intellectual growth, part of which is the development of critical judgment and self-determination. A prominent professed educational goal is that of promoting in students increased capacity for reasoning and abstraction. In many ways the textbook, lecture, and testing format is at odds with this laudable ideal. Too often perhaps, in the instructor's zeal and excitement over ideas, he forgets to permit students to be anything but passive recipients of information. We instructors are frequently long on presentation of "facts" and short on exposure of the multifaceted nature of problems and the contradictory evidence surrounding them. All too often "reality" is presented in packaged form, with no latitude for judgment and evaluation on the part of students. Granted, an important role of the teacher is to provide conclusions and offer generalizations based on his or her professional evaluation of the literature. But

---

A somewhat different version of this introduction also appears in *Organizational Issues in Industrial Society* (Englewood Cliffs, N. J.: Prentice-Hall, 1972). Used by permission of the publisher.

knowledge comes into existence only to be modified or abandoned in a short time. Students leave the academic setting with considerable knowledge that is impermanent, sometimes even irrelevant to life's pursuits; therefore, they ultimately must be capable of doing for themselves what their teachers have too often tried to do for them. Otherwise, they are at the mercy of the mass media, which is unbalanced at its best and parochial and amenable to vested interest at its worst.

Present and future generations face a society changing at such a swift pace that the answers of one generation are of questionable utility to the next. A society of this nature requires people who can meet new situations with the intellectual flexibility necessary for creative adaptation to a changing environment. Therefore, it is essential that our educational system stress the student's role in the learning process. For it is they who must learn to grapple with conflicting and inconsistent information and to sift these data until reaching their own syntheses. If this facility is not developed, the optimum benefits of education will not have been realized.

The format of this reader encourages the development of this facility by revealing the multidimensionality of sociological phenomena. Assembled in one place are writings on issues which expose gaps in knowledge and make apparent the differences in perspective, levels of analysis, and variables. Each chapter is devoted to one problem area, with the chapter titles posing issues in question form. Several selections, together reflecting various aspects of a controversy, are included in each chapter. Some selections directly disagree, while others reflect varying shades of gray.

Because selections in each chapter are related, reading any single one requires referral to others in order to arrive at a meaningful answer to the posed question and encourages examination of the question from several angles. Such "stretching" of the question should result in comprehension and perception of greater depth. Thus, in addition to exposing students to concepts and perspectives—the traditional aim of textbooks and collections of readings—this volume is intended to promote the development of critical judgment and balanced thought.

Furthermore, this design offers more than adequate stimulation as a basis for discussion in an atmosphere of debate. Its applicability to a lecture-discussion group class arrangement is obvious. Whatever the class design, student participation and intellectual involvement should be natural by-products.

To those students whose exposure to sociological thought is limited to the basic courses, it is imperative that, at the very least, they take with them some facility for applying sociological concepts in everyday life. Hopefully, this format will provide the intellectual experience inherent in the application of sociological perspectives and concepts to social problems and can stimulate them to interpret and understand their social environment long after the course is over.

The first selection, "The Promise" by C. Wright Mills, elaborates on the second premise of this reader—that sociology offers unique intellectual tools for comprehending the patterns and meanings in social life, patterns which are either undetected by the untutored mind or appear as random events. "The Promise" is an urgent and intense statement of sociology's potential. In Mills's mind, the acquisition of the *sociological imagination* reveals links between social structures and personal situations. The fact that most people cannot comprehend the interplay between society and their own lives is all the more undesirable in a society where change is the most enduring feature. Anticipating the current social problems emphasis in American society, Mills argues that the relationships between social structures, public issues, and personal difficulties should occupy centerstage in the social sciences.

Spectrum on Social Problems contains six additional chapters, each centering on a contemporary problem created by the intersection of the economy and certain social institutions. These problem areas include the locus of power in American society; the responsibility of business to society; the poor; minorities and women in the labor force; and technology, leisure and alienation. Such issues constitute arenas for the application of sociological perspectives and concepts acquired in the introductory sociology course.

C. WRIGHT MILLS

The Promise

Nowadays men often feel that their private lives are a series of traps. They sense that within their everyday worlds, they cannot overcome their troubles, and in this feeling, they are often quite correct: What ordinary men are directly aware of and what they try to do are bounded by the private orbits in which they live; their visions and their powers are limited to the close-up scenes of job, family, neighborhood; in other milieux, they move vicariously and remain spectators. And the more aware they become, however vaguely, of ambitions and of threats which transcend their immediate locales, the more trapped they seem to feel.

Underlying this sense of being trapped are seemingly impersonal changes in the very structure of continent-wide societies. The facts of contemporary history are also facts about the success and the failure of individual men and women. When a society is industrialized, a peasant becomes a worker; a feudal lord is liquidated or becomes a businessman. When classes rise or fall, a man is employed or unemployed; when the rate of investment goes up or down, a man takes new heart or goes broke. When wars happen, an insurance salesman becomes a rocket launcher; a store clerk, a radar man; a wife lives alone; a child grows up without a father. Neither the life of an individual nor the history of a society can be understood without understanding both.

Yet men do not usually define the troubles they endure in terms of historical change and institutional contradiction. The well-being they enjoy, they do not usually impute to the big ups and downs of the socie-

---

Reprinted by permission of the publisher from C. Wright Mills, *The Sociological Imagination* (New York: Oxford University Press, Inc., 1959), pp. 3-15. Copyright © 1959 by Oxford University Press, Inc.

The Promise

ties in which they live. Seldom aware of the intricate connection between the patterns of their own lives and the course of world history, ordinary men do not usually know what this connection means for the kinds of men they are becoming and for the kinds of history-making in which they might take part. They do not possess the quality of mind essential to grasp the interplay of man and society, of biography and history, of self and world. They cannot cope with their personal troubles in such ways as to control the structural transformations that usually lie behind them.

Surely it is no wonder. In what period have so many men been so totally exposed at so fast a pace to such earthquakes of change? That Americans have not known such catastrophic changes as have the men and women of other societies is due to historical facts that are now quickly becoming "merely history." The history that now affects every man is world history. Within this scene and this period, in the course of a single generation, one sixth of mankind is transformed from all that is feudal and backward into all that is modern, advanced, and fearful. Political colonies are freed; new and less visible forms of imperialism installed. Revolutions occur; men feel the intimate grip of new kinds of authority. Totalitarian societies rise, and are smashed to bits—or succeed fabulously. After two centuries of ascendancy, capitalism is shown up as only one way to make society into an industrial apparatus. After two centuries of hope, even formal democracy is restricted to a quite small portion of mankind. Everywhere in the underdeveloped world, ancient ways of life are broken up and vague expectations become urgent demands. Everywhere in the overdeveloped world, the means of authority and of violence become total in scope and bureaucratic in form. Humanity itself now lies before us, the super-nation at either pole concentrating its most co-ordinated and massive efforts upon the preparation of World War Three.

The very shaping of history now outpaces the ability of men to orient themselves in accordance with cherished values. And which values? Even when they do not panic, men often sense that older ways of feeling and thinking have collapsed and that newer beginnings are ambiguous to the point of moral stasis. Is it any wonder that ordinary men feel they cannot cope with the larger worlds with which they are so suddenly confronted? That they cannot understand the meaning of their epoch for their own lives? That—in defense of selfhood—they become morally insensible, trying to remain altogether private men? Is it any wonder that they come to be possessed by a sense of the trap?

It is not only information that they need—in this Age of Fact, information often dominates their attention and overwhelms their capacities to assimilate it. It is not only the skills of reason that they need—although their struggles to acquire these often exhaust their limited moral energy.

What they need, and what they feel they need, is a quality of mind that will help them to use information and to develop reason in order to achieve lucid summations of what is going on in the world and of what may be happening within themselves. It is this quality, I am going to contend, that journalists and scholars, artists and publics, scientists and editors are coming to expect of what may be called the sociological imagination.

1

The sociological imagination enables its possessor to understand the larger historical scene in terms of its meaning for the inner life and the external career of a variety of individuals. It enables him to take into account how individuals, in the welter of their daily experience, often become falsely conscious of their social positions. Within that welter, the framework of modern society is sought, and within that framework the psychologies of a variety of men and women are formulated. By such means the personal uneasiness of individuals is focused upon explicit troubles and the indifference of publics is transformed into involvement with public issues.

The first fruit of this imagination—and the first lesson of the social science that embodies it—is the idea that the individual can understand his own experience and gauge his own fate only by locating himself within his period, that he can know his own chances in life only by becoming aware of those of all individuals in his circumstances. In many ways it is a terrible lesson; in many ways a magnificent one. We do not know the limits of man's capacities for supreme effort or willing degradation, for agony or glee, for pleasurable brutality or the sweetness of reason. But in our time we have come to know that the limits of "human nature" are frighteningly broad. We have come to know that every individual lives, from one generation to the next, in some society; that he lives out a biography, and that he lives it out within some historical sequence. By the fact of his living he contributes, however minutely, to the shaping of his society and to the course of its history, even as he is made by society and by its historical push and shove.

The sociological imagination enables us to grasp history and biography and the relations between the two within society. That is its task and its promise. To recognize this task and this promise is the mark of the classic social analyst. It is characteristic of Herbert Spencer—turgid, polysyllabic, comprehensive; of E. A. Ross—graceful, muckraking, upright;

of Auguste Comte and Emile Durkheim; of the intricate and subtle Karl Mannheim. It is the quality of all that is intellectually excellent in Karl Marx; it is the clue to Thorstein Veblen's brilliant and ironic insight, to Joseph Schumpeter's many-sided constructions of reality; it is the basis of the psychological sweep of W. E. H. Lecky no less than of the profundity and clarity of Max Weber. And it is the signal of what is best in contemporary studies of man and society.

No social study that does not come back to the problems of biography, of history and of their intersections within a society has completed its intellectual journey. Whatever the specific problems of the classic social analysts, however limited or however broad the features of social reality they have examined, those who have been imaginatively aware of the promise of their work have consistently asked three sorts of questions:

(1) What is the structure of this particular society as a whole? What are its essential components, and how are they related to one another? How does it differ from other varieties of social order? Within it, what is the meaning of any particular feature for its continuance and for its change?

(2) Where does this society stand in human history? What are the mechanics by which it is changing? What is its place within and its meaning for the development of humanity as a whole? How does any particular feature we are examining affect, and how is it affected by, the historical period in which it moves? And this period—what are its essential features? How does it differ from other periods? What are its characteristic ways of history-making?

(3) What varieties of men and women now prevail in this society and in this period? And what varieties are coming to prevail? In what ways are they selected and formed, liberated and repressed, made sensitive and blunted? What kinds of "human nature" are revealed in the conduct and character we observe in this society in this period? And what is the meaning for "human nature" of each and every feature of the society we are examining?

Whether the point of interest is a great power state or a minor literary mood, a family, a prison, a creed—these are the kinds of questions the best social analysts have asked. They are the intellectual pivots of classic studies of man in society—and they are the questions inevitably raised by any mind possessing the sociological imagination. For that imagination is the capacity to shift from one perspective to another—from the political to the psychological; from examination of a single family to comparative assessment of the national budgets of the world; from the theological school to the military establishment; from considerations of an oil industry to studies of contemporary poetry. It is the capacity to range from the most impersonal and remote transformations to the most intimate features of the human self—and to see the relations between the two. Back of its use there is always the urge to know the social and historical meaning of the individual in the society and in the period in which he has his quality and his being.

That, in brief, is why it is by means of the sociological imagination that men now hope to grasp what is going on in the world, and to understand what is happening in themselves as minute points of the intersections of biography and history within society. In large part, contemporary man's self-conscious view of himself as at least an outsider, if not a permanent stranger, rests upon an absorbed realization of social relativity and of the transformative power of history. The sociological imagination is the most fruitful form of this self-consciousness. By its use men whose mentalities have swept only a series of limited orbits often come to feel as if suddenly awakened in a house with which they had only supposed themselves to be familiar. Correctly or incorrectly, they often come to feel that they can now provide themselves with adequate summations, cohesive assessments, comprehensive orientations. Older decisions that once appeared sound now seem to them products of a mind unaccountably dense. Their capacity for astonishment is made lively again. They acquire a new way of thinking, they experience a transvaluation of values: in a word, by their reflection and by their sensibility, they realize the cultural meaning of the social sciences.

2

Perhaps the most fruitful distinction with which the sociological imagination works is between "the personal troubles of milieu" and "the public issues of social structure." This distinction is an essential tool of the sociological imagination and a feature of all classic work in social science.

Troubles occur within the character of the individual and within the range of his immediate relations with others; they have to do with his self and with those limited areas of social life of which he is directly and personally aware. Accordingly, the statement and the resolution of troubles properly lie within the individual as a biographical entity and within the scope of his immediate milieu—the social setting that is directly open to his personal experience and to some extent his willful activity. A trouble is a private matter: values cherished by an individual are felt by him to be threatened.

Issues have to do with matters that transcend these local environments of the individual and the range of his inner life. They have to do with the organization of many such milieux into the institutions of an historical society as a whole, with the ways in which various milieux overlap and interpenetrate to form the larger structure of social and historical life. An issue is a public matter: some value cherished by publics is felt to be threatened. Often there is a debate about what that value really is and about what it is that really threatens it. This debate is often without focus if only because it is the very nature of an issue, unlike even widespread trouble, that it cannot very well be defined in terms of the immediate and everyday environments of ordinary men. An issue, in fact, often involves a crisis in institutional arrangements, and often too it involves what Marxists call "contradictions" or "antagonisms."

In these terms, consider unemployment. When, in a city of 100,000, only one man is unemployed, that is his personal trouble, and for its relief we properly look to the character of the man, his skills, and his immediate opportunities. But when in a nation of 50 million employees, 15 million men are unemployed, that is an issue, and we may not hope to find its solution within the range of opportunities open to any one individual. The very structure of opportunities has collapsed. Both the correct statement of the problem and the range of possible solutions require us to consider the economic and political institutions of the society, and not merely the personal situation and character of a scatter of individuals.

Consider war. The personal problem of war, when it occurs, may be how to survive it or how to die in it with honor; how to make money out of it; how to climb into the higher safety of the military apparatus; or how to contribute to the war's termination. In short, according to one's values, to find a set of milieux and within it to survive the war or make one's death in it meaningful. But the structural issues of war have to do with its causes; with what types of men it throws up into command; with its effects upon economic and political, family and religious institutions, with the unorganized irresponsibility of a world of nation-states.

Consider marriage. Inside a marriage a man and a woman may experience personal troubles, but when the divorce rate during the first four years of marriage is 250 out of every 1,000 attempts, this is an indication of a structural issue having to do with the institutions of marriage and the family and other institutions that bear upon them.

Or consider the metropolis—the horrible, beautiful, ugly, magnificent sprawl of the great city. For many upper-class people, the personal solution to "the problem of the city" is to have an apartment with private garage under it in the heart of the city, and forty miles out, a house by Henry Hill, garden by Garrett Eckbo, on a hundred acres of private land. In these two controlled environments—with a small staff at each end and a private helicopter connection—most people could solve many of the problems of personal milieux caused by the facts of the city. But all this, however splendid, does not solve the public issues that the structural fact of the city poses. What should be done with this wonderful monstrosity? Break it all up into scattered units, combining residence and work? Refurbish it as it stands? Or, after evacuation, dynamite it and build new cities according to new plans in new places? What should those plans be? And who is to decide and to accomplish whatever choice is made? These are structural issues; to confront them and to solve them requires us to consider political and economic issues that affect innumerable milieux.

In so far as an economy is so arranged that slumps occur, the problem of unemployment becomes incapable of personal solution. In so far as war is inherent in the nation-state system and in the uneven industrialization of the world, the ordinary individual in his restricted milieu will be powerless—with or without psychiatric aid—to solve the troubles this system or lack of system imposes upon him. In so far as the family as an institution turns women into darling little slaves and men into their chief providers and unweaned dependents, the problem of a satisfactory marriage remains incapable of purely private solution. In so far as the overdeveloped megalopolis and the overdeveloped automobile are built-in features of the overdeveloped society, the issues of urban living will not be solved by personal ingenuity and private wealth.

What we experience in various and specific milieux, I have noted, is often caused by structural changes. Accordingly, to understand the changes of many personal milieux we are required to look beyond them. And the number and variety of such structural changes increase as the institutions within which we live become more embracing and more intricately connected with one another. To be aware of the idea of social structure and to use it with sensibility is to be capable of tracing such linkages among a great variety of milieux. To be able to do that is to possess the sociological imagination.

3

What are the major issues for publics and the key troubles of private individuals in our time? To formulate issues and troubles, we must ask what values are cherished yet threatened, and what values are cherished and supported, by the characterizing trends of our period. In the case both of threat and of support we must ask what salient contradictions of structure may be involved.

When people cherish some set of values and do not feel any threat to them, they experience *well-being*. When they cherish values but *do* feel them to be threatened, they experience a crisis—either as a personal trouble or as a public issue. And if all their values seem involved, they feel the total threat of panic.

The Promise

But suppose people are neither aware of any cherished values nor experience any threat? That is the experience of *indifference*, which, if it seems to involve all their values, becomes apathy. Suppose, finally, they are unaware of any cherished values, but still are very much aware of a threat? That is the experience of *uneasiness*, of anxiety, which, if it is total enough, becomes a deadly unspecified malaise.

Ours is a time of uneasiness and indifference—not yet formulated in such ways as to permit the work of reason and the play of sensibility. Instead of troubles—defined in terms of values and threats—there is often the misery of vague uneasiness; instead of explicit issues there is often merely the beat feeling that all is somehow not right. Neither the values threatened nor whatever threatens them has been stated; in short, they have not been carried to the point of decision. Much less have they been formulated as problems of social science.

In the 'thirties there was little doubt—except among certain deluded business circles that there was an economic issue which was also a pack of personal troubles. In these arguments about "the crisis of capitalism," the formulations of Marx and the many unacknowledged re-formulations of his work probably set the leading terms of the issue, and some men came to understand their personal troubles in these terms. The values threatened were plain to see and cherished by all; the structural contradictions that threatened them also seemed plain. Both were widely and deeply experienced. It was a political age.

But the values threatened in the era after World War Two are often neither widely acknowledged as values nor widely felt to be threatened. Much private uneasiness goes unformulated; much public malaise and many decisions of enormous structural relevance never become public issues. For those who accept such inherited values as reason and freedom, it is the uneasiness itself that is the trouble; it is the indifference itself that is the issue. And it is this condition, of uneasiness and indifference, that is the signal feature of our period.

All this is so striking that it is often interpreted by observers as a shift in the very kinds of problems that need now to be formulated. We are frequently told that the problems of our decade, or even the crises of our period, have shifted from the external realm of economics and now have to do with the quality of individual life—in fact with the question of whether there is soon going to be anything that can properly be called individual life. Not child labor but comic books, not poverty but mass leisure, are at the center of concern. Many great public issues as well as many private troubles are described in terms of "the psychiatric"—often, it seems, in a pathetic attempt to avoid the large issues and problems of modern society. Often this statement seems to rest upon a provincial narrowing of interest to the Western societies, or even to the United States—thus ignoring two-thirds of mankind; often, too, it arbitrarily divorces the individual life from the larger institutions within which that life is enacted, and which on occasion bear upon it more grievously than do the intimate environments of childhood.

Problems of leisure, for example, cannot even be stated without considering problems of work. Family troubles over comic books cannot be formulated as problems without considering the plight of the contemporary family in its new relations with the newer institutions of the social structure. Neither leisure nor its debilitating uses can be understood as problems without recognition of the extent to which malaise and indifference now form the social and personal climate of contemporary American society. In this climate, no problems of "the private life" can be stated and solved without recognition of the crisis of ambition that is part of the very career of men at work in the incorporated economy.

It is true, as psychoanalysts continually point out, that people do often have "the increasing sense of being moved by obscure forces within themselves which they are unable to define." But it is *not* true, as Ernest Jones asserted, that "man's chief enemy and danger is his own unruly nature and the dark forces pent up within him." On the contrary: "Man's chief danger" today lies in the unruly forces of contemporary society itself, with its alienating methods of production, its enveloping techniques of political domination, its international anarchy—in a word, its pervasive transformations of the very "nature" of man and the conditions and aims of his life.

It is now the social scientist's foremost political and intellectual task —for here the two coincide—to make clear the elements of contemporary uneasiness and indifference. It is the central demand made upon him by other cultural workmen—by physical scientists and artists, by the intellectual community in general. It is because of this task and these demands, I believe, that the social sciences are becoming the common denominator of our cultural period, and the sociological imagination our most needed quality of mind.

4

In every intellectual age some one style of reflection tends to become a common denominator of cultural life. Nowadays, it is true, many intellectual fads are widely taken up before they are dropped for new ones in the course of a year or two. Such enthusiasms may add spice to cultural play, but leave little or no intellectual trace. That is not true of such ways of thinking as "Newtonian physics" or "Darwinian biology." Each of these intellectual universes became an influence that reached far beyond any special sphere of idea and imagery. In terms of them, or in terms derived from them, unknown scholars as well as fashionable commentators came to re-focus their observations and re-formulate their concerns.

During the modern era, physical and biological science has been the major common denominator of serious reflection and popular metaphysics in Western societies. "The technique of the laboratory" has been the accepted mode of procedure and the source of intellectual security. That is one meaning of the idea of an intellectual common denominator: men can state their strongest convictions in its terms; other terms and other styles of reflection seem mere vehicles of escape and obscurity.

That a common denominator prevails does not of course mean that no other styles of thought or modes of sensibility exist. But it does mean that more general intellectual interests tend to slide into this area, to be formulated there most sharply, and when so formulated, to be thought somehow to have reached, if not a solution, at least a profitable way of being carried along.

The sociological imagination is becoming, I believe, the major common denominator of our cultural life and its signal feature. This quality of mind is found in the social and psychological sciences, but it goes far beyond these studies as we now know them. Its acquisition by individuals, and by the cultural community at large is slow and often fumbling; many social scientists are themselves quite unaware of it. They do not seem to know that the use of this imagination is central to the best work that they might do, that by failing to develop and to use it they are failing to meet the cultural expectations that are coming to be demanded of them and that the classic traditions of their several disciplines make available to them.

Yet in factual and moral concerns, in literary work and in political analysis, the qualities of this imagination are regularly demanded. In a great variety of expressions, they have become central features of intellectual endeavor and cultural sensibility. Leading critics exemplify these qualities as do serious journalists—in fact the work of both is often judged in these terms. Popular categories of criticism—high, middle, and low-brow, for example—are now at least as much sociological as aesthetic. Novelists—whose serious work embodies the most widespread definitions of human reality—frequently possess this imagination, and do much to meet the demand for it. By means of it, orientation to the present as history is sought. As images of "human nature" become more problematic, an increasing need is felt to pay closer yet more imaginative attention to the social routines and catastrophes which reveal (and which shape) man's nature in this time of civil unrest and ideological conflict. Although fashion is often revealed by attempts to use it, the sociological imagination is not merely a fashion. It is a quality of mind that seems most dramatically to promise an understanding of the intimate realities of ourselves in connection with larger social realities. It is not merely one quality of mind among the contemporary range of cultural sensibilities—it is *the* quality whose wider and more adroit use offers the promise that all such sensibilities—and in fact, human reason itself—will come to play a greater role in human affairs.

SOCIETY
AND
ECONOMY

II

Who Has the Power in American Society?

The question "Who has the power?" centers on the distribution and exercise of power. This question was not new when David Riesman attempted to answer it for American society early in the 1950s, but it gained in saliency when Floyd Hunter and C. Wright Mills propounded their theory of monolithic power later in the same decade. The monolithic, conspirational theory of power has the greatest appeal among those (whether on the political right or left) who view power in American society in the context of manipulative or coercive power. Those on the left, particularly radical intellectuals, find Mills's theory of *The Power Elite* graphically descriptive of the "military-industrial complex." According to Mills's theory of elite domination in American society, we no longer have separate economic and political orders, with the military capable of making only inconsequential political and financial waves. This superannuated perception of power must be replaced by the reality of a triumvirate — the top men in military, economic, and political positions have coalesced to form the power elite. In Mills's view, one must look through this lens in order to understand the distribution and exercise of power at the higher levels of American society. A flood of book reviews, articles, and books have appeared since 1956, many attempting to rebut the Millsian power elite thesis.

Liberals in American society have typically subscribed to a diffused picture of power distribution. An important early proponent of this theory of power distribution, David Riesman, argued that power in American society is exercised via "veto groups." According to this formulation, decisions on a given issue result from the exertion of power by certain groups, each of whom has a special interest in the outcome. However, rather than initiating events to attain their own ends (although this happens too), veto groups primarily maneuver to garner sufficient power to protect themselves against other interest groups which may attempt to do them harm.

In the first reading of this chapter "'Power Elite' or 'Veto Groups'?" William Kornhauser summarizes and then compares the theories of Mills and Riesman, concluding that the truth concerning the distribution and locus of power in American society lies somewhere in between the ideas of these two men.

The fires ignited by the Mills-Riesman disagreement burn yet. In the next three selections, advocates on each side of the power elite thesis present evidence in support of their interpretation.

In "The Power Structure: Introduction" and "The Power Structure: Conclusion" Arnold Rose advances the "multi-influence" hypothesis as the most accurate description of the exercise of power in American society. According to Rose, the economic elite in American society does not dominate the political elite. Those in upper economic and political echelons do influence and aid one another at particular times on specific issues, but conflict and lack of consensus are also characteristics of their relationship. In addition, each acts to a great degree independently of the other.

In explicit contrast to Rose, G. William Domhoff ("How the Power Elite Set National Goals") believes that a power elite is alive and well in America. Using two examples, Domhoff attempts to document his thesis that national policies are the product of an intricate process involving the corporate rich, major corporations, universities, foundations, the executive branch of the federal government, and certain other elite groups. According to Domhoff, the corporate rich are the prime beneficiaries of this process.

Who *does* have the power in American society?

WILLIAM KORNHAUSER

"Power Elite"
or
"Veto Groups"?

In the fifties two books appeared attempting to describe the structure of power in America. They reached opposite conclusions: where C. Wright Mills found a *power elite,* David Riesman found *veto groups.* *The Power Elite* has been most favorably received by radical intellectuals, and *The Lonely Crowd* has found its main acceptance among liberals.

I wish to enter this controversy just long enough to do two things: (1) locate as precisely as possible the items upon which Riesman and Mills disagree; and (2) formulate certain underlying issues in the analysis of power that have to be met before disagreements between Riesman and Mills can be resolved.

I will compare Mills and Riesman's ideas on power in America along five dimensions:

1.) *Structure of power:* how power is distributed among the major segments of American society.

2.) *Changes in the structure of power:* how the distribution of power has changed in the course of American history.

3.) *Operation of the structure of power:* the means whereby power is exercised in American society.

4.) *Bases of the structure of power:* how social and psychological factors shape and sustain the existing distribution of power.

5.) *Consequences of the structure of power:* how the existing distribution of power affects American society.

Adapted by permission of the author and publisher from William Kornhauser, "'Power Elite' or 'Veto Groups'?" in *Culture and Social Character,* ed. S. M. Lipset and Leo Lowenthal (New York: Free Press, 1961), pp. 252-67.

STRUCTURE OF POWER

The contrasting images of American power held by Mills and Riesman may be diagrammed as two different pyramids of power. Mills' pyramid of power contains three levels:

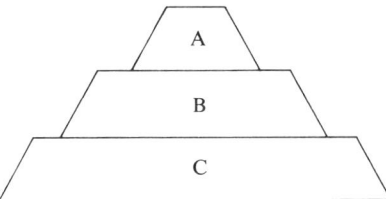

The top of the pyramid (A) is the *power elite*: a unified power group composed of the top government executives, military officials, and corporation directors. The second level (B) comprises the "middle levels of power": a diversified and balanced plurality of interest groups, perhaps most visibly at work in the halls of Congress. The third level (C) is the "mass society": the powerless maze of unorganized people who are controlled from above.

Riesman's pyramid of power contains only two major levels:

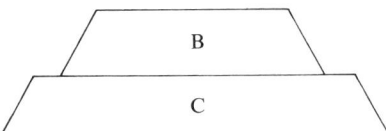

The two levels roughly correspond to Mills' second and third levels. The obvious difference between the two pyramids is the presence of a peak in the one case and its absence in the other. Riesman sees no *power elite,* in the sense of a single unified power group at the top, and this is the sharpest contrast between his image of power in America and Mills'. The upper level of Riesman's pyramid (B) consists of *veto groups*: a diversified and balanced plurality of interest groups, each of which is primarily concerned with protecting its interests by blocking efforts of other groups that seem to threaten those interests. There is no one ruling group, but an undefined structure of power with interplay among interest groups. The lower level of the pyramid (C) is the more or less unorganized public, which is sought as an ally (rather than dominated) by the interest groups in their maneuvers against actual or threatened encroachments on the interests each seeks.

CHANGES IN THE STRUCTURE OF POWER

Riesman and Mills agree that the American power structure has gone through four major periods. They disagree on the present and future: Mills judges the present to represent a fifth period, Riesman judges it to be a continuation of the fourth.

The first period, according to Mills and Riesman, extended roughly from the founding of the republic to the Jacksonian era. During this period, Riesman believes America possessed a clearly defined ruling group, composed of a "landed-gentry and mercantilist-money leadership" (239).[1] According to Mills, "the important fact about these early days is that social life, economic institutions, military establishment, and political order coincided, and men who were high politicians also played key roles in the economy and, with their families, were among those of the reputable who made up local society" (270).[2]

The second period extended roughly from the decline of Federalist leadership to the Civil War. During this period power became more widely dispersed, and it was no longer possible to identify a sharply defined ruling group. "In this society," Mills writes, "the 'elite' became a plurality of top groups, each in turn quite loosely made up" (270). Riesman notes that farmer and artisan groups became influential, and "occasionally, as with Jackson, moved into a more positive command" (240).

The third period began after the Civil War and extended through McKinley's administration in Riesman's view (240) and until the New Deal according to Mills (271). They agree that the era of McKinley marked the high point of the one-sided supremacy of corporate economic power. During this period, power once more became concentrated, but unlike the Federalist period and also unlike subsequent periods, the higher circles of economic institutions were dominant.

The fourth period took definite shape in the 1930s. In Riesman's view this period marked the rise of the veto groups, and rule by coalitions rather than by a unified power group. Mills judges it to have been so only in the early and middle Roosevelt administrations: "In these years, the New Deal as a system of power was essentially a balance of pressure groups and interest blocs" (273).

Up to World War II, then, Mills and Riesman view the development of power relations in America similarly. Their sharply contrasting pictures of present-day American power relations begin with their diverging assessments of the period beginning about 1940. Mills sees World War II and its aftermath as the beginning of a new era in American power relations. With war as the major problem, there arose a new power group composed of corporate, governmental, and military directors.[3] Where Mills sees the rise of a power elite, Riesman sees the opposite tendency toward the dispersal of power among a number of organized interest groups (239, 246-247).

OPERATION OF THE STRUCTURE OF POWER

Mills believes the power elite sets all important public policies, especially foreign policy. Riesman, on the other hand, does not believe that the same group or coalition of groups sets all major policies, but rather that the question of who exercises power varies with the issue at stake: most groups are inactive on most issues, and all groups are active primarily on those issues that vitally affect their central interests. There are as many power structures as there are distinctive spheres of policy (256).

Both Mills and Riesman point to increasing *manipulation,* rather than command or persuasion, as the favored form of power play. Mills emphasizes the secrecy behind important policy-determination. Riesman stresses not so much manipulation under the guise of secrecy as manipulation under the guise of mutual tolerance for one another's interests and beliefs. Manipulation occurs, according to Riesman, because each group is trying to hide its concern with power in order not to antagonize other groups. Thus both believe the play of power takes place to a considerable extent backstage; but Mills judges this power play to be under the direction of one group, while Riesman sees it as controlled by compromise among many groups.

Mills maintains that the mass media are important instruments of manipulation: the media lull people to sleep by suppressing political topics and by emphasizing entertainment. Riesman says that the mass media give more attention to politics and problems of public policy than their audiences actually want, and convey the false impression that there is more interest in public affairs than really exists in America. Where Mills judges the mass media to be powerful political instruments in American society (315-316), Riesman argues that they have relatively little significance in this respect (228-231).

BASES OF THE STRUCTURE OF POWER

To Mills, the power elite reflects the consolidation of a *coincidence of interests* among the economic, political, and military elites. For Riesman there is an undefined power structure, which reflects a *diversity of interests* among the major organized groups. The power structure of veto groups rests on the divergent interests of political parties, business groups, labor organizations, farm blocs, and other organized groups (247).

In addition to interests power also rests on the capabilities and opportunities for cooperation among those who have similar interests, and for confrontation among those with opposing interests. Mills argues that the power elite rests not merely on the coincidence of interests among major institutions but also on the "psychological similarity and social intermingling" of those persons in high military, economic, and political positions (19). By virtue of similar social origins (old family, upper-class background), religious affiliations (Episcopalian and Presbyterian), education (Ivy league college or military academy), and the like, those who head up the major institutions share values as well as material interests. This makes for easy communication, especially when many of these people either already know one another, or know many of the same people. They share a common way of life, and therefore have both the will and the opportunity to coordinate their lines of action as representatives of key institutions.

Riesman and Mills agree that there is widespread political apathy in American society, but they disagree on its social distribution. Mills locates the apathetic primarily among the lower social strata, whereas Riesman finds extensive apathy in higher as well as lower strata. Part of the difference rests on the different standards they use. Mills sees apathy as the failure to see that what happens in politics is related to personal troubles.[4] Riesman extends the notion of apathy to include the politically uninformed as well as the politically uncommitted.[5] Riesman judges political apathy to be an important *basis* for shifting and undefined power relations. Mills, on the other hand, treats political apathy primarily as a *result* of the concentration of power.

CONSEQUENCES OF THE STRUCTURE OF POWER

Four parallel sets of consequences of the structure of power for American society may be taken from the writings of Mills and Riesman. The first concerns the impact of the power structure on the interests of certain groups or classes in American society. Mills asserts that the existing power arrangements enhance the interests of the major institutions whose directors constitute the power elite (276 ff). Riesman asserts the contrary: no one group or class is decisively favored over others by the decisions on public issues (257).

The second set of consequences concerns the impact of the structure of power on the quality of politics in American society. Here Mills and Riesman are in closer agreement. Mills maintains that with the concentration of power in a small circle, and the use of manipulation as the favored manner of exercising power, people at the middle and lower strata are decreasingly capable of grasping political issues, and of relating them to personal interests.[6] Riesman also believes that politics has declined in meaning for large numbers of people. This is not due simply to the rise of veto groups. More important, the increasing complexity and remoteness of politics make political self-interest obscure and aggravate feelings of powerlessness even when self-interest is clear.[7]

The third set of consequences of the American power structure concerns its impact on the quality of power relations themselves. Mills contends that the concentration of power has taken place without shift in the bases of legitimacy of power: power is still supposed to reside in the public and its elected representatives, but in reality it is in the hands of those heading key bureaucracies. As a consequence, men of power are neither responsible nor accountable for their power (316-317). Riesman also implies that there is a growing discrepancy between the facts of power and the images of power, but for the opposite reason from Mills: power is more widely dispersed than is generally believed (257-258).

Finally, a fourth set of consequences concerns the impact of the power structure on democratic leadership. If power tends to be lodged in a small group that is not accountable for its power, and if politics no longer involves genuine public debate, then there will be a *severe weakening of democratic institutions*. Mills claims that power in America has become so concentrated that it increasingly resembles the Soviet system of power.

If power tends to be dispersed among groups that are primarily concerned with protecting their own interests, and if at the same time politics has declined as an area of participation, then there will be a severe weakening of leadership. Yet Riesman does not claim that the decline of leadership directly threatens American democracy. At least in the short run the dispersion of power among a wide variety of veto groups supports democratic institutions even as it inhibits effective leadership. The long-run prospects of a leaderless democracy are of course less promising.

SUMMARY OF TWO PORTRAITS OF THE AMERICAN POWER STRUCTURE

	Mills	Riesman
Levels	a. Unified power elite b. Diversified and balance plurality of interest groups c. Mass of unorganized people who have practically no power over elite	a. No dominant power elite b. Diversified and balanced plurality of interest groups c. Mass of unorganized people who have some power over interest groups
Changes	a. Increasing concentration of power	a. Increasing dispersion of power
Operation	a. One group determines all major policies b. Manipulation of people at the bottom by group at the top	a. Who determines policy shifts with the issue b. Monopolistic competition among organized groups
Bases	a. Coincidence of interests among major institutions (economic, military, governmental)	a. Diversity of interests among major organized groups. b. Sense of weakness and dependence among those in higher as well as lower status
Consequences	a. Enhancement of interests of corporations, armed forces, and executive branch of government b. Decline of politics as public debate c. Decline of responsible and accountable power — loss of democracy	a. No one group or class is favored significantly over others b. Decline of politics as duty and self-interest c. Decline of capacity for effective leadership

NOTES

1. Page references in the text for remarks by David Riesman refer to *The Lonely Crowd* (New York: Doubleday Anchor, 1953).

2. Page references in the text for remarks by C. Wright Mills refer to *The Power Elite* (New York: Oxford University Press, 1956).

3. C. Wright Mills, "The Power Elite," in A. Kornhauser (ed.), *Problems of Power in American Society* (Detroit: Wayne State University Press, 1957), p. 161.

4. *White Collar* (New York: Oxford University Press, 1951), p. 327.

5. David Riesman and Nathan Glazer, "Criteria for Political Apathy," in Alvin W. Gouldner (ed.), *Studies in Leadership* (New York: Harper & Brothers, 1950).

6. *White Collar*, pp. 342-350.

7. "Criteria for Political Apathy," p. 520.

ARNOLD M. ROSE

The Power Structure: Introduction

The belief that an "economic elite" controls governmental and community affairs, by means kept hidden from the public, is one than can be traced at least as far back in American history as the political attacks of some Jeffersonians on some Hamiltonians at the end of the eighteenth century. Scarcely any lower-class political movement in the United States has failed to express the theme that the upper classes successfully used nondemocratic means to thwart democratic processes. Perhaps the widest popular use of the theme was achieved by the Populist movement in the decades following 1890. Anarchism and Marxism were imports from Europe that accepted the theme as one of the essential elements of their ideologies.[1] The history of the United States also provides ample factual examples to strengthen credence in the theme. The literature of exposure, especially that of the "muckrakers" in the first decade of the twentieth century, provides details as to how economically privileged individuals and groups illegally bought and bribed legislators, judges, and executive heads of government to serve their own desires for increased wealth and power.

The belief is not entirely wrong. But it presents only a portion of relevant reality and creates a significant misimpression that in itself has political repercussions. A more balanced analysis of the historical facts would probably arrive at something like the following conclusion: Segments of the economic elite have violated democratic political and legal processes, with differing degrees of effort and success in the various

---

Reprinted by permission of the publisher from *The Power Structure: Political Process in American Society* (New York: Oxford University Press, 1967), pp. 1-3. Copyright © 1967 by Oxford University Press, Inc.

periods of American history, but in no recent period could they correctly be said to have controlled the elected and appointed political authorities in large measure. The relationship between the economic elite and the political authorities has been a constantly varying one of strong influence, co-operation, division of labor, and conflict, with each influencing the other in changing proportion to some extent and each operating independently of the other to a large extent. Today there is significant political control and limitation of certain activities over the economic elite, and there are also some significant processes by which the economic elite uses its wealth to help elect some political candidates and to influence other political authorities in ways which are not available to the average citizen. Further, neither the economic elite nor the political authorities are monolithic units which act with internal consensus and coordinated action with regard to each other (or probably in any other way). In fact there are several economic elites which only very rarely act as units within themselves and among themselves, and there are at least two political parties which have significantly differing programs with regard to their actions toward any economic elite, and each of them has only a partial degree of internal cohesion.[2] On domestic issues, at least, it is appropriate to observe that there are actually four political parties, two liberal ones and two conservative ones, the largest currently being the national Democratic party, which generally has a domestic policy that frustrates the special interests of the economic elite. This paragraph states our general hypothesis, and we shall seek to substantiate it with facts that leave no significant areas of omission. Merely to provide it with a shorthand label, we shall call it the "multi-influence hypothesis," as distinguished from the "economic-elite-dominance" hypothesis.

NOTES

1. That the orthodox communist viewpoint regarding power in the United States today is still in terms of dominance by an economic elite was made evident in a series of interviews Walter Lippmann had with Premier Nikita Khrushchev in April 1961. When Lippmann said that decisions regarding foreign policy would be made by President Kennedy, "Khrushchev insisted that the forces behind the President would determine his policy. These forces behind the Kennedy administration he summed up in the one word: Rockefeller." It was also Khrushchev's opinion that Kennedy could not accelerate American economic growth "because of Rockefeller" and then added, "DuPont. They will not let him." (Walter Lippmann, syndicated columns, *Minneapolis Morning Tribune*, April 17, 18, 1961).

2. The two political parties sometimes agree on almost identical specific pieces of legislation, but mainly in the areas of foreign policy and national defense, practically never in regard to their programs or actions with respect to an economic elite.

ARNOLD M. ROSE

The Power Structure: Conclusion

Political power in the United States, like any other social phenomenon, is changing its locus of concentration, its distribution, and its manifestations constantly.[1] Some of the observations and generalizations made in this book will be out of date by the time the reader is able to analyze and criticize them. Recent changes, for example, have occurred in the rural-urban distribution of power in state legislatures, in the strength of the Republican-Southern Democratic "coalition" in Congress, and in the extent to which businessmen are to be found in key positions in the national Administration. Nevertheless, most aspects of power have remained sufficiently stable for a student of the power structure to draw generalizations and to note slow-moving trends. In contrast to the major theses of C. Wright Mills and Floyd Hunter—that there is a secret, hierarchical, and unified power structure in the United States headed by an economic elite, that the political elite occupies only a secondary position in the power structure, and that the masses are apathetic and act in terms of false consciousness of their interests—we would assert the following propositions. Most of them are based on studies reported or summarized in this book; others are based merely on general or participant observation.

1. There is a power structure in every organized activity of American life and at every level—national, regional, state, and local. Power is the major means used by a large, heterogeneous society to effect or to resist change, and—except in simple face-to-face relations—power is

---

Reprinted by permission of the pubisher from *The Power Structure: Political Process in American Society* (New York: Oxford University Press, 1967), pp. 483-93. Copyright © 1967 by Oxford University Press, Inc.

structured, which is to say that there are different roles and role relationships, and a pattern into which these roles and relationships fit.

2. There are varying degrees of relationship and agreement among these varied power structures. They are certainly not unified into a simple power structure, even *within* the categories of the economic and the political, although occasionally semi-permanent liaisons develop among them. Nor are they usually countervailing, because each operates primarily within its own sphere of influence, although countervailing (or check-and-balance) relationships occasionally do occur. The political party power structures—there are at least four major ones on the national level alone—probably have the largest number of relationships with other power structures, both because one of their specific roles is to mediate conflicts and because they have a large degree of control over the bureaucratic machinery of government, which—in turn—monopolizes most of the instruments of organized physical force.

3. Within each power structure, a small number of persons hold the largest amount of power. In community studies, this has been estimated to constitute less than 1 per cent of the population, but such estimates refer to those who lead in community-wide political decisions, and not to power *within* the spheres of business, unions, voluntary associations, schools, churches, etc. While in any sphere of activity there are "leaders," who constitute a tiny proportion of all those affected by the activity, this does not mean that the others have no power whatsoever. Opposition groups occasionally form, and sometimes succeed in overturning the existing elite. In all cases where there are elections, the rank-and-file voters exercise some restraining and modifying power over the elite. Their power is a function of the extent to which they have interacted to create a public opinion, the extent to which the election machinery is honest, and the extent to which voters are equal. Under these criteria, most governmental elections accord a good deal of power to the electorate, most business corporation elections accord practically no power to the electorate, and labor union and voluntary association elections vary between these two poles. But even in government and in actively democratic trade unions, there is an ever-changing elite which exercises most of the power at any given moment.

4. Each elite manifests its power mainly within its own domain. That is, the strongest powers of businessmen are exercised within their own businesses, and the strongest powers of politicians and public administrators are exercised within government. But particularly the political and economic elites, among all the elites, influence each other's spheres. Especially since the 1930's the government has set various restrictions and controls on business, and has heavily taxed business and the public

to carry out purposes deemed to be for the general good—welfare programs, education programs, highways, war and military defense activities, etc. Business leaders use lobbyists, "business representatives" in legislatures, contributions to campaign funds, publicity designed to influence public opinion, the "political strike," and other lesser techniques to influence government. Businessmen influence government more effectively than most non-businessmen—not only because they can afford lobbyists, advertisements and other costly techniques—but also because they are more educated, more knowledgeable, more articulate, and more activist than average citizens. The latter qualities give them an advantage quite compatible with a democratic society.

5. The economic elite has its greatest success in influencing government where there are no counter-pressures—from other sectors of the economic elite, from other non-economic elites, and from public opinion. The result has been that the economic elite has been relatively successful in influencing government purchasing agents and the independent regulatory commissions. This is not quite an accurate way of stating the facts, however, since individual businesses often compete strongly with each other in influencing these factors of government, and there is a considerable turnover in the individual businesses benefited by these sectors of government. In pressuring or appealing to the top levels of the federal administration, to the Congress, or even to many state legislatures (especially outside the South), businessmen have been much less successful since the 1930's. In fact, as far as general legislation is concerned, they have had an almost unbroken series of defeats, although they have succeeded in *delaying* the passage of certain bills for years. Thus, while businessmen have gained certain economic benefits from government, their typical ideology—in favor of businessman leadership in the society and of a minimum of government activity for the benefit of other segments of the population—has made no progress.[2]

6. While the federal government has been gaining ascendancy over the state and local governments, and while the office of the President has been gaining power at the expense of Congress, it is far from true that the state governments and the Congress are powerless. Rather, it could be said that the "balance of power" doctrine envisaged in the Constitution has come into operation only since 1933, because the federal government (except for military activities) and the presidency (except in wartime) were relatively weak institutions before then. These two trends in political power have reduced the influence of the economic elite, for the federal government is less susceptible to influence from businessmen than are most of the state governments, and the presidency is less susceptible to such influence than are many of the congressmen.

The Power Structure: Conclusion 33

7. In the early 1960's a coalition of several decades' duration between two major political power structures—the conservative leadership of the Republican party and the Democrats in power in most of the Southern states—largely broke down. The Southern Democrats, changing in membership and reduced in number by Republican inroads on their constituencies, drew closer to the Northern Democrats, except publicly over the issue of civil rights. The South was rapidly becoming like the North— in its industrialization, urbanization, patterns of race relations permitted by Negro voting, and development of a two-party system.[3] The Republican party was sharply divided between its conservatives and liberals, on the one hand, and a smaller group of right-wing extremists with a vigorous ideology who seized control of the party's grassroots structures in the majority of states. The extremists—while occasionally ideologically supportive of business—were not as willing to make political compromises in behalf of business or as willing to trust leading businessmen, as had been the previous conservative leaders of the Republican party. All these developments, coupled with the political skill of President Lyndon B. Johnson, permitted the passage of a great deal of "liberal" legislation in the 1964–65 sessions of Congress—including "Medicare" for the elderly . . ., federal aid to education, the anti-poverty program, tax reduction without a balanced budget, a comprehensive civil rights act, a voting rights act, elimination of national quotas for immigrants, creation of a new Department of Housing and Urban Development, aid to urban mass-transit programs and to highway and city beautification efforts, and a National Foundation on the Arts and Humanities. Further, the President had an unofficial price control policy which worked for a few years to keep major industries from raising prices.

8. In the passage of the above-mentioned legislation, interested economic elite pressure groups were mostly defeated. On the other hand, the major legislation sought by organized labor—repeal of Section 14(b) of the Taft-Hartley Act—was also defeated in the Senate. The one economic elite group that continued to reap major economic benefits from government activity was the armaments and space-exploration supply industries, although the Secretary of Defense made certain decisions on procurement—such as in favor of competitive bidding rather than cost-plus contracts—even in this area which were not favored by the leading manufacturers.

9. Through the Voting Rights Act of the Congress and the *Baker* v. *Carr* and *Reynolds* v. *Sims* decisions of the United States Supreme Court —including the giving of permission to the Attorney General to seek a Court review of the poll tax (which was consequently outlawed by the Supreme Court)—a major democratization of voting for state legislatures

was occurring in many states. Both state and local government activities were increasingly influenced by standards set by federal aid programs that covered ever wider spheres.

10. The pattern of legislation at both federal and state levels revealed the emergence of new popular pressure groups with considerable power, partly because of demographic shifts and partly because of growing political consciousness among these groups. These groups are the elderly, a portion of whom are now organized into many associations, the most politically active of which is the National Association of Senior Citizens; the Negroes, possibly a majority of whom are organized into various civil rights associations and activist churches; and the "resentful disaffecteds," practically all organized into a variety of leftist and rightist extremist organizations, of which the John Birch Society is the largest and the wealthiest. The political organization of voluntary associations representing these three categories of the "masses" provides increasing evidence of a thesis expounded in an earlier section on "Reactions against the Mass Society"....

11. The major area of small-group control of national policy remaining in the country was that of foreign policy. The most powerful arm of this small group—namely the President and his official advisers—are quite exposed to the public. But there are secret decision-makers operating in this area also—secret in that their influence and processes of decision-making are not accessible to the public. These decision-makers are the CIA, the foreign policy "experts" in the universities and in such organizations as the Foreign Policy Association and the Council on Foreign Relations, and the military supplies industrialists who exert their influence mainly through the military leaders. The last-named are the ones whom Mills placed at the pinnacle of the power elite in the United States; we identify them rather as one influence among several affecting the nation almost exclusively in the area of foreign policy. We are entirely skeptical about Mills's contention that the other "members" of the economic elite—say, for example, those organized in the Chamber of Commerce—have more influence on foreign policy than the workers organized into trade unions, especially when they engage in shipping boycotts.

12. Despite the fact that the Republican party's ideological move to the right after 1962 left the Democrats securely in command of the center, the program of the Democratic party remained as liberal as it had ever been. This can be seen not only by comparing national party platforms over the years, but by reviewing the legislation supported (and usually passed) by the majority of Democrats in Congress and by the Democratic Presidents Kennedy and Johnson. This can be explained either as a long-run trend—in terms of the increasing strength of voters

who favor liberal measures and generally support the Democratic party as the instrument to achieve them—or as part of a structural cycle. Lipset specifies a version of the latter theory:[4] Republican Presidents seek center support and so force Republican congressmen from safe conservative seats to behave in a more liberal fashion. When a Republican holds the presidency, the Southern contingent of conservative Democrats have more power in their party. Thus, in a Republican presidency, the two congressional parties are not so far apart. But when a Democrat holds the presidency, he pulls his congressmen to the left, to respond to the needs of the greater number of voters there, while the Republican congressmen are free to follow their ideological inclination toward the right, and the two parties are quite far apart. It is difficult to judge from the facts which theory is correct, but this author tends to regard the former theory as more persuasive, especially in view of the decline of differences between South and North. In any case, there has been a significant difference between the platforms and policies of the two national parties at least since 1932,[5] and the difference in the mid-1960's was as great as could be found between democratic political parties anywhere in the Western world. The increasing number of differences between the two major political parties, and the growing ideological framework for those differences, will probably have profound implications for the political future of the United States—but it is still too early to foresee the future development. Nevertheless, from the standpoint of the thesis of this book, we can say that there is little evidence that business is playing any significant role in the development of these trends. Business is a declining influence on the political power structures, except in the narrow area of its relationship to government procurement officials and the independent regulatory commissions—largely because business exerts its strongest efforts on these and because there are few countervailing influences on them. . . .

13. The public's and the formal leadership's image of the power structure—if we can generalize from a study of the one state of Minnesota—does not include many people as seeing the economic elite as all-powerful, although the extent to which they do see business as influential may be somewhat exaggerated in terms of the facts. Judging from their public pronouncements, it is the political extremist—of both the right and the left—whose image of the American power structure includes a conspiratorial and all-powerful role for the economic elite. The extremist groups have different names for this "all-powerful group" but they refer to the same business elite: The "lunatic fringe" rightists call them "the hidden group behind the communists," the more rational extreme rightists call them "the Establishment"; the more rational ex-

treme leftists also call them "the Establishment" or "Wall Street," but are more likely to use the Mills-Hunter terms "the power elite" or "the power structure," while the less rational extreme leftists either use the same terms or refer bluntly to "the big business conspiracy." While it is of considerable interest that the political extremists of both right and left—apparently along with many non-extremist intellectuals influenced by Mills and Hunter—have the same image of the top business elite as being all-powerful, it is of greater importance to note that the majority of the people and of the positional leaders of American organized society do not have this image. We have adduced much evidence in this book that the top business elite are far from having an all-powerful position; that power is so complicated in the United States that the top businessmen scarcely understand it, much less control it; and that since 1933 the power position of businessmen has been declining rather than growing.

14. Because the spheres of their organizations have grown in recent decades, the elites of the federal administration (including the military), of the federal courts, of certain voluntary associations, and of certain education and scientific institutions, have grown more powerful. While on rare occasions they supersede in power the top political elites—as when the United States Supreme Court ordered the state governments to end racial segregation and to reapportion their legislatures in accord with population, or when the same Court declares unconstitutional a federal statute, or when the civil rights associations pressure Congress into voting for a statute as sweeping as the Civil Rights Act of 1964, or when the labor and old-age groups pressure Congress into voting for a statute as sweeping as the Medicare Act of 1965 (although both these statutes had the full support of that significant political elite—the President)—the political elites are usually ascendent over them. The political elites control the agencies of force and the instruments of legislation, have considerable access to the mass media, and have the support of public opinion. The political elites—the two major parties, the President, the factions in the houses of Congress, the executives and legislatures of the states and large cities—are not unified of course, and they check-and-balance each other to a considerable extent.

15. While the two major political parties are listed by us as among the most powerful groups in the United States, their structures are quite generally misunderstood by the public and by nonspecialized intellectuals and other leadership groups. They are structured mainly as voluntary associations, with grass-roots elections that range from being wholly democratic to being "controlled" from a self-perpetuating group at the top. In some states (e.g. Texas) they are highly fractionated and schismatic. They are structured on the layer principle: ward or county, mu-

nicipality, district, and state. They scarcely exist as voluntary associations at the national level—except for the quadrennial national nominating conventions—but they exist in the caucuses of Congress, where they are the most important single influence on congressmen's voting behavior despite the bifurcation within both political parties.

16. While money in the hands of rich people opens special opportunities to democratic political processes—such as through the use of lobbyists, advertisements, and campaign contributions—these processes are by no means closed to poor people. A volunteer campaign worker for a congressman will have more influence on him than most lobbyists, and as much influence on him as a campaign contribution equivalent to the voluntary labor, roughly speaking. The fact that the political party in most states is an open, if not entirely democratic, voluntary association, and the fact that it is the single most important influence on most elected officials, also gives the non-wealthy citizen access to political power often greater than that of the wealthy, but not politically active, citizen. In this context it should be understood that most elected officials, especially at higher levels, are only partially open to pressures of any kind. Practically all congressmen, and probably most state legislators, vote for bills in accord with their own personal convictions—when they have convictions with regard to specific bills—most of the time. Where they do not have convictions regarding a specific bill, the most important influence on them are the caucus leaders or committee chairmen of their own political party who are representing the party leadership's position. The "personal convictions" factor suggests that the *initial* selections of candidates and the means which they use to get elected to Congress are the two most important links in the chain leading to the passage of bills where influence can be most effectively applied. It is for this reason that we say that voluntary campaign labor, participation in the grass-roots party (as voluntary association), and monetary campaign contributions are the most powerful instruments to influence a legislator (or probably any other elected official).

In sharper summary, the conclusions of this book—in contrast with those of Mills and Hunter—are that power structure of the United States is highly complex and diversified (rather than unitary and monolithic), that the political system is more or less democratic (with the glaring exception of the Negro's position until the 1960's), that in political processes the political elite is ascendant over and not subordinate to the economic elite, and that the political elite influences or controls the economic elite, at least as much as the economic elite controls the political elite. To arrive at such conclusions we must in part have a contrast conception: What should the American political power structure be compared to? We believe that Mills has implicitly compared the existing American power structure to some populist or guild socialist ideal, which has never existed and which we believe could never exist considering basic sociological facts—such as the existence of culture, of the value of money to most people, etc. Our implicit comparison in this book has been to any known other society—past or present (with the possible exception of the contemporary Scandinavian countries). We do not say that the multi-influence hypothesis is entirely the fact, or that the United States is completely democratic; we simply say that such statements are more correct for the United States today than for any other society.

While the whole first chapter of this book might be repeated in the summary, we wish merely to repeat in conclusion the statement of the multi-influence hypothesis which has guided the studies reported in this book: Segments of the economic elite have violated democratic political and legal processes, with differing degrees of effort and success in the various periods of American history, but in no recent period could they correctly be said to have controlled the elected and appointed political authorities in large measure. The relationship between the economic elite and the political authorities has been a constantly varying one of strong influence, co-operation, division of labor, and conflict, with each group influencing the other in changing proportion to some extent, and each operating independently of the other to a large extent. Today there is significant political control and limitation of certain activities of the economic elite, and there are also some significant processes by which the economic elite use their wealth to help elect some political candidates and to influence other political authorities in ways which are not available to the average citizen. Further, neither the economic elite nor the political authorities are monolithic units which act with internal consensus and co-ordinated action with regard to each other (or probably in any other way): in fact, there are several economic elites, which only very rarely act as units within themselves and among themselves, and there are at least two (we prefer to think of them as four) political parties which have significantly differing programs with regard to their actions toward any economic elite and each of these parties has only a partial degree of internal cohesion.

The power structure of the United States is indeed so complex that this book only touches on certain aspects of it, rather than providing full empirical evidence for these aspects. We believe, however, that enough empirical documentation has been provided to give basic support to the multi-influence hypothesis as a general statement about what is true of the power structure of the United States.

NOTES

1. Even from the time the present study was begun, in 1960, until it was sent to the publishers, in 1966, there were so many significant changes that additions, corrections, and qualifications had to be made regularly in the manuscript.

2. It has been argued that this businessman's ideology represents a "false consciousness"—that is, it claims to represent an economic interest, but is in fact, contrary to the economic interest of businessmen. The factual argument is that businessmen gain most economic benefits when the government actively promotes the welfare and education of even its poorest citizens, when it maintains a regularly unbalanced budget, and when it reduces tariffs—all policies which most businessmen oppose.

3. The decline in the number of "safe" Democratic House seats has been documented by Raymond E. Wolfinger and Joan Heifetz, "Safe Seats, Seniority, and Power in Congress," *American Political Science Review,* 59 (June 1965), 337-49.

4. Seymour Martin Lipset, *Political Man* (New York: Doubleday, 1960), pp. 306-7.

5. The basic ideological difference between the leadership of the two parties, on the average, has been demonstrated by Herbert McClosky, Paul J. Hoffman, and Rosemary O'Hara, "Issue Conflict and Consensus Among Party Leaders and Followers," *American Political Science Review,* 54 (June 1960), 406-27. The public, also, sees ideological differences between the two parties. See, for example, the report of the Minnesota Poll in the *Minneapolis Sunday Tribune,* November 3, 1963, p. UM2.

G. WILLIAM DOMHOFF

How the Power Elite Set National Goals

There are those who think that specific priorities in America are created in the political process via elections, debates in Congress, and discussions in the White House. I also have heard it said that everybody is in on the setting of priorities—consumers, laborers, voters, businessmen, farmers, and so on. I disagree with these views except in the obvious sense that such factors have some part to play. Rather, it is my belief that the national goals are set by those who have been the best at making profits, that is, by the wealthy—who are the winners by the American rules of the game of life.

The wealthy in this country are the owners and managers of the large corporations, banks, insurance companies, and finance houses. Making up perhaps 0.2–0.3 percent of the population, these corporate rich possess about 25 percent of all the privately held wealth in the United States. More importantly, they own perhaps 60–70 percent of all privately held corporate wealth, from whence derives the dividends that underwrite their fabulous life style and the private schools, debutante balls, gentlemen's clubs, summer resorts, and overseas vacations that help to weld the group together as an interacting and intermarrying social class.

I am aware that not all members of this privileged class involve themselves in governing, managing, and goal setting. Some are merely jetsetters, sportsmen, or clotheshorses. However, many do so involve

---

Reprinted by permission of the publisher and author from G. William Domhoff, "How the Power Elite Set National Goals," in *National Priorities,* ed. Kan Chen (San Francisco: San Francisco Press, 547 Howard Street, San Francisco, Calif., 1970), pp. 51-60.

themselves, and these members of the upper class are at the core of a power elite that is the "operating arm" or "leadership group" or "executive committee" that manages the affairs of the corporate rich as a whole. This inner core is filled out and aided in its work by high-level employees in institutions controlled by members of the upper class, which means top-level corporation managers, foundation officials, and university presidents. These latter members of the power elite, I believe, are advanced in terms of their ability to deal with the problems of an economic system that does very nicely by its richest members.

The power elite (which I prefer to think of in the plural rather than the singular because there are some differences of emphasis and style among them) set priorities in two different places. The first is the corporate board room, which is the meeting place of bankers, financiers, corporate lawyers, and businessmen from all over the country. The interlocking and overlapping of these boards almost defies description. Suffice it to say that everybody in this little world is in touch with everybody else through a variety of people and pipelines. As to what priorities are set by this closely knit group—they make investment decisions, decide plant locations, determine the size and shape of the work force, and other such seemingly mundane things that provide the context within which the political process operates.[1]

Important as corporate board rooms and counting houses are as meeting places for the setting of goals and priorities by the power elite, there is yet a second location for such activity that is perhaps even more important, for it concerns the corporate system as a whole, not just the fortunes of a given company or interest group. This priority-setting process is at its crucial points connected to the government, but it has nothing at all to do with electoral politics and congressional debates.

The process has four or five stages. For simplicity's sake, and as a starting point for discussion, I would diagram the process as in Figure 1.

The Archimedian point in this little "model" is in the groups I call the *consensus-seeking* or *policy-planning groups* of the power elite. It is in these groups that wealthy men from all over the country get together to try to figure out how to react to the general problems facing the corporate system. And I should add, of course, that they have a little bit of help from their friends, the academic experts, particularly the economists, who are well financed via the foundations and enormously flattered by all the attention and acclaim they receive. Some of them even think that experts such as themselves run the country.[2]

Among the most important of the organizations I have in mind are the Council on Foreign Relations, the Committee for Economic Development, and the American Assembly, but there are others, some old, some new, some waning in importance, some just coming into their own. There are many things that could be said about these organizations, but I want to emphasize only those aspects germane to goal setting:

1. They bring together big business leaders from all over the country to discuss issues of importance.
2. They retain academic experts housed in corporate and foundation-financed think tanks to serve as consultants to these groups.
3. They receive much of their financial support from power-elite foundations such as Ford, Rockefeller, and Carnegie.
4. Most importantly, members and advisers of these organizations are often called to government service or asked to serve on special "blue-ribbon" commissions or "task forces" concerned with the issues already dealt with in the discussion groups of the policy-planning organizations.

It turns out that this model even applies to the framework within which national goals are being discussed. The story begins in the second half of the 1950s when the concerns were not overpopulation, environmental pollution, and youthful disenchantment but diversifying the military to fight against nationalist uprisings, rebuilding national prestige and morale in the face of Russia's firsts in space, combatting recession and a generally sluggish economy, and bolstering the nation's vigilance against international communism. The anti-communist crusade was especially important, for the Soviets looked like they might be able to make good on their goal of burying the United States economically, the Sino-Soviet split had not developed to a very great extent, and the possibility of wars of liberation not amenable to treatment by A-bombs and H-bombs was making international bankers and businessmen jittery over President Eisenhower's reliance on "massive retaliation" at the expense of conventional forces.

Because I think these concerns could be traced to corporate board rooms and discussion within the consensus-seeking groups, I am being slightly arbitrary in starting a detailed account of events with a special panel convened by the Rockefellers in late 1956 under the auspices of one of their foundations, the Rockefeller Brothers Fund. The "panel," which constitutes a consensus-seeking group consisted of about 85 people organized into six groups of from 10 to 30 participants. Members were predominantly corporate leaders, foundation officials, and leading members of the various policy-planning and discussion organizations, along with several academic advisers and a few labor leaders and jour-

FIGURE 1

The Power-Elite Policy-Making Process

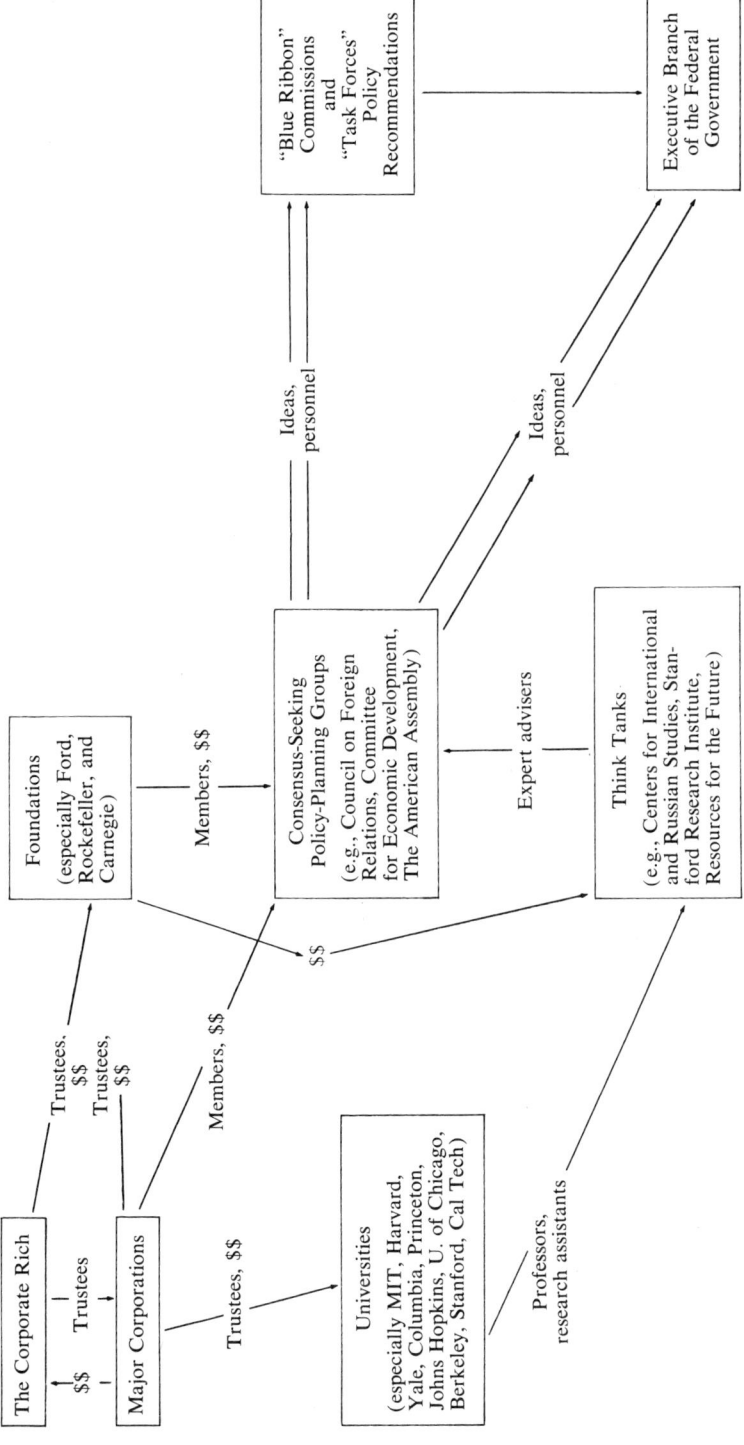

nalists. The task of the panels was to take stock of America in such areas as foreign policy, international security, economic policy, and education, and to make recommendations for the future.

Some of the panels also availed themselves of special consultants who, in two or three cases, helped to write the final report. For example, Henry Kissinger, later to be a Kennedy and Nixon adviser on foreign affairs, helped with two of the reports, while a Chase Manhattan Bank official and a Columbia University law professor helped with another.

Four of the panel reports appeared in the first half of 1958. They had two recorded effects in the world of government and politics. First, one of the members of the overall panel guiding the Rockefeller studies, Charles Percy (then president of Bell and Howell, now a senator from Illinois), was named head of a GOP Goals Committee. Second, President Eisenhower announced in his 1959 State of the Union message that he was going to set up a special commission on national goals. According to *The New York Times*, it was Percy who convinced the President to make such a move: "In an interview, White House sources report, Mr. Percy convinced President Eisenhower of the need for a nonpartisan document defining great national goals the country should move toward in the next decade."[3] Important as this explicit connection is between the Rockefeller studies and the national-goals commission, the assertion of a causal relationship does not hang on such a narrow reed as Percy talking to President Eisenhower. There are innumerable connections that could be drawn between the Rockefeller group and several of the most important lawyers, bankers, and businessmen working in the Eisenhower Administration. There is also, as we shall now see, some overlap in personnel between the two groups.

Due to difficulties in picking personnel and in making the plan acceptable for private funding (which Eisenhower insisted upon), the President's Commission on National Goals was not announced until January 1960. The details of the commission's situation are quite interesting. First, it was administered by the American Assembly, a discussion organization of big businessmen and their advisers that was set up at Columbia University in 1950 (and which served as a base from which to tout Columbia University President Eisenhower for President of the United States). After accepting its official charge from the President, the American Assembly then received its funding from several private foundations. The foundations read like a Who's Who of the big business world, and, not incidentally, of the Rockefeller panels: the Carnegie Corporation, which had five trustees involved in the Rockefeller panels; the Ford Foundation, which had one trustee involved in the Rockefeller panels; the Rockefeller Foundation, which had two trustees involved in the Rockefeller panels; and the Alfred P. Sloan Foundation, which had two trustees involved in the Rockefeller panels. Four foundations whose trustees were not involved in any of the panels also contributed: the Maurice and Laura Falk Foundation, the Johnson Foundation (Racine), the Richardson Foundation, and the U.S. Steel Foundation.

The commission itself, as of course are all government commissions, was drawn from all walks of life. *The New York Times* tells us that "Included are a jurist, a scientist, a labor leader, four educators, a retired general, two corporation executives, and an editor."[4] Accurate though that statement may be in a narrow sense, I don't think it captures the reality of the matter. True enough, the venerable George Meany of the AFL-CIO was seated at the table, as he so often is on these official blue-ribbon occasions, but the rest of the group has a rather strong power-elite flavor. Seven of the eleven members were in 1960-61 members of one organization alone, the Council on Foreign Relations. Here is the lineup:

Henry M. Wriston, chairman. At the time Wriston was the president of both the American Assembly and the Council on Foreign Relations. He was formerly president of Brown University.

Frank Pace, Jr., vice chairman. Pace was the chairman of General Dynamics and sat on other corporate boards. (A senior vice president from General Dynamics was on one of the Rockefeller panels.)

Erwin D. Canham, editor of the *Christian Science Monitor*, president of the United States Chamber of Commerce for 1959-60. (The managing editor of the same newspaper was on one of the Rockefeller panels.)

James B. Conant, retired president of Harvard University.

Colgate W. Darden, Jr., retired president of the University of Virginia. He is married to a daughter of Irenée duPont and sits on the boards of duPont, U.S. Rubber, Life Insurance Company of Virginia, and Newport News Shipbuilding and Dry Dock Company.

Crawford H. Greenewalt, also married to a duPont, and president of E. I. duPont de Nemours & Company. He was also an MIT trustee at the time, which is interesting in light of the fact that a member of the commission yet to be introduced is the chairman of MIT.

Alfred M. Gruenther, retired general, president of the American Red Cross. His brother was on the White House staff during the Eisenhower Administration.

Learned Hand, a retired judge who was 88 years of age and took no part in the writing of the final report.

Clark Kerr, president of the University of California.

James R. Killian, Jr., chairman of MIT, a member of the Rockefeller panels, and a director of General Motors and IBM.

George Meany, president of the AFL-CIO.

The commission asked fourteen "distinguished Americans" to write papers on various problems for its consideration. In addition to Wriston and Kerr, who were on the commission itself, the writers include the president of the Carnegie Corporation (who played an important role in the Rockefeller panels), the vice president of the Alfred P. Sloan Foundation, a director of the Twentieth Century Fund (who helped write the sixth and final Rockefeller panel report), the president of IBM, two economists from the Committee for Economic Development, an editor from the Des Moines *Register* and *Tribune* (whose publisher was on the Rockefeller panel), the chairman of the Chase Manhattan Bank (who was also chairman of the Council on Foreign Relations and the Ford Foundation trustees), and five academicians.

The commission also had a staff. It was headed by William P. Bundy, brother of McGeorge, son-in-law of Dean Acheson, and a member of the Council on Foreign Relations. He was "on leave" from the Board of National Estimates of the Central Intelligence Agency, which makes it somewhat academic that the commissioners themselves had "no connection with the government."[5]

I present these details as evidence that the commission is perhaps the inside job that I believe it to be. In any event, it must have had a meeting of minds rather quickly, for its report was available in book form in early December even though it was not appointed until January. The report, published by Prentice-Hall under the title *Goals for Americans*, was publicized widely as a public service by the Advertising Council, which is yet another outpost of the power elite. And, as the preface duly notes, "The book will also provide a basis for deliberations by regional, state and municipal sessions of the American Assembly as well as by civic groups, classes and discussion meetings." In short, the goals were to be communicated to the underlying population.[6]

The possible impact of the Eisenhower Commission report was undoubtedly muted by the election of John F. Kennedy in 1960, for no Democratic president is going to openly embrace the suggestions of even a "nonpartisan" commission that was set up by an outgoing Republican president. However, it is likely that the effects of the report and the Rockefeller panels could be traced into the special "task forces" that were established by Kennedy in the months before his inauguration, for there is overlap in personnel between the Rockefeller panels and the task forces on foreign and educational policies, while two of those who wrote reports for the Eisenhower Commission also served on task forces. More generally, six Rockefeller panelists served President Kennedy in defense and foreign-policy matters, and two of those who wrote reports for the Eisenhower Commission had assignments in the Kennedy Administration. From this point the influence of these reports would have to be traced into specific policy decisions, a difficult task which is not our concern here. However, I cannot pass up the opportunity to note that President Kennedy said the following in announcing his task force on "defense frontiers":

The committee will not make another sweeping investigation or study of defense, military policies and resources such as has been so ably and thoroughly done in recent years by various House and Senate Committees, and by such private groups as the Gaither and Rockefeller Committees, the Council on Foreign Relations, the Foreign Policy Association, the Carnegie Corporation, the great universities, and others. Rather it will utilize their splendid work as its primary source for facts, analyses and informed opinion on the narrower field of defense management and administration with which it is called upon to deal.[7]

Returning to the framework of goal setting, the next development concerns the establishment in 1962 of a Center for Priority Analysis by the National Planning Association. This is noteworthy first because the committee "overseeing" the project for the NPA includes one of the fourteen contributors to the commission as well as numerous power-elite types and one or two labor leaders. It is also interesting because the top three officers in the NPA were also members of the Council on Foreign Relations and the Committee for Economic Development (and one of those three served on a Rockefeller panel). However, it is mostly noteworthy because the Center for Priority Analysis explicitly used the framework provided by the Eisenhower Commission report: "For the list of goals to be studied, the report of President Eisenhower's Commission on National Goals was taken as a point of departure."[8] The objective was to put dollars-and-cents figures by each of the goals so decision makers could decide among various alternatives on a more factual basis. A main finding, in addition to "costing out" each goal, was that all the goals could not be pursued at once. In the NPA, which may be of waning importance, we see a nice example of how the power elite provide themselves with the facts and figures necessary to operate their complex corporate system.

The matter does not end here. As problems multiply, the need for rational planning and goal-setting increases. Thus we find retired Ford Motor Company president Arjay Miller calling for a permanent goals institute within the federal government.[9] Thus we hear of Thomas J. Watson of IBM (one of the fourteen contributors to the Eisenhower Commission) calling in early 1970 for a new government agency to be concerned with national goals. And thus we see President Nixon, with whom corporate leaders and foundation officials have conferred so often about so many things, making a first move in this direction with the creation, in July 1969, of a National Goals Research Staff within the White House. In announcing the new group, President Nixon said "the staff would forecast future developments, assess longer-range consequences of present social trends, estimate the range of alternate goals that would be feasible and measure the probable future impact of alternative courses of action to meet anticipated problems."[10] Headed by former Nixon law partner Leonard Garment, the staff includes Raymond Bauer of the Harvard Business School, Anthony Wiener of the Hudson Institute (still another think tank), and experts brought in from such government outposts as HEW and OEO. The staff is concerned with drawing together what has been done on these problems by the government and "private institutions." I take the latter to be the Committee for Economic Development, the National Bureau of Economic Research, Resources for the Future (which has two directors from the goals commission), The Brookings Institution, the National Planning Association, and other power-elite organizations.

Now, the National Goals Research Staff may not grow into anything bigger, but I think it is the straw in the wind that will complete the circuit from corporation to foundation to policy-planning group to blue-ribbon commission to government agency. Speeches at gentlemen's clubs, conferences at elite campuses like Stanford, reports by government groups and commissions, discussions at the American Assembly, a small goals staff in the White House, a friendly editorial about the goals staff in *The New York Times* (July 17, 1969)—soon the word will be out to all nooks and crannies of the big-business community that a new agency is needed, at which time the whole thing can be moved through a stodgy Congress which harbors many resisters who are from the "old school" of thought, worlds apart from the sophisticated circles of internationally minded corporate leaders and their academic advisers.

In closing this discussion of how the power elite set national goals, I want to comment on the question that is so often raised: So what? Does it make any difference? For it goes without saying, at least in business and academic circles, that American leaders act in the interest of all of us when they make their decisions. Sociologist Arnold M. Rose assures us, for instance, that the kind of evidence I have presented "does not prove that the business appointees are running the government for the benefit of business;" to the contrary, his own opinion is that decision makers with business backgrounds promote "their conception of the national interest [in the case of foreign affairs]."[11] Unfortunately, I don't think it is all that straightforward and clear-cut. However much the power elite may try to take us into account (and that is being generous), they have—like all of us—biases, implicit assumptions, and narrowed outlooks based upon their upbringings and their occupations. Psychology and sociology have documented this in detail for the middle and lower levels of Western societies—surely it could not be claimed that it is otherwise among the very affluent, who have a different (and more bountiful) source of income than the rest of us, not to mention a rather unique life style.

Indeed, to even raise the question of "So what?" in the face of the wealth and income distributions—not to mention the ugly statistics on infant mortality, educational opportunities, health and disease, unemployment, housing, and life span—is to make a cruel joke. The power elite set priorities through the mechanisms I have outlined, and the wealth and well-being statistics suggest that they set them for the benefit of the corporate rich.

NOTES

1. Andrew Hacker, "Power to Do What?," in Irving L. Horowitz (ed.), *The New Sociology* (New York: Oxford Univ. Press, 1964).

2. However, as Arjay Miller mentioned in a discussion after his talk, you can buy 24 economists with the salary of the chairman of General Motors. But I digress.

3. Russell Baker, "Funds' Wariness Blocks U.S. Study," *The New York Times* (October 29, 1959), p. 19.

4. "Goals Group Led by Educator, Long Interested in Government," *The New York Times* (November 28, 1960), p. 24.

5. *Goals for Americans* (Englewood Cliffs, N.J.: Prentice-Hall, 1960), p. xi.

6. *Goals for Americans* was not the only study on priorities to appear in 1960. A few months earlier the "capstone" report in the Rockefeller series had appeared. Entitled *The Power of the Democratic Ideal*, its writing committee included a Carnegie Corporation vice president and the Twentieth Century Fund director who wrote a paper for the goals commission. Other authors included a Columbia University philosophy professor, a counselor for Radio Free Europe (which is in part supported by the CIA), and the president of the Social Science Research Council (which is a whole story of foundation financing in itself).

7. *New Frontiers of the Kennedy Administration* (Washington, D.C.: Public Affairs Press, 1961), p. 21; on the importance of task forces see Norman C. Thomas and Harold L. Wolman, "The Presidency and Policy Formation: The Task Force Device," *Public Administration Review* (September-October, 1969).

8. Leonard Lecht, *Goals, Priorities, and Dollars* (New York: Free Press, 1966), Appendix B, p. 341.

9. Actually, Miller's contribution to this seminar, with its mentions of the Ford Foundation, The Brookings Institution, the Center for Priority Analysis, the Urban Coalition, and special government committees and agencies, is a nice presentation of the process this paper tries to describe.

10. "White House Panel to Study Problems," *The New York Times* (July 13, 1969), p. 51; John Herbers, "U.S. Unit at Work on Social Report," *The New York Times* (December 24, 1969), p. 11.

11. Arnold M. Rose, *The Power Structure* (New York: Oxford Univ. Press, 1967), pp. 23, 93.

Does Business Have a Responsibility to Society?

Debate on the role of private enterprise in society is not new. From the beginning of the Industrial Revolution, challenges have been issued to the ideological tenet that the production of goods, services, and profits constitutes the only responsibility of business to society. The recent environmental concern and the revelations of the consumer movement have rejuvenated the attack on the "what's good for business is good for society" philosophy. As will be apparent from reading the next three selections, the debate thus far rests less on evidence than on values.

Albert Carr entitles his contribution in question form: "Can An Executive Afford a Conscience?" His answer is unmistakable—an executive cannot afford to be without a conscience because a perfectly possible alternative to the solution of current social problems is the destruction of political democracy and capitalism. Recognizing that corporate environments are hostile to social action which conflicts with profits, Carr nevertheless outlines some steps toward social responsibility which the morally responsive executive can take. In Carr's mind the solution of our social problems cannot await the formation of a new business ideology encompassing genuine corporate social responsibility.

George Cabot Lodge ("Top Priority: Renovating Our Ideology") also considers social responsibility a legitimate function of business. However, he invests little faith in individual executive action. According to Lodge, a successful assault on social problems requires that business transcend its traditional pragmatism; that is, business must abandon its posture of "that which works is good." Pressure must be exerted on government to engage in ideological thought which would culminate in a philosophy defining societal goals and the roles to be assumed by business and government in achieving the "good society." Lodge believes we must be willing to jettison some long-valued ideas regarding private property and private enterprise if a new public-private alliance is to be forged.

It would be difficult to find a statement more opposed to Lodge's position than the following one by Theodore Levitt ("The Dangers of Social Responsibility") written twelve years earlier. "What is bad for this or any country is for society to be consciously and aggressively shaped by a single functional group or a single ideology, whatever it may be." This statement reflects Levitt's perception of danger flowing from the concern of business with social problems—Levitt fears the creation of a monolithic society controlled by a coalition of business and government. Levitt's prescription is to let business focus on long-run profit maximization while government attends to the general social welfare. Further, Levitt expresses a strong conviction that a commitment to social responsibility by business seriously threatens capitalism. Levitt believes that business—for its own safety—should adhere to the basic principles of profit-maximization.

What form *should* the responsibility of business to society take?

ALBERT Z. CARR

Can an Executive Afford a Conscience?

Ask a business executive whether his company employs child labor, and he will either think you are joking or be angered by the implied slur on his ethical standards. In the 1970's the employment of children in factories is clearly considered morally wrong as well as illegal.

Yet it was not until comparatively recently (1941) that the U.S. Supreme Court finally sustained the constitutionality of the long-contested Child Labor Act, which Congress had passed four years earlier. During most of the previous eight decades, the fact that children 10 years old worked at manual jobs for an average of 11 hours a day under conditions of virtual slavery had aroused little indignation in business circles.

To be sure, only a few industries found the practice profitable, and the majority of businessmen would doubtless have been glad to see it stopped. But in order to stop it the government had to act, and any interference with business by government was regarded as a crime against God, Nature, and Respectability. If a company sought to hold down production costs by employing children in factories where the work did not demand adult skills or muscle, that was surely a matter to be settled between the employer and the child's parents or the orphanage.

To permit legitimate private enterprise to be balked by unrealistic do-gooders was to open the gate to socialism and anarchy—such was the prevailing sentiment of businessmen, as shown in the business press, from the 1860's to the 1930's.

Reprinted by permission of the author's estate and Marie Rodell, Literary Agent, from Albert Z. Carr, "Can an Executive Afford a Conscience?," *Harvard Business Review* 48 (July-August 1970): 58-64.

Every important advance in business ethics has been achieved through a long history of pain and protest.[1] The process of change begins when a previously accepted practice arouses misgivings among sensitive observers. Their efforts at moral suasion are usually ignored, however, until changes in economic conditions or new technology make the practice seem increasingly undesirable.

Businessmen who profit by the practice defend it heatedly, and a long period of public controversy ensues, climaxed at last by the adoption of laws forbidding it. After another 20 or 30 years, the new generation of businessmen regard the practice with retrospective moral indignation and wonder why it was ever tolerated.

A century of increasingly violent debate culminating in civil war had to be lived through before black slavery, long regarded as an excellent business proposition, was declared unlawful in the United States. To achieve laws forbidding racial discrimination in hiring practices required another century. It took 80 years of often bloody labor disputes to win acceptance of the principle of collective bargaining, and the country endured about 110 years of flagrant financial abuses before enactment of effective measures regulating banks and stock exchanges.

In time, all of these forward steps, once bitterly opposed by most businessmen, came to be accepted as part of the ethical foundation of the American private enterprise economy.

JESSE JAMES VS. NERO

In the second half of the twentieth century, with the population, money supply, military power, and industrial technology of the United States expanding rapidly at the same time, serious new ethical issues have arisen for businessmen—notably the pollution of the biosphere, the concentration of economic power in a relatively few vast corporations, increasing military domination of the economy, and the complex inter-relationship between business interests and the threat of war. These issues are the more formidable because they demand swift response; they will not wait a century or even a generation for a change in corporate ethics that will stimulate businessmen to act.

The problems they present to business and our society as a whole are immediate, critical, and worsening. If they are not promptly dealt with by farsighted and effective measures, they could even bring down political democracy and the entrepreneurial system together.

In fact, given the close relationship between our domestic economic situation and our military commitments abroad, and the perils implicit

Can an Executive Afford a Conscience? 55

in the worldwide armaments buildup, it is not extreme to say that the extent to which businessmen are able to open their minds to new ethical imperatives in the decade ahead may have decisive influence in this century on the future of the human species.

Considering the magnitude of these rapidly developing issues, old standards of ethical judgment seem almost irrelevant. It is of course desirable that a businessman be honest in his accountings and faithful to his contracts—that he should not advertise misleadingly, rig prices, deceive stockholders, deny workers their due, cheat customers, spread false rumors about competitors, or stab associates in the back. Such a person has in the past qualified as "highly ethical," and he could feel morally superior to many of those he saw around him—the chiselers, the connivers, the betrayers of trust.

But standards of personal conduct in themselves are no longer an adequate index of business ethics. Everyone knows that a minority of businessmen commit commercial mayhem on each other and on the public with practices ranging from subtle conflicts of interest to the sale of injurious drugs and unsafe automobiles, but in the moral crisis through which we are living such tales of executive wrongdoing, like nudity in motion pictures, have lost their power to shock.

The public shrugs at the company president who conspires with his peers to fix prices. It grins at the vice president in charge of sales who provides call girls for a customer. After we have heard a few such stories, they become monotonous.

We cannot shrug or grin, however, at the refusal of powerful corporations to take vigorous action against great dangers threatening the society, and to which they contribute. Compared with such a corporation or with the executive who is willing to jeopardize the health and well-being of an entire people in order to add something to current earnings, the man who merely embezzles company funds is as insignificant in the annals of morality as Jesse James is compared with Nero.

The moral position of the executive who works for a company that fails in the ethics of social responsibility is ambiguous. The fact that he does not control company policy cannot entirely exonerate him from blame. He is guilty, so to speak, by employment.

If he is aware that the company's factories pollute the environment or its products injure the consumer and he does not exert himself to change the related company policies, he becomes morally suspect. If he lends himself to devious evasions of laws against racial discrimination in hiring practices, he adds to the probability of destructive racial confrontations and is in some degree an agent of social disruption. If he knows that his company is involved in the bribery of legislators or government officials, or makes under-the-table deals with labor union officials, or uses the services of companies known to be controlled by criminal syndicates, he contributes through his work to disrespect for law and the spread of crime.

If his company, in its desire for military contracts, lobbies to oppose justifiable cuts in the government's enormous military budget, he bears some share of responsibility for the constriction of the civilian economy; for price inflation, urban decay, and shortages of housing, transportation, and schools; and for failure to mitigate the hardships of the poor.

From this standpoint, the carefully correct executive who never violates a law or fails to observe the canons of gentlemanly behavior may be as open to ethical challenge as the crooks and the cheaters.

"TOXINS OF SUPPRESSED GUILT"

The practical question arises: If a man in a responsible corporate position finds that certain policies of his company are socially injurious, what can he do about it without jeopardizing his job?

Contrary to common opinion, he is not necessarily without recourse. The nature of that recourse I shall discuss in the final section of this article. Here, I want to point out that unless the executive's sense of social responsibility is accompanied by a high degree of realism about tactics, then he is likely to end in frustration or cynicism.

One executive of my acquaintance who wrote several memoranda to his chief, detailing instances of serious environmental contamination for which the company was responsible and which called for early remedy, was sharply rebuked for a "negative attitude."

Another, a successful executive of a large corporation, said to me quite seriously in a confidential moment that he did not think a man in a job like his could afford the luxury of a conscience in the office. He was frank to say that he had become unhappy about certain policies of his company. He could no longer deny to himself that the company was not living up to its social responsibilities and was engaged in some political practices that smacked of corruption.

But what were his options? He had only three that he could see, and he told me he disliked them all:

If he argued for a change in policies that were helping to keep net earnings high, he might be branded by his superiors as "unrealistic" or "idealistic"—adjectives that could check his career and might, if he pushed too hard, compel his resignation.

Continued silence not only would spoil his enjoyment of his work, but might cause him to lose respect for himself.

If he moved to one of the other companies in his industry, he would merely be exchanging one set of moral misgivings for another.

He added with a sigh that he envied his associates whose consciences had never developed beyond the Neanderthal stage and who had no difficulty in accepting things as they were. He said he wondered whether he ought not to try to discipline himself to be as indifferent as they to the social implications of policies which, after all, were common in business.

Perhaps he made this effort and succeeded in it, for he remained with the company and forged ahead. He may even have fancied that he had killed his conscience—as the narrator in Mark Twain's symbolic story did when he gradually reached the point where he could blithely murder the tramps who came to his door asking for handouts.

But conscience is never killed; when ignored, it merely goes underground, where it manufactures the toxins of suppressed guilt, often with serious psychological and physical consequences. The hard fact is that the executive who has a well-developed contemporary conscience is at an increasing disadvantage in business unless he is able to find some personal policy by which he can maintain his drive for success without serious moral reservations.

DISTRUSTFUL PUBLIC

The problem faced by the ethically motivated man in corporate life is compounded by growing public distrust of business morality.

The corporation executive is popularly envied for his relative affluence and respected for his powers of achievement, but many people deeply suspect his ethics—as not a few successful businessmen have been informed by their children. Surveys made in a number of universities across the country indicate that a large majority of students aiming at college degrees are convinced that business is a dog-eat-dog proposition, with which most of them do not want to be connected.

This low opinion is by no means confined to youngsters; a poll of 2,000 representative Americans brought to light the belief of nearly half of them that "most businessmen would try anything, honest or not, for a buck."[2] The unfairness of the notion does not make it less significant as a clue to public opinion. (This poll also showed that most Americans are aware of the notable contributions of business to the material satisfactions of their lives; the two opinions are not inconsistent.)

Many businessmen, too, are deeply disturbed by the level of executive morality in their sphere of observation. Although about 90% of executives in another survey stated that they regarded themselves as "ethical," 80% affirmed "the presence of numerous generally accepted practices in their industry which they consider unethical," such as bribery of government officials, rigging of prices, and collusion in contract bidding.[3]

The public is by no means unaware of such practices. In conversations about business ethics with a cross-section sampling of citizens in a New England town, I found that they mentioned kickbacks and industrial espionage as often as embezzlement and fraud. One man pointed out that the kickback is now taken so much for granted in corporations that the Internal Revenue Service provides detailed instructions for businessmen on how to report income from this source on their tax returns.

The indifference of many companies to consumers' health and safety was a major source of criticism. Several of the persons interviewed spoke of conflicts of interest among corporation heads, accounts of which had been featured not long before in the press. Others had learned from television dramas about the ruthlessness of the struggle for survival and the hail-fellow hypocrisy that is common in executive offices.

Housewives drew on their shopping experience to denounce the decline in the quality of necessities for which they had to pay ever-higher prices. Two or three had read in *Consumer Reports* about "planned obsolescence."

I came to the conclusion that if my sample is at all representative—and I think it is—the public has learned more about the ways of men in corporate life than most boards of directors yet realize.

These opinions were voiced by people who for the most part had not yet given much thought to the part played by industrial wastes in the condition of the environment, or to the inroads made on their economic well-being by the influence of corporation lobbyists on military decision makers. It is to be expected that if, as a result of deteriorating social and economic conditions, these and other major concerns take on more meaning for the public, criticism of business ethics will widen and become sharper.

If the threats of widespread water shortage in the 1970's and of regional clean air shortages in the 1980's are allowed to materialize, and military expenditures continue to constrict civilian life, popular resentment may well be translated into active protest directed against many corporations as well as against the government. In that event, the moral pressure on individual executives will become increasingly acute.

Regard for public opinion certainly helped to influence many companies in the 1950's and 1960's to pledge to reduce their waste discharges

Can an Executive Afford a Conscience? 59

into the air and water and to hire more people with dark skins. Such declarations were balm for the sore business conscience.

The vogue for "social responsibility" has now grown until, as one commentator put it, "pronouncements about social responsibility issue forth so abundantly from the corporations that it is hard for one to get a decent play in the press. Everybody is in on the act, and nearly all of them actually mean what they say!"[4] More than a few companies have spent considerable sums to advertise their efforts to protect a stream, clean up smokestack emissions, or train "hardcore unemployables."

These are worthy undertakings, as far as they have gone, but for the most part they have not gone very far. In 1970 it has become obvious that the performance of U.S. corporations in the area of social responsibility has generally been trivial, considering the scope of their operations.

BEHIND THE BOARDROOM DOOR

No company that I have ever heard of employs a vice president in charge of ethical standards; and sooner or later the conscientious executive is likely to come up against a stone wall of corporate indifference to private moral values.

When the men who hold the real power in the company come together to decide policy, they may give lip service to the moral element in the issue, but not much more. The decision-making process at top-management levels has little room for social responsibilities not definitely required by law or public opinion.

Proposals that fail to promise an early payoff for the company and that involve substantial expense are accepted only if they represent a means of escaping drastic penalties, such as might be inflicted by a government suit, a labor strike, or a consumer boycott. To invest heavily in antipollution equipment or in programs for hiring and training workers on the fringe of employability, or to accept higher taxation in the interest of better education for the children of a community—for some distant, intangible return in a cloudy future—normally goes against the grain of every profit-minded management.

It could hardly be otherwise. In the prevailing concept of corporate efficiency, a continual lowering of costs relative to sales is cardinal. For low costs are a key not only to higher profits but to corporate maneuverability, to advantage in recruiting the best men, and to the ability to at least hold a share of a competitive market.

Of the savings accruing to a company from lowered costs, the fraction that finds its way into the area of social responsibility is usually miniscule. To expend such savings on nonremunerative activities is regarded as weakening the corporate structure.

The late Chester A. Barnard, one of the more enlightened business leaders of the previous generation and a man deeply concerned with ethics, voiced the position of management in the form of a question: "To what extent is one morally justified in loading a productive undertaking with heavy charges in the attempt to protect against a remote possibility, or even one not so remote?"[5] Speaking of accident prevention in plants, which he favored in principle, he warned that if the outlay for such a purpose weakened the company's finances, "the community might lose a service and the enterpreneur an opportunity."

Corporate managers apply the same line of reasoning to proposals for expenditure in the area of social responsibility. "We can't afford to sink that amount of money in nonproductive uses," they say, and, "We need all our cash for expansion."

The entrepreneur who is willing to accept some reduction of his income—the type is not unknown—may be able to operate his enterprise in a way that satisfies an active conscience; but a company with a competitive team of managers, a board of directors, and a pride of stockholders cannot harbor such an unbusinesslike intention.

Occasionally, statesmen, writers, and even some high-minded executives, such as the late Clarence B. Randall, have made the appeal of conscience to corporations. They have argued that, since the managers and directors of companies are for the most part men of goodwill in their private lives, their corporate decisions also should be guided by conscience.

Even the distinguished economist A. A. Berle, Jr. has expressed the view that the healthy development of our society requires "the growth of conscience" in the corporation of our time.[6] But if by "conscience" he meant a sense of right and wrong transcending the economic, he was asking the impossible.

A business that defined "right" and "wrong" in terms that would satisfy a well-developed contemporary conscience could not survive. No company can be expected to serve the social interest unless its self-interest is also served, either by the expectation of profit or by the avoidance of punishment.

"Gresham's law" of ethics

Before responsibility to the public can properly be brought into the framework of a top-management decision, it must have an economic justification. For instance, executives might say:

Can an Executive Afford a Conscience? 61

"We'd better install the new safety feature because, if we don't, we'll have the government on our necks, and the bad publicity will cost us more than we are now saving in production."

"We should spend the money for equipment to take the sulfides out of our smokestacks at the plant. Otherwise we'll have trouble recruiting labor and have a costly PR problem in the community."

It is worth noting that Henry Ford II felt constrained to explain to stockholders of the Ford Motor Company that his earnest and socially aware effort to recruit workers from Detroit's "hard-core unemployed" was a preventive measure against the recurrence of ghetto riots carrying a threat to the company.

In another situation, when a number of life insurance companies agreed to invest money in slum reconstruction at interest rates somewhat below the market, their executives were quick to forestall possible complaints from stockholders by pointing out that they were opening up future markets for life insurance. Rationally, the successful corporate manager can contemplate expense for the benefit of society only if failure to spend points to an eventual loss of security or opportunity that exceeds the cost.

There can be no conscience without a sense of personal responsibility, and the corporation, as Ambrose Bierce remarked, is "an ingenious device for obtaining individual profit without individual responsibility." When the directors and managers of a corporation enter the boardroom to debate policy, they park their private consciences outside.

If they did not subordinate their inner scruples to considerations of profitability and growth, they would fail in their responsibility to the company that pays them. A kind of Gresham's Law of ethics operates here; the ethic of corporate advantage invariably silences and drives out the ethic of individual self-restraint.

(This, incidentally, is true at every level of the corporate structure. An executive who adheres to ethical standards disregarded by his associates is asking for trouble. No one, for example, is so much hated in a purchasing department where graft is rife as the man who refuses to take kickbacks from suppliers, for he threatens the security of the others. Unless he conforms, they are all too likely to "get him.")

The crucial question in boardroom meetings where social responsibility is discussed is not, "Are we morally obligated to do it?" but, rather, "What will happen if we don't do it?" or, perhaps, "How will this affect the rate of return on investment?"

If the house counsel assures management that there will be no serious punishment under the law if the company does not take on the added expense, and the marketing man sees no danger to sales, and the public relations man is confident he can avoid injury to the corporate image, then the money, if it amounts to any considerable sum, will not be spent—social responsibility or no social responsibility.

Even the compulsion of law is often regarded in corporate thinking as an element in a contest between government and the corporation, rather than as a description of "right" and "wrong." The files of the Federal Trade Commission, the Food and Drug Administration, and other government agencies are filled with records of respectable companies that have not hesitated to break or stretch the law when they believed they could get away with it.

It is not unusual for company managements to break a law, even when they expect to be caught, if they calculate that the fine they eventually must pay represents only a fraction of the profits that the violation will enable them to collect in the meantime. More than one corporate merger has been announced to permit insiders to make stock-market killings even though the companies concerned recognized that the antitrust laws would probably compel their eventual separation.

WHAT CAN THE EXECUTIVE DO?

One can dream of a big-business community that considers it sound economics to sacrifice a portion of short-term profits in order to protect the environment and reduce social tensions.

It is theoretically conceivable that top managers as a class may come to perceive the profound dangers, for the free-enterprise system and for themselves, in the trend toward the militarization of our society, and will press the government to resist the demand for nonessential military orders and overpermissive contracts from sections of industry and elements in the Armed Services. At the same level of wishfulness, we can imagine the federal government making it clear to U.S. companies investing abroad that protection of their investments is not the government's responsibility.

We can even envisage a time when the bonds of a corporation that is responsive to social needs will command a higher rating by Moody's than those of a company that neglects such values, since the latter is more vulnerable to public condemnation; and a time when a powerful Executive League for Social Responsibility will come into being to stimulate and assist top managements in formulating long-range economic policies that embrace social issues. In such a private-enterprise utopia the executive with a social conscience would be able to work without weakening qualms.

Can an Executive Afford a Conscience? 63

In the real world of today's business, however, he is almost sure to be a troubled man. Perhaps there are some executives who are so strongly positioned that they can afford to urge their managements to accept a reduced rate of return on investment for the sake of the society of which they are a part. But for the large majority of corporate employees who want to keep their jobs and win their superiors' approbation, to propose such a thing would be inviting oneself to the corporate guillotine.

He is not powerless

But this does not necessarily mean that the ethically motivated executive can do nothing. In fact, if he does nothing, he may so bleach his conception of himself as a man of conviction as to reduce his personal force and value to the company. His situation calls for sagacity as well as courage. Whatever ideas he advocates to express his sense of social responsibility must be shaped to the company's interests.

Asking management flatly to place social values ahead of profits would be foolhardy, but if he can demonstrate that, on the basis of long-range profitability, the concept of corporate efficiency needs to be broadened to include social values, he may be able to make his point without injury—indeed, with benefit—to his status in the company. A man respected for competence in his job, who knows how to justify ethically based programs in economic terms and to overcome elements of resistance in the psychology of top management, may well be demonstrating his own qualifications for top management.

In essence, any ethically oriented proposal made to a manager is a proposal to take a longer-range view of his problems—to lift his sights. Nonethical practice is shortsighted almost by definition, if for no other reason than that it exposes the company to eventual reprisals.

The longer range a realistic business projection is, the more likely it is to find a sound ethical footing. I would go so far as to say that almost anything an executive does, on whatever level, to extend the range of thinking of his superiors tends to effect an ethical advance.

The hope and the opportunity of the individual executive with a contemporary conscience lies in the constructive connection of the long economic view with the socially aware outlook. He must show convincingly a net advantage for the corporation in accelerating expenditures or accepting other costs in the sphere of social responsibility.

I was recently able to observe an instance in which an executive persuaded his company's management to make a major advance in its antipollution policy. His presentation of the alternatives, on which he had spent weeks of careful preparation, showed in essence that, under his plan, costs which would have to be absorbed over a three-year period would within six years prove to be substantially less than the potential costs of less vigorous action.

When he finished his statement, no man among his listeners, not even his most active rivals, chose to resist him. He had done more than serve his company and satisfy his own ethical urge; he had shown that the gap between the corporate decision and the private conscience is not unbridgeable if a person is strong enough, able enough, and brave enough to do what needs to be done.

It may be that the future of our enterprise system will depend on the emergence of a sufficient number of men of this breed who believe that in order to save itself business will be impelled to help save the society.

NOTES

1. For amplifications of this view, see Robert W. Austin, "Responsibility for Social Change," HBR July-August 1965, p. 45; and Theodore Levitt, "Why Business Always Loses," HBR March-April 1968, p. 81.

2. Louis B. Harris and Associates, in a survey reported at a National Industrial Conference Board meeting, April 21, 1966.

3. Raymond C. Baumhart, S.J., "How Ethical Are Businessmen?" HBR July-August 1961, p. 6.

4. Theodore Levitt, "The Dangers of Social Responsibility," HBR September-October 1958, p. 41.

5. *Elementary Conditions of Business Morals* (Berkeley, Committee on the Barbara Weinstock Lectures, University of California, 1958).

6. *The Twentieth Century Capitalist Revolution* (New York, Harcourt, Brace & Company, 1954), pp. 113-114.

GEORGE CABOT LODGE

Top Priority: Renovating Our Ideology

We are living in a time of growing suspicion about the purposes and effectiveness of the major institutions of the United States—business, government, the universities, and the churches, among others. We are also living in a time when great things must be done quickly. We are confronted with social problems on an unprecedented scale—so large a scale, in fact, that we now use the all-embracing term "environmental crisis" to describe them as a group.

To many people, it seems that it is business's job to meet this crisis —to bring to bear its particular skills, its huge resources, and its unique talent for getting the job done. The social responsibility of business is assumed today, not merely discussed or suggested; and few seem to doubt that if U.S. business were to concentrate its power on the body of the problems of U.S. society, those problems would yield to its assault.

Can business make such a unified assault? As matters stand today, I do not believe it can do so directly. Disunity and alienation abound. The ideological bridgework that related the timeless values of our Western civilization to the real world and guided the activities of our institutions has become palsied and obscure.

This is not new. As a nation we have tended to be unmindful of our ideology and we have allowed it to degenerate. Some social commentators, most notably Daniel Bell, have even said it is dead.[1] In spite of

---

Reprinted by permission of the author and publisher from George Cabot Lodge, "Top Priority: Renovating Our Ideology," *Harvard Business Review* 48 (September-October 1970): 43-55. © 1970 by the President and Fellows of Harvard College; all rights reserved.

the profound effect of this degeneration on the U.S. community, we have deferred the renovation of our ideology. We have been able to do this, in part, because its function has been filled, on a temporary basis, by a continuous series of national crises—the great depression, World War II, the threat of communism, and so on—each of which evoked in its turn a degree of unity in the community.

Today, surely, we are in a crisis, but its exact nature is more controversial than earlier ones; its challenge is less clear; it is hardly unifying. To bring the community together so it can work on our problems in concert, we need a unifying vision. We need to examine and renovate our ideology.

Thus there is something business must do before it can make a broad attack on our social problems; it must press for a renovated ideology in the United States—a new, dynamic vision of the community and how it ought to operate. Without such guiding principles, any actions business can take to benefit the society at large are likely to lead to confusion and anarchy, an overall fragmentation of our efforts.

Before discussing this challenge to business in more detail, let me offer an example of a company that, by virtue of the business it is in, is under heavy pressure to take radical action, while its ideological context and foundation constrict or prohibit it from taking any radical action at all.

CON EDISON POWERLESS?

Consolidated Edison Company of New York is a privately owned utility that provides electricity, gas, and steam to some 9 million people in metropolitan New York and Westchester County. This company is an integral part of that vast community:

It sells $70 million worth of electricity a year to the City of New York alone.

It pays the City roughly $140 million a year in taxes.

It spends an average of $250 million a year on construction in the City, providing 20% of all the employment in the building trades in New York.

It is the second largest employer in the metropolitan area.

With the lowest rate of return of any private utility in the country, it has been plagued with myriad difficulties: power shortages causing blackouts and brownouts, high rates, customer complaints, and continued wrangling with government officials. At this writing, Charles Luce, Chairman of the Board of Con Edison, says that the company may well be unable to supply sufficient power to meet the demand it expects during the summer. It faces the need to ration power, to decide who will get it and who will not. To say that it is difficult to find a politically acceptable formula for rationing electricity in New York is to understate the case.

This shortage is hardly the result of mismanagement—the company is headed by exceptionally intelligent and competent managers. Instead, this problem and the other pressing problems of the company derive from the political structures that surround it and the tension, confusion, and competition of interests they embody. The ideological underpinning of these structures—the whole community and the company within it— is the real villain of the piece.

For example, the company is squeezed between its expenses and income. Company costs and services are determined by the City, directly or indirectly, while its rates—i.e., income—are subject to approval by a board at the state level.

Again, it badly needs a very large, new plant to keep pace with the demand, but completion of a 2-million kilowatt plant at Cornwall-on-the-Hudson has been blocked since 1965 by the court action of the Scenic Hudson Preservation Conference. It also needs additional nuclear-power facilities badly, but these are subject to the sometimes erratic determination of the AEC, which is concerned, among other things, with the public safety.

The matter of new power plants reduces to this: the area needs and wants more power, but it does *not* want, and perhaps cannot safely tolerate, any more plants. Years of debate in the courts have done nothing to erode this impasse.

When one looks at this situation in the context of the power needs of the northeastern United States over the next 50 years, and from the point of view of Con Edison's customers (not to mention its stockholders), one cannot help asking whether the company is properly constituted, in political terms. Would it not make more sense for the New York State Power Authority or a new northeast regional public power authority to be charged with the task of power production, leaving to private companies the distribution of power on a decentralized basis to meet local consumer needs?

The problems are too complex to do more than raise the question here. But if the answer to this question is *yes,* as it seems it might well be, then we must confront the task of forcing this change through the enormous tangle of political jurisdictions and interests which must be consolidated and rationalized for such a change to take place. Robert Wood, the noted urbanologist, for example, tells us that from the top of the Empire State Building on a clear day, one can see 1,400 political jurisdictions.

There is also the formidable ideological obstacle which any notion of "public power" causes in the mind of Con Edison itself. Formed in 1936 by a group of powerful New York financiers, the company has religiously opposed any and all suggestions that any of its operations be governmentally controlled. In earlier times, it had sufficient political clout to make its will felt. Today the old religion survives, but the clout is fast disappearing. Not only is efficient service to the community involved, but also return to Con Edison shareholders. It may well be that by turning power production over to a public authority the company would be more profitable. We face an odd irony: the company may be willing to sacrifice profits for a noble ideology of privacy.

Hence, it is in the interest of Con Edison and of business in general to press and assist government to come to this confrontation. Any lingering delay out of affection for the status quo would seem to be unprofitable folly.

Origins of impotence

How has it happened that a dynamic utility, whose services are necessary to the very continuance of life in New York City, has been shackled into impotence? Its problems, which are also its community's problems, it apparently cannot solve. We ought to ask why this situation exists, how it could have come about. The answer will help explain what business can do, and *must* do, before it can cope effectively in today's environment.

Finding the answer to this question entails some discussion of "official" American political and social theory—ideology—and of our practical way of life, which has, especially for the businessman, usually been at variance with the theory. This kind of discussion is ordinarily distasteful to the businessman, who prefers to leave ideology strictly alone and to concentrate on the practical question of how to get something done. His implicit pragmatism leads him away from theories in general. Interestingly, it is in large part exactly this pragmatic approach that has undercut our ideology to the point where business lacks an exact idea of what its social responsibility is; and this has deprived business, even if it *did* have such an idea, of knowing how to fulfill it.

LOCKE, PROPERTY AND 1776

Our Protestant beginnings, the challenges and opportunities of our national geography, indeed our entire national experience, have made us what we are: "primarily a people for whom the deed to be done strikes us first, and the theory for doing it comes along afterward, if at all."[2] This national predilection has been a great strength, but also a weakness. We have moved fast and far, relatively unencumbered by fear of inconsistency with political doctrine or theory, but in the process we have become increasingly confused about what we have done and where we are going.

Often, when an American is "up against it" ideologically—when he is abroad, say, and must describe the United States to a foreigner—this confusion becomes dramatically evident. The man will lapse into a quasi-official, ideological jargon that seriously misrepresents reality. He will speak of "capitalism" and "private enterprise," of "individualism" and "initiative," to people for whom these words may well mean abusive exploitation, selfishness, monopoly, imperialism, and worse.

Rarely does one hear an American abroad speak of his country as a social unit or hear him mention the vast array of restrictions, curbs, supports, subsidies, controls, bargains, and pressures—both governmental and nongovernmental—which we have installed to ensure that our "private enterprise system" maintains harmony with the public consensus concerning the nation's good. These measures, we feel, are vaguely un-American; they seem inconsistent with our image of ourselves; we see them as unavoidable, but somehow not entirely legitimate, necessities.

This formalistic jargon has its source in an ideology that lies deep within the U.S. community, an ideology which we have regularly and consistently ignored in working out the practical mechanics of our political, social, and economic order, but which we have never explicitly rejected or replaced, and which therefore retains a moral and political force. It is time that we identified and examined this ideology and its effect on us.

It comes to us from European political thought of the seventeenth century, via the Declaration of Independence of July 4, 1776. It is there that we find set down the inalienable rights of man which we believe it is the function of our government to safeguard. This Declaration asserts the primacy of *individual* rights and the quality of *individuals,* and limits the role of government to just those functions necessary to protect the individual and his property.

The utopian ideal our Declaration and Constitution thus represent had been formulated a century earlier by European philosophers, the most important of whom was John Locke. F.S.C. Northrop, Yale professor of law and philosophy, writes: "The traditional culture of the United States is an applied utopia in which the philosophy of John Locke defines the idea of the good."[3] Harvard's Louis Hartz says:

"Locke dominates American political thought as no thinker anywhere dominates the political thought of a nation. He is a massive national cliché."[4]

The influence of Locke's thought on American life has been various and profound. Indeed, more fertile soil for his philosophy could scarcely have been cultivated. The American had left the organic society of Europe for the atomistic one of America. Liberated from the feudal tradition and structures of Europe, he lived in the free air of a vast new frontier. He was indeed an individual, equal to all other individuals and able to feel his equality. There was property enough for all. As Jefferson wrote to John Adams: "Here everyone owns property or has a sufficient interest in it to guarantee its protection."[5]

Our national preoccupation with this strain of political thought has had three important consequences that relate to our present dilemma.

1. Government should exist, we believe, solely to protect the individual and his property.

Locke, significantly, said nothing about the relations between individuals; he therefore prescribed no social laws, either of God or of nature. The laws of civil and ecclesiastical government were for Locke mere conventions deriving their entire authority from the private opinions of the independent individuals in a society and their joint majority consent.[6] In Locke there are none of the organic social principles of Plato and Aristotle, for whom man was, in his essential nature, a "political animal." There is none of the idealism of Kant. Indeed, he sets out no criteria for communitarian existence.

Thus the two basic premises of Locke's theory of government and the Declaration of Independence arose in their familiar form: all men are born free and equal, and the origin and basis of government is "the consent of the governed."

Where the individual is his own concern and government's chief business is to protect him and his property, it is difficult for government to place the rights of society at large—human rights, if you will— above property rights. This is a consequence that we must hold in serious question today.

Do we really intend that any vote, no matter how democratic or consonant with the public needs, shall be unconstitutional if it violates the principles of private property? In our official tradition, we have intended exactly this. "The justification for the doctrine of private property is not democratic processes," writes Northrop. "Instead the preservation of private property is the justification for the existence of any government whatever, even a democratic one."[7]

The transcendent importance of property was appropriate and natural in the American ideology in 1776. But is it still effective today? What, for example, will be the sense of our political philosophy when most Americans are renters?

And again, how shall we define "property"? Surely Locke and the founding fathers did not have in mind the large publicly held corporations and conglomerates when they used the word. There is little private about such companies in the Lockean sense. Indeed, Adam Smith, following the spirit of Locke directly, had profound distrust for the British joint-stock companies, which he conceived as essentially public bodies; "being the managers of other people's money than their own [they] cannot well be expected to watch over it" with the "same anxious vigilance" as an individual over his property. "Negligence and profusion, therefore, must always prevail, more or less, in the management of the affairs of such a company."[8]

2. Hence, we believe, the least government is the best government.

The assumption, implicit in Locke, that the least (and weakest) government is the best, is at the root of Americans' suspicion and disrespect for government, particularly central government. Although this suspicion is apt to be submerged in times of crisis, as it was in World War II, for example, it quickly surfaces in normal times. But the ˙pattern of practical action we have built up for dealing with crises is extremely important in this connection, especially since we seem to live and act today in an atmosphere of "total" crisis.

Originally, we had only a small, weak government. Lockean influence in the United States impeded the establishment of a strong federal principle in the Constitution and strengthened the notion of states' rights. In the early days of the Republic, Hamilton and Jay were forced to bring forth new arguments, different from those of Jefferson and his Lockean followers, for the establishment of a federal system. These included the cultural unity of the colonies, the geographic unity of the country, and the aristocratic, elitist, thoroughly non-Lockean conception of government as planner and developer of the resources of an underdeveloped nation.

It is significant that Hamilton and Jay, like those who followed them, supported their position with *pragmatic*—not ideological—arguments. Neither they nor any of their successors challenged the rightness of Locke directly.

In the crisis of the Civil War the great test came, when Hamilton's admirer, Lincoln, took up the cause of the Union against the Lockean notion that the consent of the governed gave the South the right to secede. Lincoln victoriously pressed a pragmatic federalism that weakened forever the Lockean principle of "the less government, the better." The phrase lost none of its currency, but it did lose a large measure of its applicability.

Lincoln introduced another anti-Lockean concept which was to be carried forward and developed by Theodore Roosevelt, Woodrow Wilson, and Franklin D. Roosevelt; namely, the idea of the good state having a responsibility for the human and social welfare of the people and for planning the allocation of power and resources accordingly.

Again, however, it is significant how gingerly these men proceeded with their radical view, even in the midst of the crises of war and depression. They did not hesitate to take strong executive action, but they were very careful to justify it on the basis of public exigency; they avoided constitutional—*ideological*—questions as much as possible.

Even F.D.R. did not confront Locke and the Constitution directly. Hartz refers to "the experimental mood of Roosevelt, in which Locke goes underground, while problems are solved often in a non-Lockean way."[9] He goes on to say that "what makes the New Deal 'radical' is the smothering by the American Lockean faith of the socialist challenge to it." Roosevelt did not need and did not want a new ideology. Indeed, the last thing he would like to have been called was an ideologist, a socialist, or whatever.

Thus, the traditional ideology, as a concept, has repeatedly survived the onslaughts of pragmatic wisdom, although its practical force was continually diminished as the country grew through its crises and strengthened the federal principle.

3. This Lockean ideology has been thoroughly subverted by our pragmatic approach to both government and business.

When a problem presents itself, the typical American response is to improvise a workable solution pragmatically.

Considered in a body, a batch of solutions of this kind may lack ideological consistency, but, the pragmatist argues, no ideological bridgework is necessary for right action. Indeed, he says it is downright harmful; it tends to be rigid, artificial, authoritarian, confusing, and quickly outdated. He believes that the individual (or a group) can at any time apply values to the world almost intuitively—experimenting, testing, and modifying until he achieves a proper fit. To oversimplify, the pragmatist believes: that which works is good and true. Or, to put it in more specialized form, what works for one individual is good, presumably, for all.

But pragmatism slowly and steadily destroys Lockean thinking. As Hartz puts it, "Pragmatism...feeds on the Lockean settlement."[10]

Locke's laissez-faire, individualistic doctrine can be very easily adjusted to the notion that what works for the individual in experience and experiment, is useful and good.

If we combine this vulnerability with (a) the Darwinian lesson that only the fit survive and (b) the Protestant premise that success in the marketplace is a sign of God's blessing, we have the energetic ideology underlying traditional American business practice. That it is a gross perversion of Locke is obvious, since it has frequently entailed serious curtailment of the freedom and equality of individuals, which he held paramount.

The inequities of this perversion as well as the interests of business itself caused the emergence of interest groups as a vital part of the American political process. Seeking to press government to provide whatever supports served their cause at the moment—be it subsidies, protection, or regulation and control—interest groups have further compounded the break between American political practice and the Lockean view of government and democratic individualism. That our times ring with the charge of hypocrisy is not surprising.

Interest group pluralism. While pragmatism has strengthened the federal principle, it has also contributed heavily to our tradition of interest group pluralism. America's central political problem has been the classical liberal dilemma of majority rule versus minority rights. Interest group pluralism partially resolves this dilemma by playing on the power consoles of government to bring about the balanced change. The well-known pendulum effect produced by the interests of business and labor is a good example.

In spite of the undoubted practicality—the essential *pragmatism*—of interest group pluralism, however, it has today left us with profound distortions. Two of these distortions seem particularly relevant here:

First, and most important, it has brought us into conflict with our basic ideology, the freedom and equality of the individual—particularly the black American, the Mexican-American, the American Indian, and other such groups, which have been denied not only the opportunity to form effective interest groups but also the right of access to the political process itself.

The power, force, and necessity of radical black organizations, for example, are perfectly consistent with the demands of interest group pluralism. The American system invites the crises which such movements evoke—crises which, in turn, it has hitherto resolved by its pragmatic improvisations, which, in *their* turn, laid the foundations for the additional splintering of the society. "Today's solution to today's problem" is not a prescription that conduces to far-sighted statesmanship.

Second, interest group pluralism has also seriously warped the activities of government, directing them toward whatever interest group has the most compelling force. Theodore J. Lowi persuasively documents the effects, for example, of farmers on the Agriculture Department and its programs, of business on the Commerce Department, of labor on the Labor Department, and of other interests on specialized agencies of the government.[11] He argues that during the last 40 years government has taken onto itself virtually unlimited scope of power, but at the same time has reaffirmed and expanded the notion of interest group pluralism. Thus government has become powerful but formless, a victim of the "pulling and hauling among competing interest groups."[12]

The liberal state, he contends, has a weakened thrust and has become essentially amoral. It has diminished the power and meaning of law by leaving the power to make public policy to private interests. For the requirements of standards it has substituted the requirement of participation. It has solidified bureaucratic conservatism and all in all created a "crisis of public authority . . . [and] the crisis deepens because its nature has not yet been discovered. . . . The zeal of pluralism for the group and its belief in a natural harmony of group competition has tended to break down the very ethic of government by reducing the essential conception of government to nothing more than another set of mere interest groups."[13]

The failure is particularly notable when important segments of society—blacks, militant youth, or whatever—are excluded from prevailing interest groups or when public problems, such as environmental pollution and the complex of urban difficulties, are not solvable through interest group activity.

Consolidated Edison, to return to my opening example, is a company hedged in by many interest groups in a free-for-all in which the only winner can be the principle that a society divided against itself cannot stand. This is no time to assume that "something can be worked out" by all the competing groups. It is a time to think seriously about the shape we want the solution to take.

THE VESTIGE OF IDEOLOGY . . .

Our ideology has always remained largely inexplicit. Our pragmatic preference has caused us to avoid any rigorous or continuing formulation of ideology. We have preferred to remain flexible.

Equally, the pragmatic enlargement and extension of the role and function of government by every powerful President has been profoundly discordant with the Lockean ideology with which we were founded as a nation—that government is a necessary evil, an unfortunate infringement on individual freedom, and best when it governs least.

The vestige of this ideal, as it exists today, is still surrounded with and bolstered by a body of myths—of the frontiersman, who tames the wilderness and is a law unto himself; of Horatio Alger, who can rise from rags to riches by virtue of his own effort; of the founding fathers, as "men of superhuman wisdom and courage whose deeds correspond to the work of Theseus in founding Athens";[14] of nationalism, which so often has manifested itself in the notion that the American people have a mission or destiny that the nation as a whole has an obligation to fulfill; and, among all these others, of the near omnipotence of American business.

Although these myths have been profoundly useful in uniting our social and political order, they have also been profoundly misleading in some ways. Notably, they have retarded and restrained sober and realistic thought about the need to reform our ideology. Today American ideology and the myths surrounding it are under attack.

...and the demand for change

This attack is aimed primarily at the two most significant embodiments of American ideology, government and business. It is ill-formed and contradictory, like the interest groups from which it emanates. Individualistic assertions are mixed with broad demands of the community; complaints about the power, size, and bureacracy of government are interspersed with calls for more powerful and far-reaching government; and, most relevant for my purposes here, in many instances the assault on business raises issues which business itself is powerless to resolve.

The attack takes the form of a demand for change—rapid, radical, revolutionary change. In presupposing that the direction which the change is to follow is clear or determined, the attackers confuse themselves. The direction is unclear, as are the priorities of change, the speed with which it should be made, and the means to be used. Further, we can no longer attempt to deal with radical change pragmatically because the distinction between what is "desirable" change and what is "undesirable" change is *fundamentally an ideological distinction.* For example:

We hold abolition of or infringement on private property to be undesirable change, and yet pressures grow to control and regulate the uses of property ever more stringently in accordance with certain public goals, such as clean air and water, urban development, and improved transportation systems.

Full employment is desirable, according to the Employment Act of 1946, but its achievement will conflict with several components of traditional ideology, particularly the notions of the limited role of government in planning the allocation of resources and of manpower and the freedom of individuals and of enterprises to locate where they choose and produce what the market will buy at any point in time.

Competition is held to be ideologically desirable, and yet increasingly it appears that consumers are better served in many instances by economies of scale that restrain competition.

The concept of profit, which is profoundly ideological, raises other conflicts. In the abstract, profitability is the best measure we have of effective economic employment of economic resources. It objectively tests business's performance; it provides business with its singular strength as an economic institution, namely, its capacity to go out of business.

On the other hand, profit is really a somewhat ineffective measure of business's social and political effectiveness. If profit, therefore, is taken as the sole or major aim of business, other social and political relationships between business and the surrounding environment may be neglected, and business may ultimately be denied even its objective of profit.

It is these "other relationships," concerning business's purpose, function, and role in the community, that rest on and are derived from ideology. They evolve out of the social and political order through the priorities it sets and the rules it adopts for fulfilling its fundamental values. Unless we explicitly describe the comprehensive vision of a functioning ideology, we cannot see these relationships clearly as they affect each other in their combinations in the real world.

Therefore, it is no longer realistic to suppose that the old ideology can remain part of the substratum of American life while pragmatic adjustments are made on the surface. The speed and profundity of change required are too great to allow for the short-term experimentation of the pragmatist; we need some new and more explicit framework to bring basic values to bear directly on the world around us.

MAIN CHALLENGE TO BUSINESS

What can business do in this situation—what *should* it do? Let us first look at the ways in which ideology and pragmatism have affected business's capabilities in promoting change, and then at business's specific efforts in three directions (black urban areas, ecology, and transportation). I hope to make it clear that many people, including many businessmen, have misconceived the kind of response which business can and ought to make.

The calls for help

As I said before, there is a disposition to suppose that U.S. business can solve the social and socio-technological problems of our time. The opinion is heard that if business wanted to—if it were "socially responsible"—it could effectively address the problems that plague our major cities, such as poverty, housing, unemployment, and even transportation and education; it could wipe out the dreadful blight of pollution; and it could even set about the establishment of a new world order through the workings of multinational enterprises.[15] Business, it is said, is engaged in a war with the evils of our time, a war it must win.[16] This view which is held, oddly enough, by government leaders, businessmen, liberals, conservatives, and bomb-throwing extremists alike, is a reflection of the traditional American myth that business is nearly omnipotent.

"The new demand," Peter Drucker says, "is for business to *make* social values and beliefs, *create* freedom for the individual, and *altogether produce* the good society."[17] The readiness of business to respond to such a call is understandable—after all, the quality of life in our society is obviously connected to the interests of business. Business cannot sell to a sick society, and improving the general quality of life offers business new and rewarding opportunities. Businessmen are mindful of their consciences and their images. Also, the penalty for neglect is high in terms of public outcry and government reaction.

The historical efficiency and effectiveness with which business has responded to various national calls for help is in all our memories. Indeed the techniques and systems of American management are among our most renowned achievements. Hence the demand that business apply its techniques to problems which government is finding it increasingly difficult to manage is not only understandable but profoundly harmonious with traditional ideology, which limits the role of government and glorifies the individual, his initiative, and his property, and, by extension, the "private" sector.

The dangers in making an oversimplified response to this siren call, however, are manifold. Businessmen and the technical experts under their command are frequently unprepared to deal with the political questions involved, and the community is unwilling to relinquish such authority to them.

Those who would have business rush into the breach often cite the ability of business to muster tremendous support for wars and defense. Why, they ask, cannot business do the same in the sphere of social problems? The analogy between business action to improve the quality of life and war is imprecise and misleading. In a war (at least a war like World War II) the political and ideological cast within which all operations take place is clearly set out by the government and accepted by the community. Purposes and priorities are explicit: the production of guns, tanks, bullets, and airplanes to be used for the conquest of the enemy, the capture of his territory—of Berlin, Tokyo, or wherever.

Business participation in such an activity is, of course, politically and ideologically pure and simple, as it is in the space program; it works harmoniously within a structured setting to meet explicit needs and objectives. (The Viet Nam war is a different case, of course; the purposes of the war and of the political structure which the government has set up to execute it are neither clear nor acceptable to large portions of the community. Business participation in this effort has therefore been correspondingly messy.)

But if we are speaking about a war to remake our domestic society in the United States, then the initial prerequisite for its successful conduct is the definition of the struggle, the establishment of goals and priorities, and criteria for measuring victory. When such a political or ideological framework is in place, business can work efficiently within it. For unelected businessmen, however, to suppose that they can erect such a framework, is a suggestion of anarchy.

This truth is particularly relevant when the authority of government is in question as it is today. When a Senator or Cabinet officer comes to business and says: "The job of transforming our cities is yours, employing the great genius of American business," it is hard to say: "No, my friend. That is your job; we can only help when you have decided what will be the direction, the speed, and the design—the ideological basis—of the transformation. You are the politician; you are the elected ruler of the community; you are the sovereign state; you speak for the people. We serve you."

If business makes any answer other than this one, however, government is further weakened and distracted from its task, its authority further undermined, its power further dissipated. Perhaps, most important, if business responds by assuming this initiative, the planning processes of government are weakened and delayed, and the energy and effort of the society are further splintered and, finally, frustrated.

Helping urban black communities

There are inexorable, rapid, and unplanned changes taking place today in our cities. They result from the natural play of a wide variety of forces—the flow of jobs, the yearning of individuals for a better neighborhood, and the working of the community and the world.

Professor David L. Birch of the Harvard Business School has been using census data to measure what has been actually happening in our cities and what is happening today. He sees a process at work wherein the central portions of many older cities are slowly emptying of blacks who are going to the suburbs where jobs are more plentiful and living is better. The neighborhoods which they are abandoning are becoming the sites for high-cost office and apartment buildings.

Such a process does not happen quickly or uniformly. It is uneven; it involves critical questions of justice. Who, for example, should benefit from the rapid rise in land value resulting from this transformation—the city, the state, the rich whites, the poor blacks, the black community as a whole, or who? In many cases, the poorest, most hopeless, and least skilled are left behind in these areas, in desperate need of motivation and organization, of hope, mobility, and power. How is their future to be planned?

Overall, this is the question: In planning the transformation of our cities, do we harmonize all activities with natural demographic flows, do we resist these flows, or do we disregard them, opting for short-term, pragmatic responses to crises as they emerge?

The latter is the traditional course, as I have said, and experience shows us that it is filled with danger. In response to the turmoil in the ghettos in 1965 and 1966, a number of large corporations established some 25 plants in black areas of major cities, creating perhaps 8,000 new jobs.[18] It is too early to know definitely what the effect of this action has been. It lies athwart the natural flow which Birch has projected, since it aims at keeping blacks in the ghettos rather than helping them out. It is apparent that some of these plants are in extreme difficulty, falling far short of both economic and social goals.

Investments in such plants have been small, and companies may be willing to charge them off to "social responsibility." But these operations may prove to have been socially detrimental if it turns out that they have retarded a more effective, long-term community development.

Black capitalism. The encouragement of "black capitalism" through a variety of relatively undernourished and underplanned government programs aimed at helping individual blacks to own and operate ghetto businesses has also been disappointing. There is probably no part of the United States in which it is harder to run an effective, profitable business than the black communities of our cities. Is this where we should encourage relatively inexperienced and rare black managers to try their hand? Perhaps the wiser course would be to find ways in which black business can gain access to white markets where the money and the opportunities are more plentiful. More analysis, more planning, a broader vision, and better ideology are needed to provide the answers.

Government at the federal, state, city, and (eventually) regional levels has a capacity for community analysis and planning which business does not and cannot have. It is urgent that government perform this task. Business can encourage and assist it in doing so. The Committee for Economic Development (CED), which is itself an unusual agency for business-government planning, spoke of the need in its statement of July 1966:

"The bewildering multiplicity of small, piece-meal, duplicative, overlapping jurisdictions cannot cope with the staggering difficulties encountered in managing modern urban affairs. The fiscal effects of duplicate suburban separatism create great difficulty in the provision of costly central city services benefiting the whole urbanized area. If local governments are to function effectively in metropolitan areas, they must have sufficient size and authority to plan, administer, and provide significant financial support for solutions to area-wide problems."[19]

Black education. In a study of the education difficulties of our country, the CED comments:

"The schooling of deprived minorities in the slums and ghettos and in many poor rural areas has been a tragic failure and one that will not be corrected without a major revolution in the objectives, methods, and organization of the schools."[20]

Proposals have been made by both businessmen and black militants that education should be made competitive and turned over to private business. Perhaps, but before such a step is taken seriously, a sequence of profound and radical political and ideological decisions must be taken. If business moves haphazardly into the "education business," thus removing some pressure from government to do what the CED says it must, the results are likely to be chaotic and disappointing.

Had our ideology sprung more from Mill, Burke, Rousseau, or Hegel than from Locke, we might at this point readily assert that government has the responsibility and should have the capacity to perform the task of community analysis and planning as well as the task of determining priorities and allocating resources accordingly. We should contend that this is not a job which the unelected leaders of business can or should undertake. We might then argue as to what level of government would be most useful—federal, state, city, or some new regional form—and how government should be organized for the task.

Enchanted as we are by the Lockean myth, however, we cannot get over the very first hurdle. We are semiconsciously and inexplicitly bent on limiting the role of government, on keeping it haphazard and ad hoc, in the hope that we can somehow pull ourselves out of our troubles through an unplanned collection of pragmatic public and private actions as we have always done before, and still emerge with our Lockeanism intact.

Ideological backfires. I think it is worth pointing out that when the traditional ideology is applied more or less intact to our problems today (as it occasionally is), there is a chance that it will show itself a thoroughly inadequate tool.

The Urban Coalition can provide us with an example of overreliance on traditional ideology. The Urban Coalition was built on a combination of traditional Lockean individualism—the idea that private efforts can solve enormously complex public problems—and charity, which in many instances bordered on paternalism. In some cities (in Boston, in particular), the Coalition failed to appreciate the extent to which the black problem is one of power and that, consistent with the American way, power cannot be bestowed but must be won. To win it, the blacks must organize and participate in the political processes of the society as an interest group.

Organizing urban blacks is an enormously difficult task. They are short of leaders; they lack trust, confidence, and hope; and they are convinced of their weakness and vulnerability. They require unusually high levels of agitation before they can achieve the motivation needed to organize successfully. In many instances, the Urban Coalition found itself at loggerheads with those who were fostering this necessary agitation. Unable to see the nature of the political process required, the white leadership of the Coalition was repelled, embittered, and defeated.

Responding to our ecology

"Our cities," wrote Mayor John Lindsay, "have developed their own perverse ecology, each problem feeding another, often attracting 'solutions' which merely shift the crisis from one area to another. The need now is to think in terms of total environment."[21]

The ecological crisis of which we are becoming chaotically aware involves a web of values. To sort them, we require rigorous priorities and criteria for measuring our progress toward the good community. "Ours is an age," writes Lewis Mumford, "in which the increasingly automatic processes of production and urban expansion have displaced the human goals they are supposed to serve. Quantitative production has become . . . the only imperative goal."[22]

Consider air and water pollution—the green slime which the $1.5-billion U.S. detergent industry is spreading generously over lakes, rivers, and swamps; the noxious fumes from automobiles and factories; the hot water from nuclear power stations; and nuclear wastes themselves.

A *Fortune* survey of 250 top business executives reveals an understandably equivocal reaction to the problem of environmental pollution. Businessmen know they must do something, but they are not sure what. They are vaguely aware that business alone cannot possibly cope with the problem. They acknowledge the necessity for government initiative and leadership to "set the standards, regulate all activities pertaining to the environment and help finance the job with tax incentives," but, on the other hand, they are concerned lest government action "sap their financial vigor."[23]

They are deeply uncertain about the legitimacy and capacity of government to undertake "to regulate all activities pertaining to the environment," because the traditional American ideology and its companion political syndromes have created government singularly unprepared for the job.

Here is a case where the nation and every important interest group in it accept the necessity of radical action, but do not know how it should be taken. Each powerful group is afraid that it will be "hurt" more than others, and none of them—the conservationists and so on—is sufficiently strong and cohesive to have direct influence. Government, with its current ideological basis and pragmatic preferences, will find it difficult to act fast enough, and particularly if it is not pressed to do so by an interest group strong enough to make the point stick; and business is the only group powerful enough to do so. The main challenge to business is to do exactly this—to press government into taking a forceful lead.

The task of taking the lead is, of course, fundamentally ideological in the purest sense. It involves the vision which we have of the community which is in its becoming—a framework of ideas by which we connect accepted values to the real world of production and technology, and set the priorities and criteria by which we allocate resources. It is an ideology, however, which must be radically different from the individualistic Lockean notions with which we were born because it must, in very essence, be concerned with the community as a whole and with the interlocking web of forces and interests which compose and wrack it.

High among the priorities of the new ideology will be establishing the requirement of harmony between man and nature. Note the conflict between such a notion and traditional Western religion and myth, which emphasize control and exploitation of nature by man. The appeal of Eastern religions to youth foreshadows things to come.

We must now induce the political leadership to formulate such a new ideological framework.

Planning for transportation

In the early 1960's Mark Cresap, then president of Westinghouse Electric Corporation, heard a speech by President Kennedy about urban transportation—the evils of automobile traffic and pollution, the need for low-cost urban transit to move men from home to job, and the like. He responded to the Presidential call for help.

His response crystallized when Patrick J. Cusick, Jr., executive director of the Pittsburgh Regional Planning Association, challenged local industry—including Westinghouse—to provide a modern transit system that could effectively compete with the automobile and reduce rush-hour traffic. Funds were allocated to design an urban transit system, to be called Transit Expressway, which would be useful for medium-sized U.S. cities like Pittsburgh. As designed, the expressway offered fast, frequent, safe, and comfortable service at minimum cost. The transit line was to be constructed overhead, in the median strip, or beside automobile lanes.

Four different groups combined to put up $5 million for a test and demonstration in Pittsburgh: the Federal Housing and Home Finance Agency (now HUD), the Port Authority of Allegheny County, the Pennsylvania State Department of Commerce, and Westinghouse. As it turned out, the cost was considerably more than estimated; but Westinghouse, convinced that it had a good idea for meeting a grave national problem, made up the difference out of its own pocket.

The tests went well. The demonstration did show that Transit Expressway was indeed a relatively flexible way to meet the transit needs of medium-sized cities. The company found mayors and transit authorities in other cities generally enthusiastic, but it discovered that these officials weren't really the customers for the system. "The consultant to the authority is normally the real customer, and it's a rare consultant who will take a risk on an innovative system," said a Westinghouse executive. "The architects and city planners will accept the risk but they don't have the influence."

The company also encountered problems with bidding procedures; it seemed necessary to interest other companies in inventing transit systems in order to provide competition or else to turn Transit Expressway over to some sort of public body. Furthermore, with cities depending on dwindling real estate taxes for revenue, it became apparent that federal funds would be necessary to build transit expressways, and the federal government was neither organized nor prepared to consider such funding. Also, of course, the powerful highway and gasoline lobbies were still to be reckoned with. Westinghouse came to learn that there was some truth in Andrew Carnegie's warning that "pioneering don't pay." It persevered, however, and has sold several systems for use in airports and amusement parks. Meanwhile, the problem of urban transit gets worse.

It is possible to criticize Westinghouse for inadequate environmental analysis, but one cannot help but admire its motivation. The lesson we should learn here is that business cannot meet the transformational social needs of this country until political leadership provides the necessary ideology and structure. There is danger to itself, to the community, and to government in asking and expecting it to do so.

It is true that business may well be able to carry on more effectively a variety of activities previously undertaken by government, but it is equally possible that some activities of business are better performed by government. The critical questions of which activities, how controlled, for what purposes, in whose interests are, finally, political or ideological questions having to do with the basic values of the community and its ends. They are questions for politicians to decide, preferably with the strong support and assistance of business. Business depends for its life and profits on the answers, and answers there must be, or there will be chaos for which business itself will receive—perhaps unfairly—much of the blame.

SOCIAL RESPONSIBILITY?

The urgent and essential social responsibility of business and all other institutions in American life is to contribute to the building of a more adequate political structure and authority based on a clearer, more explicit, and more realistic ideology. The task is fundamentally political and requires the renovation of the authority and strength of government at all levels. As a political force, business can play an important role; but it will only delay the process and tempt disaster if it seeks to take on the task itself before the way is clear.

Business can and should finance and assist those who are working to design a new and more useful ideology and those who are prepared to work for its introduction. This may require modifying existing legislation governing business's political activity, and may also require changing conventional political channels and organizations, perhaps even creating new ones. There will certainly need to be changes in the structure of government and perhaps even in the Constitution itself.

In any case, business will be delaying the process and endangering itself if, with customary pragmatic ardor, it takes on the urgent task of change in the United States before the political order has produced a new and more useful ideology. Furthermore, it cannot wait for government to create such a framework. Government must be pressed to do so.

There can be no doubt that increasingly during the 1970's business will be subjected to mounting pressures to abandon "the single-minded pursuit of profits" and to take on "purposes linked with broad public responsibility."[24] These pressures will come from youth, ethnic minorities, consumer movements, antipollution groups, and the public in general. They will be intensified as government proves less and less willing or able to meet the needs of our time. It is surely in the interest and part of the purpose of business to meet community needs.

It can only do so, however, in partnership with effective government, in conformity with a new ideology which will better define and order the task at hand and set forth the criteria for the partnership itself. Otherwise, business will fail in doing what needs to be done and in failing will be blamed not only for its own inadequacy but for that of the political order as well.

In the conduct of its own affairs, of course, business also has a responsibility to obey both the spirit and the letter of the law; to have a just concern for the welfare of its employees; to be a good citizen in the community which it affects; and to use its resources, talents, and imagination to provide the goods and services which the community needs.

When business fails to hire a young graduate of the Harvard Business School or other such schools because he is black, as some painful evidence suggests was the case in the spring of 1970, business is not only acting irresponsibly and in violation of the law but is also gravely disloyal to the morality of individualism and equality which it pretends to extol. In such disloyalty lies disaster, because we are coming into a time—perhaps a dreadful time—when man is going to take his ideology seriously.

NOTES

1. Daniel Bell, *The End of Ideology: On the Exhaustion of Political Ideas in the Fifties* (New York, The Free Press of Glencoe, Inc., 1959).

2. F.S.C. Northrop, *The Meeting of East and West* (New York, The Macmillan Company, 1960), p. 67.

3. Ibid., p. 71.

4. Louis Hartz, *The Liberal Tradition in America* (New York, Harcourt, Brace and World, Inc., 1955), p. 140.

5. Ibid., p. 130.

6. Northrop, op. cit., p. 87.

7. Ibid., p. 97.

8. Adam Smith, *Wealth of Nations,* Book V, Chapter I, Part III, Article 1st, 2nd Section.

9. Hartz, op. cit., p. 260.

10. Ibid., p. 10.

11. Theodore J. Lowi, *The End of Liberalism: Ideology, Policy & the Crisis of Public Authority* (New York, W.W. Norton and Company, Inc., 1969).

12. Ibid., Preface, p. x.

13. Ibid., Preface, p. xiii; see also Arthur Schlesinger, Jr., *Washington Monthly,* January 1970, pp. 59-61.

14. Carl J. Friedrich, *Man and His Government* (New York, McGraw-Hill Book Company, Inc., 1963), p. 96.

15. See Frank Tannenbaum, "Survival of the Fittest," *Columbia Journal of World Business,* March-April 1968, p. 13.

16. See "The War That Business Must Win," *Business Week,* November 1, 1969, p. 63; and Irwin Miller, "Business Has a War to Win" (Thinking Ahead), HBR March-April 1969, p. 4.

17. Peter F. Drucker, editor, *Preparing Tomorrow's Business Leaders Today* (Englewood Cliffs, New Jersey, Prentice-Hall, Inc., 1969), p. 81; italics added.

18. William F. Haddad and G. Douglas Pugh, *Black Economic Development* (Englewood Cliffs, New Jersey, Prentice-Hall, Inc., 1969), pp. 151-152.

19. *Modernizing Local Government* (New York, Committee for Economic Development, July 1966), p. 44.

20. *Innovation in Education: New Dimensions for the American School* (New York, Committee for Economic Development, July 1968), p. 12.

21. John Lindsay, "The Plight of the Cities," *The Progressive,* April 1970, p. 29.

22. Lewis Mumford, *The City in History* (New York, Harcourt, Brace and World, Inc., 1961), p. 570.

23. Robert S. Diamond, "What Business Thinks: The Fortune 500-Yankelovich Survey," *Fortune,* February 1970, pp. 118 and 119.

24. *Fortune,* September 1969, p. 95.

THEODORE LEVITT

The Dangers of Social Responsibility

Concern with management's social responsibility has become more than a Philistinic form of self-flattery practiced at an occasional community chest banquet or at a news conference celebrating a "selfless example of corporate giving" to some undeserving little college in Podunk. It has become more than merely intoning the pious declarations of Christian brotherhood which some hotshot public relations man has pressed into the outstretched hands of the company president who is rushing from an executive committee meeting to a League of Women Voters luncheon. It has become a deadly serious occupation—the self-conscious, soul-searching preoccupation with the social responsibilities of business, with business statesmanship, employee welfare, public trust, and with all the other lofty causes that get such prominent play in the public press.

Contrary to what some uncharitable critics may say, this preoccupation is not an attitudinizing pose. Self-conscious dedication to social responsibility may have started as a purely defensive maneuver against strident attacks on big corporations and on the moral efficacy of the profit system. But defense alone no longer explains the motive.

THE NONPROFIT MOTIVE

When outnumbered by its critics at the polls, business launched a counterattack via the communications front. Without really listening to what

Reprinted by permission of the author and publisher from Theodore Levitt, "The Dangers of Social Responsibility," *Harvard Business Review* 36 (September-October 1958): 41-50. © 1958 by the President and Fellows of Harvard College; all rights reserved.

the critics alleged, business simply denied all that they were saying. But a few executives did listen and began to take a second look at themselves. Perhaps this criticism was not all captious. And so they began to preach to their brethren.

Before long something new was added to the ideological stockpile of capitalism. "Social responsibility" was what business needed, its own leaders announced. It needed to take society more seriously. It needed to participate in community affairs — and not just to take from the community but to give to it. Gradually business became more concerned about the needs of its employees, about schools, hospitals, welfare agencies, and even aesthetics. Moreover, it became increasingly clear that if business and the local governments failed to provide some of the routine social-economic amenities which people seemed clearly intent on getting, then that Brobdingnagian freewheeling monster in far-off Washington would.

So what started out as the sincere personal viewpoints of a few selfless businessmen became the prevailing vogue for them all. Today pronouncements about social responsibility issue forth so abundantly from the corporations that it is hard for one to get a decent play in the press. Everybody is in on the act, and nearly all of them actually mean what they say! Dedication reverberates throughout the upper reaches of corporate officialdom.

Happy New Orthodoxy

This, it is widely felt, is good. Business will raise itself in the public's esteem and thereby scuttle the political attacks against it. If the public likes big business, nobody can make capital by attacking it. Thus social responsibility will prolong the lifetime of free enterprise. Meanwhile, the profit motive is compromised in both word and deed. It now shares its royal throne with a multitude of noncommercial motives that aspire to loftier and more satisfying values. Today's profits must be merely adequate, not maximum. If they are big, it is cause for apologetic rationalization (for example, that they are needed to expand the company's ability to "serve" the public even better) rather than for boastful celebration. It is not fashionable for the corporation to take gleeful pride in making money. What *is* fashionable is for the corporation to show that it is a great innovator; more specifically, a great public benefactor; and, very particularly, that it exists "to serve the public."

The mythical visitor from Mars would be astonished that such a happy tableau of cooperative enterprise can create such vast material abundance. "People's Capitalism" is a resounding success. The primitive principle of aggrandizing selfishness which the Marxists mistakenly contend activates capitalism does not count at all. What we have instead is a voluntary association of selfless entrepreneurs singularly dedicated to creating munificence for one and all—an almost spiritually blissful state of cooperative and responsible enterprise. We are approaching a jet-propelled utopia. And, unlike some other periods in the short and turbulent history of capitalism, today has its practicing philosophers. These are the men busily engaged in the canonistic exposition of a new orthodoxy—the era of "socially responsible enterprise."

A Lonely Crowd

Occasionally some big business representative does speak less sanctimoniously and more forthrightly about what capitalism is really all about. Occasionally somebody exhumes the apparently antique notion that the business of business is profits; that virtue lies in the vigorous, undiluted assertion of the corporation's profit-making function. But these people get no embossed invitations to speak at the big, prestigeful, and splashy business conferences — where social responsibility echoes as a new tyranny of fad and fancy.

About a year ago, Frank O. Prior, then president and now board chairman of Standard Oil Company (Indiana), made a speech that was in part reminiscent of the late but apparently unlamented tycoon:

> Without terminological pretensions, pseudodialectical profundity, or rhetorical subtlety, he called on his big business colleagues to run their businesses as they are intended to be run — for profit. Regarding people who publicly consider profit making a doubtful morality, he called on his colleagues to "move over to the offensive," "to stand up and fight," to talk about profits in terms of their central function, and to throw all sentiment to the wolves.

His remarks must have sounded strange and harsh to people accustomed to a decade of viewing the corporation as a sort of miniature welfare state. Good human relations, he said, makes sense only when it "rests on a foundation of economic good sense and not just on sentiment. Sentiment has a tendency to evaporate whenever the heat is on. Economic good sense is durable."

Then he said: "You aren't supposed to use language like that these times. You're supposed to talk about high ideals using high-flown words. You're expected to be mainly aware of what they call social responsibility. . . . This is fine, but I still say management's No. 1 problem is profits."

And where was this vigorous affirmation of no-nonsense capitalism made? Was it Chicago, the seat of Standard's home office and one of the few places where some think the old orthodoxy retains some semblance of primeval integrity? No. This was too unreconstructed a view even for Chicago, the city of broad shoulders. So the Chamber of Commerce of distant and isolated Casper, Wyoming, provided the platform. And even there Prior could not afford to let his forthright remarks stand as bodly as he started out. The corporation, he allowed, must develop "a fuller sense of responsibility and a much broader outlook on the facts of life" — and prices should be "fair."[1]

The fact is, the profit motive is simply not fashionable today among emancipated conferees of the Committee for Economic Development or even in the National Association of Manufacturers. It has been dying a lingering, unmourned death for ten years. Rarely can a big business leader eulogize it today without being snubbed by his self-consciously frowning peers.

Things have come to a remarkable pass. And if anyone doubts it, let him contemplate the spectacle of a recent NAM convention interrupting its urgent deliberations to hear Siobhan McKenna reading Yeats's poetry, presumably to set an appropriate tone of cultural emancipation and dedication. Can anybody picture this happening 25 years ago? Or the board chairman of Sears, Roebuck & Co., stating, as he did last year, that not only is business's first responsibility social but business executives, like Secretary Benson's farmers, should look less to their pocketbooks and more to their spirits? Not even his suggestion that the top brass are overpaid ruffled any managerial feathers.[2]

The Self-Persuaders

There is nothing mysterious about the social responsibility syndrome. It does not reflect a change in businessmen's nature or the decay of self-interest. Quite to the contrary, often it is viewed as a way of maximizing the lifetime of capitalism by taking the wind out of its critics' sails. Under direct questioning it will be confessed that activities such as supporting company intramural athletic programs, hiring a paid director for a company choral society, or underwriting employee dramatic performances (even on company time) are not charity. They are hard-headed tactics of survival against the onslaught of politicians and professional detractors. Moreover, they build morale, improve efficiency, and yield returns in hard cash.

In other words, it pays to play. If it does not pay, there is no game. For instance, when it comes to choosing between the small Arkansas supplier whose town would be ruined if orders stopped and the Minneapolis supplier who can make it cheaper, there is no doubt that even the most socially responsible corporation will take the latter. It can always fall back on responsibility to its employees, stockholders, or customers, and still pretend it is being fashionable.

The Dangers of Social Responsibility

In some respects, therefore, all this talk *is* merely talk. It stops at the pocketbook. How, then, can it be dangerous? I think the answer is very simple: what people say, they ultimately come to believe if they say it enough, and what they believe affects what they do. To illustrate how innocent talk, intended in some respects simply for show, can haunt and change the very people who make it, look at what has happened to the Republican Party in the last few years. The example is only too painfully obvious to many executives:

For years the party fought the New Deal tooth and claw. Ultimately, in order to turn the Democrats out, it began matching the New Deal promise for promise. Republicans, it said, were not opposed to these measures; they simply wanted to do everything better and cheaper. The welfare state, it was emphasized, was lacking in sound business management.

Having finally ascended to office and proposing to stay in, a good many Republicans are now surprised to find themselves actually *doing* what they had promised during the election campaign. Some of the stalwarts who had lowered themselves to making expedient panegyric speeches about Modern Republicanism are now fighting a losing battle against its implementation.

The talk about social responsibility is already more than talk. It is leading into the believing stage; it has become a design for change. I hope to show why this change is likely to be for the worse, and why no man or institution can escape its debilitating consequences.

A NEW FEUDALISM

The function of business is to produce sustained high-level profits. The essence of free enterprise is to go after profit in any way that is consistent with its own survival as an economic system. The catch, someone will quickly say, is "consistent with." This is true. In addition, lack of profits is not the only thing that can destroy business. Bureaucratic ossification, hostile legislation, and revolution can do it much better. Let me examine the matter further. Capitalism as we like it can thrive only in an environment of political democracy and personal freedom. These require a pluralistic society—where there is division, not centralization, of power; variety, not unanimity, of opinion; and separation, not unification, of workaday economic, political, social, and spiritual functions.

We all fear an omnipotent state because it creates a dull and frightening conformity—a monolithic society. We do not want a society with one locus of power, one authority, one arbiter of propriety. We want and need variety, diversity, spontaneity, competition — in short, pluralism.

We do not want our lives shaped by a single viewpoint or by a single way of doing things, even if the material consequences are bountiful and the intentions are honorable. Mussolini, Stalin, Hitler, Franco, Trujillo, Peron, all show what happens when power is consolidated into a single, unopposed, and unopposable force.

We are against the all-embracing welfare state not because we are against welfare but because we are against centralized power and the harsh social discipline it so ineluctably produces. We do not want a pervasive welfare state in government, and we do not want it in unions. And for the same reasons we should not want it in corporations.

Dangerous Power

But at the rate we are going there is more than a contingent probability that, with all its resounding good intentions, business statesmanship may create the corporate equivalent of the unitary state. Its proliferating employee welfare programs, its serpentine involvement in community, government, charitable, and educational affairs, its prodigious currying of political and public favor through hundreds of peripheral preoccupations, all these well-intended but insidious contrivances are greasing the rails for our collective descent into a social order that would be as repugnant to the corporations themselves as to their critics. The danger is that all these things will turn the corporation into a twentieth-century equivalent of the medieval Church. The corporation would eventually invest itself with all-embracing duties, obligations, and finally powers — ministering to the whole man and molding him and society in the image of the corporation's narrow ambitions and its essentially unsocial needs.

Now there is nothing wrong as such with the corporation's narrow ambitions or needs. Indeed, if there is anything wrong today, it is that the corporation conceives its ambitions and needs much too broadly. The trouble is not that it is too narrowly profit-oriented, but that it is not narrowly profit-oriented *enough*. In its guilt-driven urge to transcend the narrow limits of derived standards, the modern corporation is reshaping not simply the economic but also the institutional, social, cultural, and political topography of society.

And there's the rub. For while the corporation also transforms itself in the process, at bottom its outlook will always remain narrowly materialistic. What we have, then, is the frightening spectacle of a powerful economic functional group whose future and perception are shaped in a tight materialistic context of money and things but which imposes its narrow ideas about a broad spectrum of unrelated noneconomic subjects on the mass of man and society.

Even if its outlook were the purest kind of good will, that would not recommend the corporation as an arbiter of our lives. What is bad for

The Dangers of Social Responsibility

this or any other country is for society to be consciously and aggressively shaped by a single functional group or a single ideology, whatever it may be.

If the corporation believes its long-run profitability to be strengthened by these peripheral involvements — if it believes that they are not charity but self-interest — then that much the worse. For, if this is so, it puts much more apparent justification and impulse behind activities which are essentially bad for man, bad for society, and ultimately bad for the corporation itself.

Example of Labor

The belief that one institution should encompass the complete lives of its members is by no means new to American society. One example can be taken from the history of unionism:

> In the latter part of the nineteenth century America's budding labor unions were shaken by a monumental internal struggle for power. On the one side were the unctuous advocates of the "whole man" idea of the union's function. For them the union was to be an encompassing social institution, operating on all conceivable fronts as the protector and spokesman of the workingman at large. In the process they acknowledged that the union would have to help shape and direct the aspirations, ideas, recreations, and even tastes — in short, the lives — of the members and the society in which they functioned.
>
> Opposing this view were the more pragmatic "horny-handed sons of toil," the "bread and butter" unionists. All they wanted, in the words of Samuel Gompers, was "more, more, more." At the time it was widely believed that this made Gompers a dangerous man. Lots of pious heads shook on the sidelines as they viewed the stark contrast between the dedicated "uplifters" and Gompers' materialistic opportunism. Who would not side with the "uplifters"? Yet Gompers won, and happily so, for he put American unionism on the path of pure-and-simple on-the-job demands, free of the fanciful ideological projects and petty intellectualism that drain the vitality of European unions.
>
> As late as the early 1930's the American Federation of Labor remained true to Gompers' narrow rules by opposing proposed Social Security legislation. And when, in the 1930's, the communists and the pseudo humanitarians pushed the "whole man" concept of unionism, they also lost. Today, however, without ideologically sustained or conscious direction, the more "progressive" unions have won the battle for what the nineteenth century ideologists lost. With all their vast might and organizational skill, these unions are now indeed ministering to the whole man:
>
> > Walter Reuther's United Auto Workers runs night schools, "drop-in" centers for retired members, recreation halls; supports grocery cooperatives; publishes and broadcasts household hints, recipes, and fashion news; and runs dozens of social, recreational, political, and action pro-

grams that provide something for every member of the family every hour of the day.

David Dubinsky's International Ladies' Garment Workers' Union has health centers, citizenship and hobby classes, low-cost apartment buildings, and a palatial summer resort in the Poconos.

A Toledo union promotes "respectability" in clothes and hair styles among teenagers as a way of counteracting leather-jacketed, duck-tail, rock-'n-roll delinquency.

Thus, the union is transformed in such cases from an important and desirable economic functional group into an all-knowing, all-doing, all-wise father on whom millions become directly dependent for womb-to-tomb ministration.

Toward a Monolithic Society

This is the kind of monolithic influence the corporation will eventually have if it becomes so preoccupied with its social burden, with employee welfare, and with the body politic. Only, when the corporation does this, it will do a much more thorough job than the union. For it is more protean and potentially more powerful than any democratic union ever dreamed of being. It is a self-made incubator and instrument of strength, more stable and better able to draw and hold a following than is the union. It creates its own capital and its own power by the sheer accident of doing what it is expected to do. (By contrast, the union can do nothing unless the corporation has done its job first. The union is essentially a luxury institution, not a necessity.)

I think it is significant that the right kinds of appeals to workers based on the corporation's materialistic self-interest are generally more successful than vague abstractions like "People's Capitalism." This is a truth the Soviet adherents to the materialistic philosophy stubbornly refused to learn as they tried with repeated failure to intrude ideological clack where only materialistic motives could work. Their denial of their own materialistic ideology finally surrendered to hard cash, first in the form of the "new economic policy," later through the system of "socialist competition," and now as industrial and agricultural decentralization.

If the corporate ministry of man turns out to be only half as pervasive as it seems destined to be, it will turn into a simonist enterprise of Byzantine proportions. There is a name for this kind of encircling business ministry, and it pains me to use it. The name is fascism. It may not be the insidious, amoral, surrealistic fascism over which we fought World War II, or the corrupt and aggrandizing Latin American version, but the consequence will be a monolithic society in which the essentially narrow ethos of the business corporation is malignantly extended over everyone and everything.

This feudalistic phantasmagoria may sound alarmist, farfetched, or even patently ridiculous. For one thing, it will be said, not all corporations see alike on all things. At the very least there will be the pluralism of differences arising out of corporate differences in productive functions and their differences as competitors. But look at it this way: When it comes to present-day corporate educational, recreational, welfare, political, social, and public relations programs, attitudes, ideas, promotions, and preferences, how much difference is there? Are they more alike or more unlike? Are they growing more similar or more dissimilar?

It may also be protested, "What is wrong with the corporate ideology, anyway? Who will deny the material abundance, the leisure, and even the aesthetic values it has created and fostered in the United States? Nobody!" But that is irrelevant. The point is: we do not want a monolithic society, even if its intentions are the best. Moreover, a group's behavior in the pluralistic, competitive past is no guarantee of its behavior once its reaches complete ascendance.

End of Capitalism

The power which the corporation gains as a sort of commercial demichurch it will lose as an agency of profit-motive capitalism. Indeed, as the profit motive becomes increasingly sublimated, capitalism will become only a shadow — the torpid remains of the creative dynamism which was and might have been. It will thrive in name only, at the convention rostrums and the chambers of commerce — a sort of verbal remains of the real thing, shakily sustained by pomp and ceremony. Like Rome, it will never know that when it believed itself at the height of its glory, it was undergoing its denouement. The incubus of the corporate ministry of man will be completely enthroned while capitalism withers away, a victim of its own haloed good intentions.

POWER INCORPORATED

The trouble with our society today is not that government is becoming a player rather than an umpire, or that it is a huge welfare colossus dipping into every nook and cranny of our lives. The trouble is, all major functional groups — business, labor, agriculture, *and* government — are each trying so piously to outdo the other in intruding themselves into what should be our private lives. Each is trying to mold the whole man into its own image according to its own needs and tastes. Each is seeking to extend its own narrow tyranny over the widest possible range of our institutions, people, ideas, values, and beliefs, and all for the purest motive — to do what it honestly believes is best for society.

And that is precisely what is wrong. It is this aspect of purity and service that is so nightmarish. It is perfectly legitimate for each group to fight for its survival by seeking to influence others. But somehow the past decade has produced a new twist: self-serious self-righteousness. And there is nothing more dangerous than the sincere, self-righteous, dedicated proselyte sustained by the mighty machinery of a powerful institution — particularly an economic institution. The reformer whose only aim is personal aggrandizement and whose tactics are a vulgar combination of compulsive demagoguery and opportunistic cynicism is much less dangerous than the social evangelist who, to borrow from Nietzsche, thinks of himself as "God's ventriloquist." As Greek tragedies show, there is nothing more corrupting than self-righteousness and nothing more intolerant than an ardent man who is convinced he is on the side of the angels.

When the spokesmen for such causes begin to make speeches and write books about their holy mission, to canonize their beliefs into faith, conviction, and doctrine, and to develop ways of thinking by which their particular institutional ambitions are ideologically sustained — that is the time for us to begin trembling. They will then have baptized their mission with a book — still the most powerful instrument of change devised by man.

American capitalism does not yet possess a dramatic ideological statement of the kind just described. But it is getting there. During the past decade business executives' bylines have appeared under an increasing number of book and article titles connoting a sense of mission, of reaching out—for example, *A Creed for Free Enterprise*,[3] " 'Skyhooks' (With Special Implications for Monday Through Friday),"[4] *New Frontiers for Professional Managers*,[5] and "Business Leadership and a Creative Society."[6] That such titles should be chosen and that they should appeal to the management community are, I believe, significant signs of the times. There is no doubt that the sense of zeal and social responsibility is increasing.

So far the movement is a young and rather unassuming one. But when it really gathers momentum, when its forms become crystallized and its primal innocence becomes more professionalized, its success should amaze us. The corporation is not handicapped by the cumbersome authority that has always characterized the church and the state. It can make its authority sweet as honey by making itself the embodiment of material welfare, of unbounded security, of decorous comfort, amusing diversion, healthful recreation, and palatable ideology. It can far surpass even the medieval Church in efficiency and power.

The Dangers of Social Responsibility

It may have no intention of doing this (and I firmly believe that this is the last thing that the apostles of corporate humanity want), but what we get is seldom what we want. History is fortuitous. It does not move on tracks made by rational social engineers.

Separate Functions

Business wants to survive. It wants security from attack and restriction; it wants to minimize what it believes is its greatest potential enemy — the state. So it takes the steam out of the state's lumbering engines by employing numerous schemes to win its employees and the general public to its side. It is felt that these are the best possible investments it can make for its own survival. And that is precisely where the reasoning has gone wrong. These investments are only superficially *easy* solutions, not the best.

Welfare and society are not the corporation's business. Its business is making money, not sweet music. The same goes for unions. Their business is "bread and butter" and job rights. In a free enterprise system, welfare is supposed to be automatic; and where it is not, it becomes government's job. This is the concept of pluralism. Government's job is not business, and business's job is not government. And unless these functions are resolutely separated in all respects, they are eventually combined in every respect. In the end the danger is not that government will run business, or that business will run government, but rather that the two of them will coalesce, as we saw, into a single power, unopposed and unopposable.

The only political function of business, labor, and agriculture is to fight each other so that none becomes or remains dominant for long. When one does reach overwhelming power and control, at the very best the state will eventually take over on the pretense of protecting everybody else. At that point the big business executives, claiming possession of the tools of large-scale management, will come in, as they do in war, to become the bureaucrats who run the state.

The final victor then is neither government, as the representative of the people, nor the people, as represented by government. The new leviathan will be the professional corporate bureaucrat operating at a more engrossing and exalted level than the architects of capitalism ever dreamed possible.

The functions of the four main groups in our economy — government, business, labor, agriculture — must be kept separate and separable. As soon as they become amalgamated and indistinguishable, they likewise become monstrous and restrictive.

TENDING TO BUSINESS

If businessmen do not preach and practice social responsibility, welfare, and self-restraint, how can management effectively deal with its critics, the political attacks, the confining legislation — that is, the things which have induced it to create its own private welfare state? The answer is fairly simple: to perform its main task so well that critics cannot make their charges stick, and then to assert forthrightly its function and accomplishments with the same aroused spirit that made nineteenth-century capitalism as great as it was extreme.

Present Failures

It seems clear that today's practices fall far short of this prescription. When it comes to material things, the accomplishments of American capitalism are spectacular. But the slate is not clean. American capitalism also creates, fosters, and acquiesces in enormous social and economic cancers. Indeed, it fights against the achievement of certain forms of economic and social progress, pouring millions into campaigns against things which people have a right to expect from their government and which they seem to want their government to provide. For example:

Business motives helped to create slums, and now business seems all too frequently to fight their abolition. The free operation of the profit motive has not abolished them. Indeed, it sustains them. But if abolishing slums is not a sound business proposition, business should cease its campaign against government doing a job which nobody in his right mind can deny should be done. If supporting state and federal efforts at urban renewal does not raise the public's esteem of business's good intentions, few things will. Certainly self-righteous claims of good intentions are not enough.

The same is true of health insurance, pensions, school construction, and other proposals for activities which are best handled by government (for reasons of administration as well as of ability to meet the commitments) and are therefore logical government functions. Businessmen will simply have to accept the fact that the state can be a powerful auxiliary to the attainment of the good life. This is particularly so in a free enterprise economy where there is a natural division of social and economic functions, and where this division is fortified by countervailing institutional checks and balances.

Yet in both word and deed business constantly denies the potentially beneficial role of the state. Where it does not fight the public interest, it often adopts a placid air of indifference or a vapid neutrality. Its most shameful indifference is in matters of civil rights. Although business operates in a system where the guarantee of civil rights is the bedrock of its own effective existence, management seldom raises a voice in support of civil rights — whether the issue is legislation or protecting some anonymous Joe Doakes against a Congressional kangaroo-court committee supposedly developing information for legislation.

Business must learn to speak for Joe Doakes when civil rights are involved. In doing this it would actually be speaking for itself. Civil rights are a single cloth; they cannot be curtailed for some without being curtailed for everybody. Hence to speak for Joe Doakes is to act in one's self-interest — especially in management's case, for when civil rights are gone, business loses not only freedom but also money.

Sensible Welfare

I am not arguing that management should ignore its critics. Some of them have made a good case from time to time against business's social delinquencies and against its shortsightedness in fighting practically all of Washington's efforts to provide security. (Indeed, if business had not always fought federal welfare measures, perhaps the unions would not have demanded them from business itself.)

Nor am I arguing that management has no welfare obligations at all to society. Quite to the contrary. Corporate welfare makes good sense *if* it makes good economic sense — and not infrequently it does. But if something does not make economic sense, sentiment or idealism ought not let it in the door. Sentiment is a corrupting and debilitating influence in business. It fosters leniency, inefficiency, sluggishness, extravagance, and hardens the innovationary arteries. It can confuse the role of the businessman just as much as the profit motive could confuse the role of the government official. The governing rule in industry should be that *something is good only if it pays*. Otherwise it is alien and impermissible. This is the rule of capitalism.

No matter how much business protests that saying this is redundant because it is exactly the rule being practiced, the fact is that it is *seldom* followed. Businessmen only say they practice it because it is another one of those sacred articles of the capitalist faith that must be regularly reaffirmed in speech and print. Their words are belied by some of their most common policies, such as:

The growing constellation of employee welfare programs — Do they really make good economic sense for the individual firm? I say they do not. Most company welfare measures — such as retirement, unemployment, and health benefits — are forms of mass insurance. They make economic sense only when operated on a compulsory national basis. The only conceivable basis on which it can be argued that they make economic sense when operated by individual companies is that they help attract and hold manpower. And that is seldom the primary motive. If there were adequate national mass insurance, the company that wants to attract and hold more and better manpower needs only to pay more. The whole thing would be cheaper and more efficient.

Stock purchase plans — These plans, which are one of the sacred appurtenances of "People's Capitalism," are justifiable only if they provide direct incentives to differentially superior performance. They are a menace and a drag on the economy when (as is often the case) their real object is to let the corporate insiders in on some easy capital gains gravy, or to immobilize the labor market by tying people to a particular company.

If the public wants protection against the uneven consequences of all-out capitalism, let it run to its unions and to government. If business wants protection against unions and government, let it fight for its cause on the open battlefield of manful contention — on the front of economic and political pressures. We are not back in the age of the robber barons, with its uneven matching of economic and political functional groups. Business, government, and unions are now each big and powerful enough to take care of themselves. As Mao Tse-Tung once prescribed for China, "Let all flowers bloom together; let rival schools of thought contend."

CONCLUSION

Business will have a much better chance of surviving if there is no nonsense about its goals — that is, if long-run profit maximization is the one dominant objective in practice as well as in theory. Business should recognize what government's functions are and let it go at that, stopping only to fight government where government directly intrudes itself into business. It should let government take care of the general welfare so that business can take care of the more material aspects of welfare.

The results of any such single-minded devotion to profit should be invigorating. With none of the corrosive distractions and costly bureaucracies that now serve the pious cause of welfare, politics, society, and putting up a pleasant front, with none of these draining its vitality, management can shoot for the economic moon. It will be able to thrust ahead in whatever way seems consistent with its money-making goals. If laws and threats stand in its way, it should test and fight them, relenting only if the courts have ruled against it, and then probing again to test the limits of the rules. And when business fights, it should fight with uncompromising relish and self-assertiveness, instead of using all the rhetorical dodges and pious embellishments that are now so often its stock in trade.

Practicing self-restraint behind the cloak of the insipid dictum that "an ounce of prevention is worth a pound of cure" has only limited justification. Certainly it often pays not to squeeze the last dollar out of a market — especially when good will is a factor in the long-term outlook. But too often self-restraint masquerades for capitulation. Businessmen complain about legislative and other attacks on aggressive profit seeking but then lamely go forth to slay the dragon with speeches that simply concede business's function to be service. The critic quickly pounces on this admission with unconcealed relish — "Then why *don't* you serve?" But the fact is, no matter how much business "serves," it will never be enough for its critics.

The Strenuous Life

If the all-out competitive prescription sounds austere or harsh, that is only because we persist in judging things in terms of utopian standards. Altruism, self-denial, charity, and similar values are vital in certain walks of our life — areas which, because of that fact, are more important to the long-run future than business. But for the most part those virtues are alien to competitive economics.

If it sounds callous to hold such a view, and suicidal to publicize it, that is only because business has done nothing to prepare the community to agree with it. There is only one way to do that: to perform at top ability and to speak vigorously *for* (not in defense of) what business does. Prior's stand on human relations, quoted earlier, is a good point of departure. But it is only a beginning.

In the end business has only two responsibilities — to obey the elementary canons of everyday face-to-face civility (honesty, good faith, and so on) and to seek material gain. The fact that it is the butt of demagogical critics is no reason for management to lose its nerve — to buckle under to reformers — lest more severe restrictions emerge to throttle business completely. Few people will man the barricades against capitalism if it is a good provider, minds its own business, and supports government in the things which are properly government's. Even today, most American critics want only to curb capitalism, not to destroy it. And curbing efforts will not destroy it if there is free and open discussion about its singular function.

To the extent that there is conflict, can it not be a good thing? Every book, every piece of history, even every religion testifies to the fact that conflict is and always has been the subject, origin, and life blood of society. Struggle helps to keep us alive, to give élan to life. We should try to make the most of it, not avoid it.

Does Business Have a Responsibility?

Lord Acton has said of the past that people sacrificed freedom by grasping at impossible justice. The contemporary school of business morality seems intent on adding its own caveat to that unhappy consequence. The gospel of tranquility is a soporific. Instead of fighting for its survival by means of a series of strategic retreats masquerading as industrial statesmanship, business must fight as if it were at war. And, like a good war, it should be fought gallantly, daringly, and, above all, *not* morally.

NOTES

1. Speech delivered May 6, 1957.
2. Theodore V. Houser, 1957 McKinsey Foundation Lectures, reprinted as *Big Business and Human Values* (New York, McGraw-Hill Book Company, Inc., 1957).
3. Clarence B. Randall (Boston, Little, Brown and Company, 1952).
4. O. A. Ohmann, HBR May-June 1955, p. 41.
5. Ralph J. Cordiner (New York, McGraw-Hill Book Company, Inc., 1956).
6. Abram T. Collier, HBR January-February 1953, p. 29.

IV

The Poor: Who Are They and Are They Really Different?

It has been said that the poor will always be with us. There is in the United States a strong desire for the repudiation of this historically accurate statement. Doubters (or realists depending on one's stance) argue that governmental efforts to uplift the poor are foredoomed. Lacking the aspiration and ability for self-responsibility and employment, the poor—individual cases aside—will remain in poverty. In academic circles this controversy has crystallized around Oscar Lewis's "culture of poverty" concept. In response to Lewis's thesis that the poor inherit by social transmission subcultural attitudes and behavior which make them different from the nonpoor, others argue that these apparent traits are not ingrained but situationally induced. This latter position implies changeability of the poor in the presence of opportunities.

The selections in this chapter focus on two issues: (1) Does a subculture of poverty exist? That is, does the lower class share in a subculture distinct from the larger culture, or do all members of a society, irrespective of their position in the stratification structure, share in a common cultural tradition? (2) If a subculture does exist, what are its consequences?

Clarification of some concepts is in order. While definitions of culture are many, the one most fitting in the present context states that culture encompasses those ways of thinking, believing, feeling, and behaving possessed by members of a particular society. If a subgroup of the larger society evolves certain important ways of thinking, feeling, believing, and behaving which are different from the dominant culture, a subculture is said to exist. Should the cultural traits of such a subgroup be in conflict with the larger society, a contra- or counterculture has developed.

Culture of poverty as a concept gained prominence through Oscar Lewis's anthropological accounts of life among the poor. In "The Culture of Poverty," Lewis states his brief for the existence of a subculture among the poor which is transmitted intergenerationally. Like other authors included in this chapter, Lewis sees the creation of a subculture among the poor as an adaptation, an attempt at self-defense on the part of people on the bottom of a crushing economic system. Setting Lewis apart is his belief that the subculture of poverty constitutes more than an adaptation; by his interpretation it is also perpetuated across generations. Lewis is explicit on the implications of this — by school age, children of poverty are psychologically stunted, and thus are never able to capitalize on opportunities they may encounter in later life.

In "The Lessons of Pruitt-Igoe" Lee Rainwater, like Oscar Lewis, views culture as a design for living evolved by groups in the process of adapting to their environment. Both conclude that a lower-class subculture exists as a protective alternative developed in the face of constant exclusion and deprivation. At this point agreement ends and a fundamental difference begins. According to Rainwater, the lower class merely appears to have rejected middle-class values. In fact, this apparent rejection serves as a camouflage for people whose life experiences have hammered home the inevitable failure due one who attempts to "succeed" without the requisite resources and opportunities. Correspondingly, Rainwater asserts, a radical change in the opportunity structure would reveal the true desire among lower-class persons to achieve occupational success and to live the "good life."

The writers thus far have taken diametric positions. "The Lower-Class Value Stretch" by Hyman Rodman offers an interpretation which attempts to clarify the debate on a common versus a class-differentiated value system. Rodman, too, adheres to the position that lower-class values serve an adaptive function. But our understanding of this adaptive function is advanced by Rodman's "lower-class value stretch" concept. According to this interpretation, lower-class persons who fail to live up to general societal values minimize potential pain and frustration by settling for less. For example, they do not decide that success is unimportant, just that less of it will suffice. Middle-class values are not abandoned; they are either stretched to fit the lower-class condition or alternative values are adopted. Therefore, theories of a common societal value system and of a class-differentiated value system are incomplete, but complementary explanations of reality.

Richard Ball ("The Analgesic Subculture") also sees subcultural traits among the poor as adaptations to the reality of living a denying and frustrating existence — the "analgesic" subculture soothes the pain.

However, in Ball's mind, neither the subcultural traits nor their psychological correlates such as apathy and fatalism can be explained in simple learning theory terms. According to Ball, an analgesic subculture springs from "frustration-instigated" learning, a type of learning which is nonrational and perhaps irreversible. Prediction and alteration of behavior require cognizance of the extent to which such subcultures are nonrational, intergenerationally transmitted responses to frustration. A failure to grasp this fact, contends Ball, is a mistake often committed by social change agents and social scientists trying to improve the lot of persons socialized in such subcultures. Analysis of the folk subculture of the Southern Appalachians is offered as an illustration of this interpretation.

This entire debate raises important questions. Are the poor actually socially crippled? Should poverty policies and programs be grafted onto subcultural attributes? Or do the poor share in the success and work values of American society and merely lack opportunity? The implications for poverty policy and programs are obvious. If the so-called lower class does not subscribe to the cultural values of the larger society, these attitudes must influence any action taken against poverty. For example, if the poor in America actually are a lazy lot, content to live off the labor of others, eschewing any move toward self-help, it is doubtful that manpower training programs are going to be successful. Conversely, should the lower class share in American values of independence and success, they will respond when the barriers to occupational mobility are removed.

Are the poor different?

OSCAR LEWIS

The Culture of Poverty

As an anthropologist I have tried to understand poverty and its associated traits as a culture or, more accurately, as a subculture* with its own structure and rationale, as a way of life that is passed down from generation to generation along family lines. This view directs attention to the fact that the culture of poverty in modern nations is not only a matter of economic deprivation, of disorganization, or of the absence of something. It is also something positive and provides some rewards without which the poor could hardly carry on.

In my book *Five Families: Mexican Case Studies in the Culture of Poverty,* I suggested that the culture of poverty transcends regional, rural-urban, and national differences and shows remarkable cross-national similarities in family structure, interpersonal relations, time orientation, value systems, and spending patterns. These similarities are examples of independent invention and convergence. They are common adaptations to common problems.

The culture of poverty can come into being in a variety of historical contexts. However, it tends to grow and flourish in societies with the following set of conditions: (1) a cash economy, wage labor, and production for profit;† (2) a persistently high rate of unemployment and

---

* Although the term "subculture of poverty" is technically more accurate, I shall use "culture of poverty" as a shorter form.
† Although the model presented here is concerned with conditions in contemporary urban slums, I find remarkable similarities between the culture of poverty and the way of life of Negro slaves in the antebellum South of the United States.

Reprinted by permission of the publisher from Oscar Lewis, *The Study of Slum Culture — Backgrounds for La Vida* (New York: Random House, 1968), pp. 4-21. Copyright © 1968 by Oscar Lewis.

underemployment for unskilled labor; (3) low wages; (4) the failure to provide social, political, and economic organization, either on a voluntary basis or by government imposition, for the low income population; (5) the existence of a bilateral kinship system rather than a unilateral one; and finally, (6) the existence in the dominant class of a set of values that stresses the accumulation of wealth and property, the possibility of upward mobility, and thrift and that explains low economic status as the result of personal inadequacy or inferiority.

The way of life that develops among some of the poor under these conditions is the culture of poverty. It can best be studied in urban or rural slums and can be described in terms of some seventy interrelated social, economic, and psychological traits. However, the number of traits and the relationships between them may vary from society to society and from family to family. For example, in a highly literate society, illiteracy may be more diagnostic of the culture of poverty than in a society where illiteracy is widespread and where even the well-to-do may be illiterate, as in some Mexican peasant villages before the revolution.

The culture of poverty is both an adaptation and a reaction of the poor to their marginal position in a class-stratified, highly individuated, capitalistic society. It represents an effort to cope with feelings of hopelessness and despair that develop from the realization of the improbability of achieving success in terms of the values and goals of the larger society. Indeed, many of the traits of the culture of poverty can be viewed as attempts at local solutions for problems not met by existing institutions and agencies because the people are not eligible for them, cannot afford them, or are ignorant or suspicious of them. For example, unable to obtain credit from banks, they are thrown upon their own resources and organize informal credit devices without interest.

The culture of poverty, however, is not only an adaptation to a set of objective conditions of the larger society. Once it comes into existence, it tends to perpetuate itself from generation to generation because of its effect on the children. By the time slum children are age six or seven they have usually absorbed the basic values and attitudes of their subculture and are not psychologically geared to take full advantage of the changing conditions or increased opportunities that may occur in their lifetime.

Most frequently the culture of poverty develops when a stratified social and economic system is breaking down or is being replaced by another, as in the case of the transition from feudalism to capitalism or during periods of rapid technological change. Often the culture of poverty results from imperial conquest in which the native social and economic structure is smashed and the natives are maintained in a servile colonial status, sometimes for many generations. It can also occur in the process of detribalization, such as that now going on in Africa.

The most likely candidates for the culture of poverty are the people who come from the lower strata of a rapidly changing society and are already partially alienated from it. Thus, landless rural workers who migrate to the cities can be expected to develop a culture of poverty much more readily than migrants from stable peasant villages with a well-organized traditional culture. In this connection there is a striking contrast between Latin America, where the rural population has long ago made the transition from a tribal to a peasant society, and Africa, which is still close to its tribal heritage. The more corporate nature of many of the African tribal societies as compared to Latin American rural communities and the persistence of village ties tend to inhibit or delay the formation of a full-blown culture of poverty in many of the African towns and cities. The special conditions of apartheid in South Africa, where the migrants are segregated into separate "locations" and do not enjoy freedom of movement, create special problems. Here the institutionalization of repression and discrimination tends to develop a greater sense of identity and group consciousness.

The culture of poverty can be studied from various points of view: the relationship between the subculture and the larger society; the nature of the slum community; the nature of the family; and the attitudes, values, and character structure of the individual.

The lack of effective participation and integration of the poor in the major institutions of the larger society is one of the crucial characteristics of the culture of poverty. This complex matter results from a variety of factors, which may include lack of economic resources, segregation and discrimination, fear, suspicion or apathy, and the development of local solutions for problems. However, participation in some of the institutions of the larger society — for example, in the jails, the army, and the public relief system — does not per se eliminate the traits of the culture of poverty. In the case of a relief system that barely keeps people alive, both the basic poverty and the sense of hopelessness are perpetuated rather than eliminated.

Low wages and chronic unemployment and underemployment lead to low income, lack of property ownership, absence of savings, absence of food reserves in the home, and a chronic shortage of cash. These conditions reduce the possibility of effective participation in the larger economic system. And as a response to these conditions we find in the culture of poverty a high incidence of pawning of personal goods, borrowing from local moneylenders at usurious interest rates, spontaneous informal credit devices organized by neighbors, use of secondhand clothing and furniture, and the pattern of frequent buying of small quantities of food many times a day as the need arises.

People with a culture of poverty produce very little wealth and receive very little in return. They have a low level of literacy and education, do not belong to labor unions, are not members of political parties, generally do not participate in the national welfare agencies, and make very little use of banks, hospitals, department stores, museums, or art galleries. They have a critical attitude toward some of the basic institutions of the dominant classes, hatred of the police, mistrust of government and those in high position, and a cynicism that extends even to the church. These factors give the culture of poverty a high potential for protest and for being used in political movements aimed against the existing social order.

People with a culture of poverty are aware of middle-class values; they talk about them and even claim some of them as their own, but on the whole they do not live by them.* Thus, it is important to distinguish between what they say and what they do. For example, many will tell you that marriage by law, by the church, or by both is the ideal form of marriage; but few marry. For men who have no steady jobs or other source of income, who do not own property and have no wealth to pass on to their children, who are present-time oriented and want to avoid the expense of legal difficulties involved in formal marriage and divorce, free unions or consensual marriages make a lot of sense. Women often turn down offers of marriage because they feel that it ties them down to men who are immature, punishing, and generally unreliable. Women feel that consensual union gives them a better break; it gives them some of the freedom and flexibility that men have. By not giving the fathers of their children legal status as husbands, the women have a stronger claim on their children if they decide to leave their men. It also gives women exclusive rights to a house or any other property they own.

In describing the culture of poverty on the local community level, we find poor housing conditions, crowding, gregariousness, and, above all, a minimum of organization beyond the level of the nuclear and extended family. Occasionally there are informal temporary groupings or voluntary associations within slums. The existence of neighborhood gangs that cut across slum settlements represents a considerable advance beyond the zero point of the continuum that I have in mind. Indeed,

---

* In terms of Hyman Rodman's concept of "The Lower Class Stretch," *Social Forces,* Vol. 42, No. 2 (December 1963), I would say that the culture of poverty exists where this value stretch is at a minimum, that is, where the belief in middle-class values is at a minimum.

it is the low level of organization that gives the culture of poverty its marginal and anachronistic quality in our highly complex, specialized, organized society. Most primitive peoples have achieved a higher level of sociocultural organization than our modern urban slum dwellers.

In spite of the generally low level of organization, there may be a sense of community and esprit de corps in urban slums and in slum neighborhoods. This can vary within a single city or from region to region or country to country. The major factors that influence this variation are the size of the slum, its location and physical characteristics, length of residence, incidence of homeownership and landownership (versus squatter rights), rentals, ethnicity, kinship ties, and freedom or lack of freedom of movement. When slums are separated from the surrounding area by enclosing walls or other physical barriers, when rents are low and fixed and stability of residence is great (twenty or thirty years), when the population constitutes a distinct ethnic, racial, or language group or is bound by ties of kinship or *compadrazgo*,* and when there are some internal voluntary associations, then the sense of local community approaches that of a village community. In many cases this combination of favorable conditions does not exist. However, even where internal organization and esprit de corps are at a bare minimum and people move around a great deal, a sense of territoriality develops that sets off the slum neighborhoods from the rest of the city. In Mexico City and San Juan this sense of territoriality results from the unavailability of low income housing outside of the slum areas. In South Africa the sense of territoriality grows out of the segregation enforced by the government, which confines the rural migrants to specific locations.

On the family level the major traits of the culture of poverty are the absence of childhood as a specially prolonged and protected stage in the life cycle; early initiation into sex; free unions or consensual marriages; a relatively high incidence of the abandonment of wives and children; a trend toward female- or mother-centered families, and consequently a much greater knowledge of maternal relatives; a strong predisposition to authoritarianism; lack of privacy; verbal emphasis upon family solidarity, which is only rarely achieved because of sibling rivalry; and competition for limited goods and maternal affection.

On the level of the individual the major characteristics are strong feelings of marginality, of helplessness, of dependence, and of inferiority. I found this to be true of slum dwellers in Mexico City and San Juan

---

* *Compadrazgo* is a system of relationships and obligations between godparents (*padrinos*) and godchildren (*ahijados*) and between godparents and parents, who are *compadres*.

among families who do not constitute a distinct ethnic or racial group and who do not suffer from racial discrimination. In the United States, of course, the culture of poverty of the Negroes has the additional disadvantage of racial discrimination, but as I have already suggested, this additional disadvantage contains a great potential for revolutionary protest and organization that seems to be absent in the slums of Mexico City or among the poor whites in the South.

Other traits include high incidence of maternal deprivation, of orality, and of weak ego structure; confusion of sexual identification; lack of impulse control; strong present-time orientation, with relatively little ability to defer gratification and to plan for the future; sense of resignation and fatalism; widespread belief in male superiority; and high tolerance for psychological pathology of all sorts.

People with a culture of poverty are provincial and locally oriented and have very little sense of history. They know only their own troubles, their own local conditions, their own neighborhoods, their own way of life. Usually they do not have the knowledge, the vision, or the ideology to see the similarities between their problems and those of their counterparts elsewhere in the world. They are not class conscious although they are very sensitive indeed to status distinctions.

In considering the traits discussed above, the following propositions must be kept in mind. (1) The traits fall into a number of clusters and are functionally related within each cluster. (2) Many, but not all, of the traits of different clusters are also functionally related. For example, men who have low wages and suffer chronic unemployment develop a poor self-image, become irresponsible, abandon their wives and children, and take up with other women more frequently than do men with high incomes and steady jobs. (3) None of the traits, taken individually, is distinctive per se of the subculture of poverty. It is their conjunction, their function, and their patterning that define the subculture. (4) The subculture of poverty, as defined by these traits, is a statistical profile; that is, the frequency of distribution of the traits both singly and in clusters will be greater than in the rest of the population. In other words, more of the traits will occur in combination in families with a subculture of poverty than in stable working-class, middle-class, or upper-class families. Even within a single slum there will probably be a gradient from culture of poverty families to families without a culture of poverty. (5) The profiles of the subculture of poverty will probably differ in systematic ways with the difference in the national cultural contexts of which they are a part. It is expected that some new traits will become apparent with research in different nations.

I have not yet worked out a system of weighting each of the traits, but this could probably be done and a scale could be set up for many of the traits. Traits that reflect lack of participation in the institutions of the larger society or an outright rejection—in practice, if not in theory —would be the crucial traits; for example, illiteracy, provincialism, free unions, abandonment of women and children, lack of membership in voluntary associations beyond the extended family.

When the poor become class conscious or active members of trade-union organizations or when they adopt an internationalist outlook on the world, they are no longer part of the culture of poverty although they may still be desperately poor. Any movement — be it religious, pacifist, or revolutionary — that organizes and gives hope to the poor and effectively promotes solidarity, and a sense of identification with larger groups destroys the psychological and social core of the culture of poverty. In this connection, I suspect that the civil-rights movement among the Negroes in the United States has done more to improve their self-image and self-respect than have their economic advances, although, without doubt, the two are mutually reinforcing.

The distinction between poverty and the culture of poverty is basic to the model described here. There are degrees of poverty and many kinds of poor people. The culture of poverty refers to one way of life shared by poor people in given historical and social contexts. The economic traits that I have listed for the culture of poverty are necessary but not sufficient to define the phenomena I have in mind. There are a number of historical examples of very poor segments of the population that do not have a way of life that I would describe as a subculture of poverty. Here I should like to give four examples.

1. Many of the primitive or preliterate peoples studied by anthropologists suffer from dire poverty that is the result of poor technology or poor natural resources, or both, but they do not have the traits of the subculture of poverty. Indeed, they do not constitute a subculture because their societies are not highly stratified. In spite of their poverty they have a relatively integrated, satisfying, and self-sufficient culture. Even the simplest food-gathering and hunting tribes have a considerable amount of organization, including bands and band chiefs, tribal councils, and local self-government—traits that are not found in the culture of poverty.

2. In India the lower castes (the Chamars, the leather workers, and the Bhangis, the sweepers) may be desperately poor both in the villages and in the cities, but most of them are integrated into the larger society and have their own panchayat organizations, which cut across village

lines and give them a considerable amount of power.* In addition to the caste system, which gives individuals a sense of identity and belonging, there is still another factor: the clan system. Wherever there are unilateral kinship systems or clans, one would not expect to find the culture of poverty, because a clan system gives people a sense of belonging to a corporate body that has a history and a life of its own and thereby provides a sense of continuity, a sense of a past and of a future.

3. The Jews of eastern Europe were very poor, but they did not have many of the traits of the culture of poverty because of their tradition of literacy, the great value placed upon learning, the organization of the community around the rabbi, the proliferation of local voluntary associations, and their religion, which taught that they were the chosen people.

4. My fourth example is speculative and relates to socialism. On the basis of my limited experience in one socialist country — Cuba — and on the basis of my reading, I am inclined to believe that the culture of poverty does not exist in the socialist countries. I first went to Cuba in 1947 as a visiting professor for the State Department. At that time I began a study of a sugar plantation in Melena del Sur and of a slum in Havana. After the Castro revolution I made my second trip to Cuba as a correspondent for a major magazine and I revisited the same slum and some of the same families. The physical aspect of the slum had changed very little, except for a beautiful new nursery school. It was clear that the people were still desperately poor, but I found much less of the feelings of despair, apathy, and hopelessness that are so diagnostic of urban slums in the culture of poverty. The people expressed great confidence in their leaders and hope for a better life in the future. The slum itself was now highly organized, with block committees, educational committees, party committees. The people had a new sense of power and importance. They were armed and were given a doctrine that glorified the lower class as the hope of humanity. (I was told by one Cuban official that they had practically eliminated delinquency by giving arms to the delinquents!)

It is my impression that Castro, unlike Marx and Engels, did not write off the so-called lumpen proletariat as an inherently reactionary and antirevolutionary force, but rather saw its revolutionary potential and tried to utilize this potential. In this connection, Frantz Fanon makes

---

* It may be that in the slums of Calcutta and Bombay an incipient culture of poverty is developing. It would be highly desirable to do family studies there as a crucial test of the culture of poverty hypothesis.

a similar evaluation of the role of the lumpen proletariat based upon his experience in the Algerian struggle for independence:

It is within this mass of humanity, this people of the shanty towns, at the core of the lumpen proletariat, that the rebellion will find its urban spearhead. For the lumpen proletariat, that horde of starving men, uprooted from their tribe and from their clan, constitutes one of the most spontaneous and most radically revolutionary forces of a colonized people.*

My own studies of the urban poor in the slums of San Juan do not support the generalizations of Fanon. I have found very little revolutionary spirit or radical ideology among low income Puerto Ricans. On the contrary, most of the families I studied were quite conservative politically, and about half of them were in favor of the Republican Statehood Party.† It seems to me that the revolutionary potential of people with a culture of poverty will vary considerably according to the national context and the particular historical circumstances. In a country like Algeria, which was fighting for its independence, the lumpen proletariat was drawn into the struggle and became a vital force. However, in countries like Puerto Rico in which the movement for independence has very little mass support and in countries like Mexico that achieved their independence a long time ago and are now in their post-revolutionary period, the lumpen proletariat is not a leading source of rebellion or of revolutionary spirit.

In effect, we find that in primitive societies and in caste societies the culture of poverty does not develop. In socialist, fascist, and highly developed capitalist societies with a welfare state, the culture of poverty

---

* Frantz Fanon, *The Wretched of the Earth* (New York: Grove Press, 1965), p. 103.

† "The present Partido Estadista Republicano (PER) is the inheritor of the coalition Republican Union Party of the thirties and early forties. As such it is deeply committed to the continuance of the jurisdictional presence of the United States in Puerto Rico; but this commitment has only recently been expressed exclusively in terms of statehood. . . .

". . . The Partido Estadista Republicano, unlike the Partido Popular Democrático, is formally affiliated with one of the national parties of the United States. The affiliation of the mainland and insular Republican parties dates from 1903, and, with the exception of a brief interlude between 1916 and 1919, during which the bonds were formally dissolved, the affiliation has continued uninterrupted to the present day. Federal patronage jobs in Puerto Rico now consist of only the customs collector, the United States attorney for the Puerto Rico district, two assistant federal attorneys, the federal marshal, the director of the Caribbean area office of the Production and Marketing Administration, and, when vacancies occur, postmasters and two federal district judges." From Robert W. Anderson, *Party Politics in Puerto Rico* (Stanford, Calif.: Stanford University Press, 1965), pp. 81, 91.

tends to decline. I suspect that the culture of poverty flourishes in, and is generic to, the early free-enterprise stage of capitalism and that it is also endemic to colonialism.

It is important to distinguish between different profiles in the subculture of poverty, depending upon the national context in which these subcultures are found. If we think of the culture of poverty primarily in terms of integration in the larger society and a sense of identification with the great tradition of that society or with a new emerging revolutionary tradition, then we will not be surprised that some slum dwellers with a low per capita income may have moved further away from the core characteristics of the culture of poverty than others with a higher per capita income. For example, Puerto Rico has a much higher per capita income than Mexico, yet Mexicans have a deeper sense of personal and national identity. In Mexico even the poorest slum dweller has a much richer sense of the past and a deeper identification with the great Mexican tradition than do Puerto Ricans with their tradition. In both countries I presented urban slum dwellers with the names of national figures. In Mexico City quite a high percentage of the respondents, including those with little or no formal schooling, knew about Cuauhtémoc, Hidalgo, Father Morelos, Juárez, Díaz, Zapata, Carranza, and Cárdenas. In San Juan the respondents showed an abysmal ignorance of Puerto Rican historical figures. The names of Ramón Power, José de Diego, Baldorioty de Castro, Ramón Betances, Nemesio Canales, and Lloréns Torres rang no bell. For the lower income Puerto Rican slum dweller, history begins and ends with Muñoz Rivera, his son Muñoz Marín, and *doña* Felisa Rincón!

I have listed fatalism and a low level of aspiration as key traits of the subculture of poverty. Here too, however, the national context makes a big difference. Certainly the level of aspiration of even the poorest sector of the population in a country like the United States with traditional ideology of upward mobility and democracy is much higher than in more backward countries like Ecuador and Peru, where both the ideology and the actual possibilities of upward mobility are extremely limited and where authoritarian values still persist in both the urban and the rural milieu.

Because of the advanced technology, the high level of literacy, the development of mass media, and the relatively high aspiration level of all sectors of the population, especially when compared with underdeveloped nations, I believe that although there is still a great deal of poverty in the United States (estimates range from 30 to 50 million people) there is relatively little of what I would call the culture of poverty. My rough guess would be that only about 20 percent of the population below the poverty line (from 6 to 10 million people) in the United States have characteristics that would justify classifying their way of life as that of a culture of poverty. Probably the largest sector within this group consists of very low income Negroes, Mexicans, Puerto Ricans, American Indians, and southern poor whites. The relatively small number of people in the United States with a culture of poverty is a positive factor because it is much more difficult to eliminate the culture of poverty than to eliminate poverty per se.

Middle-class people — and this would certainly include most social scientists — tend to concentrate on the negative aspects of the culture of poverty. They tend to associate negative valences to such traits as present-time orientation and concrete versus abstract orientation. I do not intend to idealize or romanticize the culture of poverty. As someone has said, "It is easier to praise poverty than to live in it"; yet some of the positive aspects that may flow from these traits must not be overlooked. Living in the present may develop a capacity for spontaneity, for the enjoyment of the sensual, for the indulgence of impulse, which is often blunted in the middle-class, future-oriented man. Perhaps it is this reality of the moment that the existentialist writers are so desperately trying to recapture but that the culture of poverty experiences as natural, everyday phenomena. The frequent use of violence certainly provides a ready outlet for hostility so that people in the culture of poverty suffer less from repression than does the middle class.

In the traditional view, anthropologists have said that culture provides human beings with a design for living, with a ready-made set of solutions for human problems so that individuals in each generation do not have to begin all over again from scratch. That is, the core of culture is its positive adaptive function. I, too, have called attention to some of the adaptive mechanisms in the culture of poverty — for example, the low aspiration level helps to reduce frustration, the legitimization of short-range hedonism makes possible spontaneity and enjoyment. Indeed, it seems that in some ways the people with a culture of poverty suffer less from alienation than do those of the middle class. However, on the whole it seems to me that it is a thin, relatively superficial culture. There is a great deal of pathos, suffering, and emptiness among those who live in the culture of poverty. It does not provide much support or satisfaction, and its encouragement of mistrust tends to magnify helplessness and isolation. Indeed, the poverty of culture is one of the crucial aspects of the culture of poverty.

The concept of the culture of poverty provides a high level of generalization that, hopefully, will unify and explain a number of phenomena that have been viewed as distinctive characteristics of racial, national, or regional groups. For example, matrifocality, a high incidence of consensual unions, and a high percentage of households headed by women, which have been thought to be distinctive characteristics of Caribbean family organization or of Negro family life in the United States, turn out to be traits of the culture of poverty and are found among diverse peoples in many parts of the world and among peoples who have had no history of slavery.

The concept of a cross-societal subculture of poverty enables us to see that many of the problems we think of as distinctively our own or as distinctively Negro problems (or as those of any other special racial or ethnic group) also exist in countries where there are no distinct ethnic minority groups. This concept also suggests that the elimination of physical poverty per se may not eliminate the culture of poverty, which is a whole way of life.

What is the future of the culture of poverty? In considering this question, one must distinguish between those countries in which it represents a relatively small segment of the population and those in which it constitutes a very large one. Obviously, the solutions will differ in these two situations. In the United States, the major solution proposed by planners and social workers in dealing with multiple-problem families and the so-called hard core of poverty has been to attempt to raise slowly their level of living and to incorporate them into the middle class. Wherever possible, there has been some reliance upon psychiatric treatment.

In the underdeveloped countries, however, where great masses of people live in the culture of poverty, a social-work solution does not seem feasible.* Because of the magnitude of the problem, psychiatrists can hardly begin to cope with it. They have all they can do to care for their own growing middle class. In these countries the people with a culture of poverty may seek a more revolutionary solution. By creating basic structural changes in society, by redistributing wealth, by organizing the poor and giving them a sense of belonging, of power, and of leadership, revolutions frequently succeed in abolishing some of the basic characteristics of the culture of poverty even when they do not succeed in abolishing poverty itself.

Some of my readers have misunderstood the subculture of poverty model and have failed to grasp the importance of the distinction between poverty and the subculture of poverty. In making this distinction I have tried to document a broader generalization; namely, that it is

---

* Indeed, it is doubtful how successful the social-work solution can be in the United States!

a serious mistake to lump all poor people together, because the causes, the meaning, and the consequences of poverty vary considerably in different sociocultural contexts. There is nothing in the concept that puts the onus of poverty on the character of the poor. Nor does the concept in any way play down the exploitation and neglect suffered by the poor. Indeed, the subculture of poverty is part of the larger culture of capitalism, whose social and economic system channels wealth into the hands of a relatively small group and thereby makes for the growth of sharp class distinctions.

I would agree that the main reasons for the persistence of the subculture are no doubt the pressures that the larger society exerts over its members and the structure of the larger society itself. However, *this is not the only reason.* The subculture develops mechanisms that tend to perpetuate it, especially because of what happens to the world view, aspirations, and character of the children who grow up in it. For this reason, improved economic opportunities, though absolutely essential and of the highest priority, are not sufficient to alter basically or eliminate the subculture of poverty. Moreover, elimination is a process that will take more than a single generation, even under the best of circumstances, including a socialist revolution.

Some readers have thought that I was saying, "Being poor is terrible, but having a subculture of poverty is not so bad." On the contrary, I am saying that it is easier to eliminate poverty than the culture of poverty. I am also suggesting that the poor in a precapitalist caste-ridden society like India had some advantages over modern urban slum dwellers because the people were organized in castes and panchayats and this organization gave them some sense of identity and some strength and power. Perhaps Gandhi had the urban slums of the West in mind when he wrote that the caste system was one of the greatest inventions of mankind. Similarly, I have argued that the poor Jews of eastern Europe, with their strong tradition of literacy and community organization, were better off than people with the culture of poverty. On the other hand, I would argue that people with the culture of poverty, with their strong sense of resignation and fatalism, are less driven and less anxious than the striving lower middle class, who are still trying to make it in the face of the greatest odds.

LEE RAINWATER

The Lessons of Pruitt-Igoe

The Pruitt-Igoe Housing Project is in St. Louis. Built in 1954, the project was the first high-rise public housing in the city. It consists of 33 eleven-story slab-shaped buildings designed to provide housing for about 2800 families. At present, it houses about 10,000 Negroes in 2,000 households. What started out as a precedent-breaking project to improve the lives of the poor in St. Louis, a project hailed not only by the local newspapers but by *Architectural Forum*, has become an embarrassment to all concerned. In the last few years the project has at all times had a vacancy rate of over 20 percent. News of crime and accidents in the project makes a regular appearance in the newspapers, and the words "Pruitt-Igoe" have become a household term — in lower class Negro homes as well as in the larger community—for the worst in ghetto living.

The description of Pruitt-Igoe which follows and the implications drawn, are based on a three-year study which I, together with a dozen colleagues, have been conducting. Pruitt-Igoe is not offered as typical of slum conditions in the ghetto — no other public housing project in the country approaches it in terms of vacancies, tenant concerns and anxieties, physical deterioration. Rather, Pruitt-Igoe is interesting precisely because it condenses into one 57-acre tract all of the problems and difficulties that arise from race and poverty, and all of the impotence, indifference, and hostility with which our society has so far dealt with these problems. Processes that are sometimes beneath the surface in less virulent slums are readily apparent in Pruitt-Igoe. And because Pruitt-

Reprinted by permission of the author and publisher from Lee Rainwater, "The Lessons of Pruitt-Igoe," *The Public Interest* 8 (Summer 1967): 116-26. Copyright© 1967 National Affairs, Inc.

Igoe exists as one kind of Federal Government response to the problems of poverty, the failure of that response is worth contemplating.

THE DUMPING GROUND

Pruitt-Igoe houses families for which our society seems to have no other place. The original tenants were drawn very heavily from several land-clearance areas in the inner city. Although there were originally some white tenants (Igoe was built for whites, Pruitt for Negroes, but a Supreme Court decision outlawing segregated public housing resulted in an "integrated" project in its earlier years), all of the whites have moved out and the population is now all Negro. Only those Negroes who are desperate for housing are willing to live in Pruitt-Igoe — over half of the households are headed by women and over half derive their principle income from public assistance of one kind or another. The project has proved particularly unappealing to "average" families, that is, families in which there is both a mother and father and a small number of children. Thus, while the overall vacancy rate has run between 20 and 25 percent for several years, the vacancy rate in two-bedroom apartments has been in the 35-40 percent range.

Life in Pruitt-Igoe, and in the St. Louis ghetto generally, is not quite as flamboyant as in Harlem, but it has the same essential characteristics. As sociologists have discovered each time they have examined a particular lower class community in detail, the lower class lives in "a world of trouble."

In the slum, people are continually confronted with dangers from both human and non-human sources. Public housing removes some of the non-human sources of danger (like rats, or faulty electrical wiring), but can replace them by others, as when children fall out of windows or into elevator shafts in Pruitt-Igoe's high-rise buildings, or burn themselves on exposed steam pipes, or cut themselves on the broken glass outside. After about two years of intensive field observation in the Pruitt-Igoe project, our research team administered a questionnaire to a representative sample of tenants to discover how extensive were some of the difficulties we had noticed. Let me list some of the troubles which over half of this representative sample of tenants characterized as "a very big problem" in the project.

A few of these problems had to do with the design and maintenance of the project:

— There's too much broken glass and trash around outside.
— The elevators are dangerous.

The Lessons of Pruitt-Igoe   121

— The elevators don't stop on every floor, so many people have to walk up or down to get to their apartments.
— There are mice and cockroaches in the buildings.
— People use the elevators and halls to go to the bathroom.

However, by far the greatest number of troubles that people complained about had as much to do with the behavior of their fellow tenants as it did with design and maintenance problems *per se:*

— Bottles and other dangerous things get thrown out of windows and hurt people.
— People who don't live in the project come in and make a lot of trouble with fights, stealing, drinking and the like.
— People don't keep the area around the incinerator clean.
— The laundry rooms aren't safe: clothes get stolen and people get attacked.
— The children run wild and cause all kinds of damage.
— People use the stairwells and laundry rooms for drinking and things like that.
— A woman isn't safe in the halls, stairways or elevators.

Given these kinds of experiences it's hardly surprising that, although the great majority of the tenants feel that their *apartments* are better than their previous dwelling units, only a minority demonstrate any real attachment to the project community, and most would very much like to move out to a neighborhood that would be nicer and safer.

It is also understandable that a good many of them develop a rather jaundiced view of the public housing program. Thus, when we asked tenants what the government was trying to accomplish by building public housing and how well this had in fact been accomplished, we got answers like these:

"They were trying to put a whole bunch of people in a little bitty space. They did a pretty good job — there's a lot of people here."

"They were trying to better poor people (but) they tore down one slum and built another; put all kinds of people together; made a filthy place and so on."

"They were trying to get rid of the slum, but they didn't accomplish too much. Inside the apartment they did, but not outside."

Other troubles also make life difficult for the project tenants. For example, we asked our sample to indicate from a list of various kinds of aggressive and deviant behaviors how serious and how frequent they felt such behavior to be. One cluster of items turned out to be judged by the tenants as both highly serious and very frequent (over half of the people characterizing these behaviors as very frequent):

— Holding somebody up and robbing them.

— Being a wino or alcoholic.
— Stealing from somebody.
— Teenagers yelling curse words at adults.
— Breaking windows.
— Drinking a lot and fooling around on the streets.
— Teenagers getting in fights.
— Boys and girls having sexual relations with a lot of different boys or girls.

In short, though some social scientists have quarreled with Kenneth Clark's emphasis on the "tangle of pathology" in the ghetto, it would seem that at least this sample from one federally-supported ghetto shares his views.

THE LOWER CLASS ADAPTATION

The observer who examines the lower class community in any detail perceives an almost bewildering variety of difficulties that confront its inhabitants. But if one wishes to move from simple observation to understanding and on to practical action, it is necessary to bring some order into this chaos of troubles, problems, pains, and failure. That is, one must move from a description of *what* lower class life is like to an understanding of *why* it is that way.

Let us start with an inventory of behavior in the lower class community that middle class people think of as hallmarks of the "tangle of pathology" of slum and ghetto worlds:

High rates of school dropouts.

Poor school accomplishment for those who do stay in.

Difficulties in establishing stable work habits on the part of those who get jobs.

High rates of dropping out of the labor force.

Apathy and passive resistance in contacts with people who are "trying to help" (social workers, teachers, etc.).

Hostility and distrust toward neighbors.

Poor consumer skills — carelessness or ignorance in the use of money.

High rates of mental illness.

Marital disruptions and female-headed homes.

Illegitimacy.

Child abuse or indifference to children's welfare.

Property and personal crimes.

Dope addiction, alcoholism.

Destructiveness and carelessness toward property, one's own and other people's.

All of this behavior is highly disturbing to middle-class people — and most of it is even more disturbing to the lower class people who must live with it. It is not necessary to assume that all lower class families engage in even some of these practices to regard such practices as hallmarks of the pathology of the lower class world. Lower class people are forced to live in an environment in which the probability of either becoming involved in such behavior, or being the victim of it, is much higher than it is in other kinds of neighborhoods. From the point of view of social epidemiology, then, this is a high-risk population.

Behavior of this kind is very difficult for most middle class observers to understand. If, however, this behavior is seen in the context of the ways of life lower class people develop in order to cope with their punishing and depriving milieu, then it becomes much easier to understand. Much of the social science research dealing with lower class life in general, or with particular forms of deviant behavior such as juvenile delinquency, has sought to place these kinds of behavior in their contexts. As a result of these studies, we now understand that the "unreasonable" behavior which so often perplexes outsiders generally arises as a logical extension of the styles of life that are available to lower class people in their efforts to adapt to their world.

The ways people live represent their efforts to cope with the predicaments and opportunities that they find in the world as they experience it. The immediately experienced world of lower class adults presents them with two kinds of problems:

1) They are not able to find enough money to live in what they, and everyone else, would regard as the average American way. Because of inability to find work or only work at very low pay, they learn that the best they can hope for if they are "sensible" is despised housing, an inferior diet, a very few pleasures.

2) Because of their poverty, they are constrained to live among other individuals similarly situated — individuals who, the experience of their daily lives teaches them, are dangerous, difficult, out to exploit or hurt them in petty or significant ways. And they learn that in their communities they can expect only poor and inferior service and protection from such institutions as the police, the courts, the schools, the sanitation department, the landlords, and the merchants.

It is to this world that they must adapt. Further, as they grow up, they learn from their experiences with those around them that persons such as they can expect nothing better. From infancy on, they begin to adapt to that world in ways that allow them to sustain themselves — but at the same time often interfere with the possibility of adapting to a different world, should such a different world become available to them. Thus, in Pruitt-Igoe, eight-year old girls are quite competent to inform the field worker that boys and men are no damn good, are not to be trusted, and that it isn't necessary to listen to or obey your mother because she's made such a mess of her life.

We know from sociological studies of unemployment that even stable or working class persons are likely to begin to show some of these lower class adaptive techniques under the stress of long-term unemployment. In the lower class itself, there is never a question of responding to the stress of sudden deprivation, since a depriving world is often all that the individual ever experiences in his life, and his whole lifetime is taken up in perfecting his adaptation to it, in striving to protect himself in that world and to squeeze out of it whatever gratification he can.

STRATEGIES FOR SURVIVAL

It is in terms of these two cardinal characteristics of lower class life — poverty and a potentially destructive community — that lower class individuals work out their strategies for living.

In most of American society two grand strategies seem to attract the allegiance of its members and guide their day-to-day actions. These are the strategies of the good life and of career-success. A good-life strategy involves efforts to get along with others and not to rock the boat; it rests on a comfortable family environment with a stable vocation for husbands which enables them to be good providers. The strategy of career-success is the choice of ambitious men and women who see life as providing opportunities to move from a lower to a higher status, to "accomplish something," to achieve greater than ordinary material well-being, prestige, and social recognition. Both of these strategies are predicated on the assumption that the world is inherently rewarding if one behaves properly and does his part. The rewards of the world may come easily or only at the cost of great effort, but at least they are there for the individual who tries.

In slum worlds, little in the experience that individuals have as they grow up sustains a belief in a rewarding world. The strategies that seem appropriate are *strategies for survival*.

Three broad categories of lower class survival strategies can be observed. One is the strategy of the *expressive life style*. In response to the fact that the individual derives little security and reward from his membership in a family which can provide for and protect him, or from his experiences in the institutions in which he is expected to achieve (the school, later the job), individuals develop an exploitative strategy toward others. This strategy seeks to elicit rewards by making oneself interesting and attractive. In its benign forms, the expressive style is what attracts so many middle class people to the lower class — the fun, the singing, the dancing, the lively slang, the spontaneous gratification of impulse. But underneath the apparent spontaneity, the expressive style of lower class people is deadly serious business. It is by virtue of their ability to manipulate others by making themselves interesting and dramatic that the individual has an opportunity to get some of the few rewards that are available to him — whether these be gifts of money, a gambling bet won, the affections of a girl, or the right to participate in a community of peers, to drink with them, bum around with them, gain status in their eyes. The individual learns by his expressive ability to "work game" on his peers, to "sound" on them, to "put them in a trick" (thereby raising his status by lowering the other fellow's). While the expressive style is central to preserving the stability and sanity of many (particularly younger) members of the lower class, the pursuit of expressive and self-dramatizing goals often results in behavior which makes trouble for the individual both from his own community and from representatives of conventional society. Dope addiction, drunkenness, illegitimacy, "spendthrift behavior," lack of interest in school on the part of adolescents — all can arise in part as a result of commitment to a strategy of "cool." For example, in Pruitt-Igoe teen-age boys drink, and some smoke marijuana, in order to be able to loosen up enough to develop a "strong game" (i.e., a really persuasive line with peers or girls).

When the expressive strategy fails — because the individual cannot develop the required skills or because the audience is unappreciative — there is a great temptation to adopt a *violent strategy* in which you force others to give you what you need. The violent strategy is not a very popular one among lower class people. There is little really cold-blooded violence either toward persons or property in the slum world; most of it is undertaken out of a sense of desperation, a sense of deep insult to the self. Yet this strategy does not seem as distant and impossible to them as it does to the most prosperous.

Finally, there is the *depressive strategy* in which goals are increasingly constricted to the bare necessities for survival (not as a social being, but simply as an organism). This is the strategy of "I don't bother anybody and I hope nobody's gonna bother me; I'm simply going through the motions of keeping body (but not soul) together." Apparently this strategy of retreat and self-isolation is one that is adopted by more and more lower class men and women as they grow older, as the pay-offs from more expressive strategies begin to decline.

HOPES AND ASPIRATIONS

And along with these survival strategies, lower class people make efforts to move in the direction of the more conventional strategies of the good life or (occasionally) of career-success. One can observe in the lives of individual families (or in whole groups, during times of extraordinary demand for lower class labor) a gradual shift away from the more destructive components of these survival strategies. It is from observations such as these, as well as from interviews about lower class people's hopes and aspirations, that one learns that lower class styles of life are pursued, not because they are viewed as intrinsically desirable, but because the people involved feel constrained to act in those ways given the deprivations and threats to which they find themselves subject. *The lower class does not have a separate system of basic values. Lower class people do not really "reject middle class values." It is simply that their whole experience of life teaches them that it is impossible to achieve a viable sense of self-esteem in terms of those values.*

But lower class people are also intimately alive to how things might be different. They know what they would like if only they had the resources of the average working class man — they would want a quiet, rather "square" life in a quiet neighborhood far from the dangers, seductions, and insults of the world in which they live. In the slums, there is no personal preference for — or sociological value attached to — matrifocal families, or a high incidence of premarital sexual relations resulting in unwanted pregnancies, or living alone as a deserted or divorced wife and having a boyfriend because you're afraid that if you remarry your welfare will be cut off or your new husband will not prove a stable provider. Lower class people are not easily confused between how they must live and how they would like to live. What they might wish to preserve from the expressive heritage of lower class ways (particularly when, as among Negroes, those ways provide a kind of ethnic identity and not just a class identity) they feel that they can preserve while living a more stable kind of life. Lower class people would not find it nearly as agonizing as some intellectuals seem to feel they would to try to reconcile their traditions and their aspirations....

HYMAN RODMAN

The Lower-Class Value Stretch

There are sharp disagreements about the nature of the values held by members of the lower class, and correspondingly, about whether a society is based upon a common value system, or a class-differentiated value system.[1] Some writers assert that the basic values of a society are common to all social classes within that society, while others assert that the values differ from class to class. Similarly, in discussing problems such as illegitimacy and juvenile delinquency, some writers assert that the lower-class values that center about these phenomena are similar to the middle-class values, while others assert that the lower-class values differ from those of the middle class. I propose to outline these contradictory points of view, as well as to suggest that we can resolve some of the apparent contradictions through the concept of lower-class value stretch.

A COMMON VALUE SYSTEM

The assumption that a common value system underlies a system of stratification has been made by Parsons, as in his reference to "a single more or less integrated system of values" in any society.[2] Merton has also assumed that a society is based upon a common value system:

Adapted by permission of the author and University of North Carolina Press from Hyman Rodman, "The Lower-Class Value Stretch," *Social Forces* 42 (December 1963): 205-15.

"It is . . . only because behavior is typically oriented toward the basic values of the society that we speak of a human aggregate as comprising a society. Unless there is a deposit of values shared by interacting individuals, there exist social relations, if the disorderly interactions may be so called, but no society."[3]

When we turn to those who have dealt specifically with illegitimacy and juvenile gang delinquency we find that certain writers imply the existence of a common value system by their contention that middle-class norms are also effective within lower-class groups. For example, Blake and Goode have discussed common-law marriage and illegitimate births in Jamaica and the Caribbean generally, and while taking note of a high rate of illegitimacy in the area (typically more than 50 percent) they nevertheless conclude that even from the point of view of the lower class this represents deviant behavior.[4] According to their interpretation the norm of legitimacy is the only norm to be found within the lower class as well as within the middle class. Although they do not address themselves to the question of whether a society is characterized by a common value system or a class-differentiated value system, we can nevertheless take their interpretation as indicative of a belief in the existence of a common value system.

In somewhat the same vein, a number of writers on juvenile gang delinquency have implied the existence of a common value system. Taft, for example, holds that juvenile delinquents share the basic values of our society.[5] Sykes and Matza have agreed with this viewpoint, but they also point out that through techniques of neutralization (for example, projecting blame upon outside forces that propel one into action, or denying one's actions have harmed anyone) the delinquent is often able to spare himself the anguish of guilt.[6] This position that the delinquents share the conventional values of the society can also be taken as evidence for a belief in the existence of a common value system.

A CLASS-DIFFERENTIATED VALUE SYSTEM

In contrast to those who support the notion that a common value system underlies a stratified society, there are others who believe that a class-differentiated value system underlies a stratified society. Herbert H. Hyman[7] gives empirical evidence that there are differences in the value systems of different classes. He examines the educational, income, and occupational aspirations of various classes, showing that, in general, level of aspiration is correlated with class level. Thus, he concludes that we have a class-differentiated value system.

Allison Davis has emphasized the differentiated values that are to be found within a society, particularly among lower-class persons who have adapted their values to their deprived circumstances. As he says, individuals of different classes are "reacting to different realistic situations. . . . Therefore their values and their social goals are different."[8]

In writing of illegitimacy in the Caribbean, Henriques has stated flatly that from a social point of view this does not represent deviance within the lower class. Rather, the values of the lower class differ from those of the middle class, and illegitimacy is acceptable and in no way stigmatized within the lower class. He believes that those who assess "the lower-class forms of the family" in terms of middle-class norms are committing a "fundamental error."[9]

In a similar vein, Walter Miller's major point about juvenile delinquency within the lower class is that it is congruent with the values to be found within the lower class, and that these lower-class values are very different from those to be found within the rest of the society. According to Miller, "the cultural system which exerts the most direct influence" upon members of delinquent gangs "is that of the lower-class community itself—a long established, distinctively patterned tradition with an integrity of its own."[10] While Miller does not specifically address himself to the general question of whether a society is characterized by a common or a class-differentiated value system, he believes that values are differentiated by class.

THE LOWER-CLASS VALUE STRETCH

To what shall we attribute these different positions? Which do we have, a common or a class-differentiated value system? We can illuminate the contradiction, by focusing upon the reactions of the members of the lower class to their deprived circumstances. I intend to discuss a type of lower-class reaction that has been hinted at but for the most part overlooked. I believe it constitutes the most important reaction to be found within the lower class. That reaction is what I call the *lower-class value stretch*. Through a consideration of this concept we can clear up some of the contradictions surrounding the question of a common versus a class-differentiated value system.

By the value stretch I mean that the lower-class person, without abandoning the general values of the society, develops an alternative set of values. Without abandoning the values placed upon success, such as high income and high educational and occupational attainment, he stretches the values so that lesser degrees of success also become desirable. Without abandoning the values of marriage and legitimate childbirth he stretches these values so that a non-legal union and legally illegitimate children are also desirable. The result is that the members of the lower class, in many areas, have a wider range of values than others within the society. They share the general values of the society with members of other classes, but in addition they have stretched these values, or developed alternative values, which help them to adjust to their deprived circumstances.

Lower-class persons in close interaction with each other and faced with similar problems do not long remain in a state of mutual ignorance. They do not maintain a strong commitment to middle-class values that they cannot attain, and they do not continue to respond to others in a rewarding or punishing way simply on the basis of whether these others are living up to the middle-class values. A change takes place. They come to tolerate and eventually to evaluate favorably certain deviations from the middle-class values. In this way they need not be continually frustrated by their failure to live up to unattainable values. The resultant is a stretched value system with a low degree of commitment to all the values within the range, including the dominant, middle-class values. This is what I suggest as the major lower-class value change, rather than a change in which the middle-class values are abandoned or flouted.[11]

Perhaps I can clarify the lower-class value stretch metaphorically by referring to the fable of the fox and the grapes. The fox in the fable declared that the unattainable sweet grapes were sour; Merton's "rebellious" fox renounces the prevailing taste for sweet grapes;[12] but the "adaptive" lower-class fox I am talking about does neither — rather, he acquires a taste for sour grapes.

If the predominant lower-class response to its situation is the value stretch, then we can immediately resolve many of the apparent contradictions described earlier. Those who hold that the basic values of the society are common to all classes are correct, because the members of the lower class do share these values with other members of society. Similarly, those who hold that the values differ from class to class are also correct, because the members of the lower class share values unique to themselves, in addition to sharing the general values of the society with others. The theories are "both correct, both incomplete, and complementary to one another."[13]

VALUES AND LEVELS OF ABSTRACTION

I want to dwell briefly upon a factor that complicates many discussions about values—the level of abstraction of the values involved. The more concrete a value, the more differentiated a society may appear. Some of the apparent contradictions about a common or class-differentiated value system must therefore be attributed to the confusion that results from the use of different levels of abstraction in talking about values.

Those who assume the existence of a common value system are talking about values at a high level of abstraction, and they may readily agree that at lower levels of abstraction there can be a great deal of differentiation.[14] It is in theoretical discussions particularly that we find contradictions about a common or class-differentiated value system stemming from different levels of abstraction.

CONCLUSION

At the heart of this controversy lies the issue of when old values die and new values develop. It is precisely because old values never die, they only fade away, and because new values only gradually appear, that it may, at times, be difficult to state that a particular value is held by a particular individual, or shared by a particular group. This is to say that people vary in their degree of commitment to a value. It is entirely possible for a lower-class person to hold middle-class values only; or he may abandon middle-class values without developing any new values; or he may abandon middle-class values while developing a new set of values.[15] I am certain that these are actual responses of many lower-class people to their deprived situation. But I am equally certain that the dominant response of the lower-class person is the lower-class value stretch. It is because the lower-class person, to a degree, typically shares the middle-class values and also holds values unique to the lower class that he is able to adapt to his circumstances without resorting to deviance or revolution. Mental disorder, juvenile delinquency, and rebellion would occur with greater frequency within the lower class without the existence of the lower-class value stretch.

Once the lower-class value stretch has been developed the lower-class person is in a better position to adapt to his circumstances because he has a wider range of values with which to operate.[16] Cultural resources, in a sense, come to compensate for his lack of social and economic resources.

NOTES

1. One could illuminate the discussion about a common or a class-differentiated value system by focusing upon any class rather than just the lower class. For example, do members of the upper class share the general values of society, or do they

hold values unique to themselves? Indeed, the whole question of the parallels between the upper class and lower class deserves a good deal more attention. Deviations from the conventional standards of society are said to occur in both of them. And there are some related and interesting findings in small group research that both low-ranking and high-ranking members of a group have greater leeway, in certain respects, to deviate from the norms of the group: See John W. Thibaut and Harold H. Kelley, *The Social Psychology of Groups* (New York: John Wiley and Sons, 1959), pp. 250-251; George C. Homans, *The Human Group* (New York: Harcourt, Brace, 1950), p. 144; Henry W. Riecken and George C. Homans, "Psychological Aspects of Social Structure," in Gardner Lindzey, ed., *Handbook of Social Psychology*, Vol. II (Cambridge, Mass.: Addison-Wesley, 1954), pp. 793-794. For an excellent discussion of the subject, which I first read after writing the above, see George C. Homans, *Social Behavior: Its Elementary Forms* (New York: Harcourt, Brace & World, 1961), pp. 336-358 *et passim*.

2. Talcott Parsons, "General Theory in Sociology," in Robert K. Merton, Leonard Broom, Leonard S. Cottrell, Jr., editors, *Sociology Today* (New York: Basic Books, Inc., 1959), p. 8.

3. Robert K. Merton, *Social Theory and Social Structure*, revised and enlarged edition (Glencoe, Ill.: Free Press, 1957), p. 141.

4. Judith Blake, "Family Instability and Reproductive Behavior in Jamaica," *Current Research in Human Fertility* (New York: Milbank Memorial Fund, 1955), pp. 34-39; William J. Goode, "Illegitimacy in the Caribbean Social Structure," *American Sociological Review*, Vol. 25 (February 1960), pp. 21-30.

5. Donald R. Taft, *Criminology*, revised edition (New York: Macmillan 1950), pp. 181-182.

6. Gresham M. Sykes and David Matza, "Techniques of Neutralization: A Theory of Delinquency," *American Sociological Review*, Vol. 22 (December 1957), pp. 664-670. [Cf. Fritz Redl and David Wineman, *Children Who Hate* (Glencoe: Free Press, 1951), pp. 158-174.] In a more recent paper Matza and Sykes have taken a somewhat different tack. In the earlier paper their position was that the delinquents shared the conventional values. In this paper they address themselves to specifically delinquent values but stress the striking similarities of these to certain subterranean values that are to be found within the society at large. This raises the question of public versus private values and the greater efficiency of the higher classes in maintaining the privacy of their private values. David Matza and Gresham M. Sykes, "Juvenile Delinquency and Subterranean Values," *American Sociological Review*, Vol. 26 (October 1961), pp. 712-719.

7. Herbert H. Hyman, "The Value System of Different Classes: A Social Psychological Contribution to the Analysis of Stratification," in Reinhard Bendix and Seymour M. Lipset, editors, *Class, Status and Power* (Glencoe: Free Press, 1953), pp. 426-442.

8. Allison Davis, "The Motivation of the Underprivileged Worker," in William Foote Whyte, editor, *Industry and Society* (New York: McGraw-Hill, 1946), p. 104.

9. Fernando Henriques, *Family and Colour in Jamaica* (London: Eyre & Spottiswoode, 1953), p. 162.

10. Walter B. Miller, "Lower Class Culture as a Generating Milieu of Gang Delinquency," *Journal of Social Issues*, Vol. 14, No. 3, 1958, p. 5.

11. This is obviously only a very sketchy account of the development of the lower-class value stretch. Tracing the historical development of lower-class values is no simple matter, especially since, in Malthus's words, "the histories of mankind that we possess are histories only of the higher classes."

Important clues to the psychological processes that accompany the development of the lower-class value stretch can be found in the literature on learning theory that has come out of the fields of animal experimentation and small group experimentation. For a demonstration of the applicability of such theory see George C. Homans, *Social Behavior: Its Elementary Forms*. See also Allison Davis, *op. cit.;* Genevieve Knupfer, "Portrait of the Underdog," *Public Opinion Quarterly*, Vol. 2 (Spring 1947), pp. 103-114.

12. Robert K. Merton, *op. cit.*, p. 156.

13. Homans makes this statement about what he refers to as the "social contract" theory and the "social mold" theory. George C. Homans, *The Human Group*, p. 330. The argument between the egg enthusiasts and the sperm protagonists is another particularly good example of the two warring sides mistaking part of the truth for the whole of it: See N. J. Berrill, *Sex and the Nature of Things* (New York: Pocket Books, 1955), pp. 1-11.

14. Talcott Parsons, "General Theory in Sociology," in Robert K. Merton, Leonard Broom and Leonard S. Cottrell, Jr., editors, *Sociology Today*, p. 8.

15. The assumption made here, as elsewhere in the discussion of the lower-class value stretch, is that the dominant, conventional, middle-class values have relevance for all members of the society, including its lower-class members. Since many middle-class values, however, are inappropriate to the conditions of lower-class life, the members of the lower class are faced with a problem. Once this value problem has been solved within the lower class—as in the development of the value stretch — then this solution is learned by many in the next generation who therefore do not face the same problem all over again. But a different kind of problem now emerges, and it is perhaps the most serious problem that practioners in the social welfare, health, educational, and vocational fields face: To what extent are lower-class individuals passing up realistic opportunities for better welfare, health, education, and jobs because of cultural resistances? And to what extent can or should these hard-to-reach lower-class individuals be induced to break away from these cultural resistances? An intriguing answer to these questions that deserves the serious attention of professional practitioners who work with lower-class individuals is given in S. M. Miller and Frank Riessman, "The Working Class Subculture: A New View," *Social Problems*, Vol. 9 (Summer 1961), pp. 86-97.

16. Members of the middle or upper class would not be under the same degree of environmental stress as lower-class members, and they would therefore not have to stretch their values to the same degree even if they did not adhere strictly to the conventional values. They would have access to resources that would permit them to retain their respectability and a seeming adherence to conventional values even in the face of deviance. Everett C. Hughes, for example, has suggested that any upper middle-class girl can get an abortion by some other name. He points out, in a personal communication, that no canon of behavior is absolutely adhered to, and that there must therefore be "a secondary set of canons of behavior—the rules which govern subsequent behavior after the first canon has been violated." This is an intriguing idea with many ramifications. The major comment suggested by a consideration of the lower-class value stretch is that secondary canons of behavior may interact with the primary canons in such a way that the primary canons are stretched.

A similar idea has been expressed by Reinhard Bendix: "Is not indeed every group in some measure engaged in a startegy of argument which seeks to maximize its self-respect in terms of the conventional standards from which behavior is bound to differ to some extent?" (personal communication).

RICHARD A. BALL

The Analgesic Subculture

Despite considerable evidence to the contrary, conventional sociology still has an essentially rationalistic view of man. Reminiscent of the eminently cool and calculating "economic man" of classical economics, the model of modern "sociologic man" is almost perfectly programmed, operating in accordance with the dictates of his culture. Any injudicious behavior on his part is typically attributed to cultural "conflicts" or "anomie." Observations suggesting that one of man's most basic attributes may be his capacity for nonrationality are largely ignored.

The best single test of the accuracy of this charge lies in close scrutiny of sociologists' handling of the critical task of diagnosing and treating "social problems." I wish to argue that considerations of the nonrational qualities of human behavior, though given lip-service, have been widely ignored in favor of the underlying assumption of rationalism. Actually, the origin, development, and continued survival of many "problem" subcultures can be better explained in terms of "nonrational" responses to environmental circumstances. The failure of planners to understand this illustrates the inadequacy of their rationalistic assumption.

One of the more serious failures has been the inability of social planners to understand and deal with widespread, apparently "irrational" stubbornness among the very people whose lives they are attempting to "improve." These "target groups" include the elderly, the Negro, and the poor. One major thread running through the experience of most persons in these heterogeneous categories is intense and prolonged frustration. It

---

Adapted by permission of the author and the American Sociological Association from Richard A. Ball, "A Poverty Case: The Analgesic Subculture of the Southern Appalachians," *American Sociological Review* 33 (December 1968): 885-95.

is my belief that to explain, predict, and alter their behavior, we must recognize that one institutionalized *nonrational* response to frustrations is what I have labeled *the analgesic subculture*.

I will focus upon only one of the many manifestations of poverty — the "folk subculture" of the Southern Appalachian Mountains. This particular example must not be considered a representative case; it is instead almost an "ideal type" illustration in support of my position.

THE FRUSTRATION-INSTIGATED BEHAVIOR CONCEPT

The distinction between frustration-instigated behavior and motivation-instigated behavior first came about as a result of Maier's (1949) experiments with rats. In most of the reported experiments, the Lashley jumping apparatus was used. This device consists of a small stand facing a wall in which there are two openings. Each "window" is covered with a card printed with its respective symbol. The animal, placed on this platform, is forced to choose one card by jumping at it and striking it with his body. If the correct card is struck, the card falls over and the animal lands on a feeding platform (reward). If the incorrect card is struck, the card remains locked in place and the animal receives a thump and falls into a net below (punishment). When one of the cards is consistently locked, and is changed to both a right and left position on different trials, the animal develops a preference for one card so that it consistently chooses the card that leads to reward and avoids the other — regardless of the side on which the reward card is placed. In experiments in which the cards are changed from side to side, and either the left or right card is consistently made correct, the animal disregards the symbol and responds to card position. These choices Maier regards as learned preferences representing goal-oriented or goal-motivated responses.

If, however, the cards are locked at random, then there is no systematic response which will permit escape from punishment. In such cases, the animal usually goes through a stage of variability in its choices, and soon refuses to jump. This resistance to jumping may be overcome by an electric shock, prodding with a stick, or blowing a blast of air on the animal. Maier speaks of this situation as the "insoluble problem" and regards it as frustrating, both because it is a problem that cannot be solved and because pressure is applied to force a response.

The behavior of the animal in these circumstances is instructive. After a short while in the "insoluble" situation, and with pressure applied to force jumping, the rat develops a response that is inadequate and inferior to any number of any other possible responses. Thus, an animal may respond by always choosing the card on its right, in spite of the fact that this position preference is punished on half the trials. Other animals respond by developing a *symbol preference* for one of the two cards, regardless of its position. The choice (either symbol or position) made by any given animal is maintained rigidly, without the animals once attempting an alternative, despite the fact that the response is punished half the time. *Even more striking is the observation that the animals will not abandon their basic responses even when punishment is received on every trial.*

Maier maintains that such behavior cannot be adequately accounted for by ordinary learning theory. His hypothesis is that motivation and frustration are qualitatively different instigators of behavior and must therefore be described by different principles. By motivation he means the process by which the expression of behavior is determined by consequences to which such behavior leads. (Maier, 1949:93). Motivation-instigated behavior is properly approached on the basis of learning theory; it is flexible and adaptive. The behavior is goal-oriented, and the learner profits from experience. *Frustration-instigated* behavior, in contrast, is not goal-oriented behavior in the usual sense. Under frustrating conditions "the consequence of the action is not a factor in the selection of behavior." (Maier, 1949:94).

Since there is no apparent goal in frustration-instigated behavior, such behavior appears senseless when regarded from the typical motivational point of view. Since behavioral science researchers and social change agents are typically products of backgrounds in which goal-orientation is a dominant theme, they find it difficult to think in less rationalistic terms. They tend to overlook the possibility that behavior resulting from extreme frustration may represent a final response to frustration rather than being a means to any end.

I feel constrained to repeat the caution against over-generalizing the results of rigidly controlled experiments with rats to account for human behavior. Still, to admit that the laboratory is not life, and that rats are not men, is not to dismiss some connections. Conclusions based on the behavior of nonhuman species can serve as valuable hypothesis in a study of man's behavior. It is ironic that the rationalistic bias, by no means restricted to sociology, has interfered with a rational evaluation of contributions such as Maier's.

ENVIRONMENTAL CHALLENGE AND CULTURAL RESPONSE

Toynbee's writings have hardly been ignored, but he has found himself subjected to unusually vehement criticism. Still, Toynbee's work is of special relevance to the problem of subcultural origin and change.

The Analgesic Subculture

Toynbee (1946), views the development of civilization as a "response" to "challenges" in both the social and natural environment. There is considerable similarity between his idea of the impossible challenge and Maier's concept of the "insoluble problem" situation, but even more significant is the close correspondence between the historian's speculations on human responses and the experimental psychologist's observations of reactions in laboratory animals. Toynbee argues, for example, that the basic contributions of the building of American civilization came from those living in the coastal region bounded by the Mason-Dixon Line to the south and a line through New England to the north. He maintains that the environmental challenge below the Mason-Dixon Line was generally insufficient to produce an energetic response, while in Maine, on the other hand, the challenge was actually too great. In his analysis of historical responses to overwhelming challenges, Toynbee (1946:147) refers to Maine as a "museum piece," remarking that, "Maine today is at once one of the longest-settled regions of the American Union and one of the least urbanized and sophisticated."

These words describe almost exactly conditions in the Southern Appalachian Mountains. In fact, closer study of the latter region discloses an even more striking correspondence between Toynbee's generalizations and the results of Maier's experiments. If the frustration-instigated behavior hypothesis is correct, the response similarities can be explained by the observation that the historical challenges faced in Appalachia approximated even more closely the conditions of Maier's experiments than did the problems encountered in Maine. Life in the Southern Appalachians has been for many almost a model of "insoluble problems," "impossible challenges," and overwhelming frustrations.

THE PROBLEMS OF APPALACHIA

Toynbee (1946:149) has set forth his view of the Appalachian challenge and the human response in no uncertain terms. He writes as follows:

> Let us next consider an instance in which the challenge has been not exclusively physical but partly physical and partly human. . . .
> The modern Ulstermen, however, are not the only surviving overseas representatives of this stock, for the Scottish pioneers who migrated to Ulster begat Scotch-Irish descendants who reimmigrated in the eighteenth century from Ulster to North America, and these survive today in the Fastnesses of the Appalachian mountains, a highland zone which runs through half a dozen states in the American Union from Pennsylvania to Georgia. . . . Obviously, this American challenge has been more formidable than the Irish challenge in both its aspects, physical and human. Has the increased challenge evoked

an increased response? If we compare the Ulstermen and the Appalachian of today, two centuries after they parted company, we shall find that the answer is once again in the negative. The modern Appalachian has not only not improved on the Ulstermen; he has failed to hold his ground and has gone downhill in the most disconcerting fashion. In fact, the Appalachian "mountain people" today are no better than barbarians. They have relapsed into illiteracy and witchcraft. They suffer from poverty, squalor, and ill health. They are the American counterparts of the latter-day white barbarians of the Old World—Rifis, Albanians, Kurds, Pathans, and Hairy Ainus; but, whereas these latter are belated survivals of an ancient barbarism, the Appalachians present the melancholy spectacle of a people who have acquired civilization and then lost it.

Toynbee has, of course, overstated the case. A closer look will usually show more differentiation than is apparent from afar, and many Southern Appalachian mountaineers have cause to resent such a blanket condemnation. Toynbee's words are more accurate when limited to what may be designated as the "folk subculture" of the area. Writers who deal with Appalachia unintentionally devote most of their attention to this particular portion of the regional population — partly because it is sizeable, partly because its existence has been defined as a "social problem," and perhaps partly because the bulk of the region's people are too much like most Americans to be considered "interesting."

These mountaineers have been subjected to a history of constant physical, economic, and social frustration. They have been repeatedly blocked, pressured, and defeated by their environment. The history of their frustration is described vividly in the following passages from Caudill's *Night Comes to The Cumberlands* (1962:ix-xi).

. . . Their past created the modern mountaineers and the communities in which they live, and resulted in a land of economic, social, and political blight without parallel in the nation. . . . Coal has always cursed the land in which it lies. When men begin to wrest it from the earth it leaves a legacy of foul streams, hideous slag heaps, and polluted air. It peoples this transformed land with blind and crippled men and with widows and orphans.

But the tragedy of the Kentucky mountains transcends the tragedy of coal. It is compounded of Indian wars, Civil war, and internecine feuds, of layered hatreds and of violent death. To its sad blend, history has added the curse of coal as a crown of sorrow. . . .

In the 1960 preferential primary, Senator—now president—John F. Kennedy campaigned across West Virginia and saw at first hand the conditions existing in the coal fields of that state. The spectacle of mass misery and of mass surrender to it appears to have deeply impressed him, because in the general election campaign he repeatedly referred to the hunger and depression he had seen there. . . . However, the fact is that a million Americans in the Southern Appalachians live today in conditions of squalor, ignorance, and ill health which could scarcely be equalled in Europe or Japan or, perhaps, in parts of mainland Asia.

Certain typical responses have resulted from these conditions. Ford (1962:9-34), interpreting data from the most comprehensive general survey of the Southern Appalachians ever conducted, lists the principal cultural themes as (1) individualism and self-reliance, (2) traditionalism and fatalism, and (3) religious fundamentalism. Weller (1965), specifically describing what he calls the "folk class" as *Yesterday's People*, gives special emphasis to individualism, traditionalism, fatalism, action-seeking, fear psychology, reference-group domination, and familism. There is now a wealth of descriptive data, and it clearly substantiates such portraits of the folk subculture. The task of explanation has proved more difficult, for the assertion that the subculture represents "tradition" is not explanation at all.

THE ANALGESIC SUBCULTURE

Research attention has been directed toward Appalachia in recent years, and specifications of the content of the Appalachian folk subculture are fairly complete, but most of the authors of these descriptions, and particularly the regional planners, admit to difficulty in understanding and dealing with the values they have described. The conduct of these people seems to them even more senseless than that of most "hard core" poverty groups. Why, it is asked, are they so little interested in improving their lives? How can they resign themselves to acceptance of minimal welfare payments and then adopt the "dole" as a permanent way of life? Why aren't they more eager to leave their hopeless environment for urban areas of greater opportunity? What, in short, explains their lack of ambition, their "episodic" view of life, and their inability to arouse themselves to sustained efforts? Admittedly, their past has been bleak and hopeless, but why should this prevent them from responding to the opportunities of the present?

As is often the case, the inability of students of Southern Appalachia to comprehend the behavior of their subjects is rooted less in faulty logic or inadequate observation than in their dubious assumptions about human behavior. One of these is the assumption that all behavior is rational or motivation-instigated. The stubbornness of the mountaineer simply resists explanation in these terms. Nor can one explain fatalism and apathy as sensible adaptations to contemporary learning situations. What the highly motivated and remarkably adaptive observer cannot easily understand is the daily experience of inexorable pressure, "insoluble problems," and absolutely overwhelming frustration. These are the life experiences of the poor generally, but they have been experienced with special intensity by the mountaineer, and it is this fact which makes his particular plight of more general relevance.

These life conditions provide the major key to the origin, development and continued existence of the Southern Appalachian folk subculture. The subculture represents to a significant degree *the institutionalization of frustration-instigated behavior*. The principal values, beliefs, and norms, formed during a long history of misfortune, are supported by the internal nature of the subculture and by the external pressures of contemporary life. These shared understandings are transmitted across generations; the young learn to anticipate defeat and to perform the subcultural rituals which reduce its impact. The frustration-instigated behaviors observable in laboratory experiments have become a thoroughgoing way of life, justified by religious doctrine and sustained by a social order. The result of this process may be conveniently labeled the *analgesic subculture*. The analgesic subculture possesses considerable durability, for not only is the expectation of defeat a self-fulfilling prophecy, but the subcultural relief behaviors tend to produce additional problems. More than a vicious circle, the consequence resembles a descending spiral.

PRINCIPAL COMPONENTS OF THE ANALGESIC SUBCULTURE

Fixation as a Subcultural Pattern

If fixation is defined as an abnormally strong and persisting response, the rigid behavior of the rats in Maier's experiments represents a clear illustration. More extreme examples are to be found in additional experiments which indicate that, even when the fixated animals have actually learned which card punishes and which does not, they are unable to respond rationally. Maier notes that this is a form of *compulsion*. That is, the animal executes an unadapted response even though it "knows better." The compulsive nature of the fixation is apparent, for example, when one places the negative card on the side to which the animal is fixated, and the other window is left open with a dish of food placed in plain view near the opening. In this case the animal goes toward the open window and sniffs toward the food; it then turns and jumps at the locked card representing the fixated response. Such behavior can hardly be described as rational or goal-oriented. It is important to recognize, however, that the fixation does appear to provide *a sort of adjustment* to the situation, thereby reducing "emotional tensions" in the animal. The conclusion is reinforced by the observation that after animals have developed a fixation response they suffer fewer seizures under pressure. Apparently the "abnormal" fixation gives the animal a way of responding to the insoluble problem, without which such situations would have remained unbearably stressful.

Much of the obstinate traditionalism of the Southern Appalachian folk subculture may be interpreted as the fixated behavior of people seeking relief from insoluble problems. What has long been criticized as an adherence to old ways which is "stubborn, sullen and perverse to a degree that others cannot comprehend" (Kephart, 1913:23), becomes more understandable in terms of the soothing qualities of ritual. Critics who complain that the tenacious adherence to custom limits the adaptability of the subculture are quite correct, but Maier's experiments indicate that such nonrational behavior may be temporarily effective in reducing anxiety. The result is that, although the opinionated, dogmatic, and argumentative behavior of the mountaineer may multiply his problems, he persists in it nevertheless. If, in the language of the subculture, he frequently "cuts off his nose to spite his face" by stubbornly insisting upon actions which are clearly against his rational self-interest, this "irrationality" is at least comprehensible as a frustration-instigated action.

Regression as a Subcultural Pattern

The frustration-instigated behavior concept also leads one to predict that the Appalachian folk subculture will exhibit patterns of regression, aggression and resignation.

Many of the behaviors commonly cited in descriptions of the folk subculture can be taken as examples of regression induced by frustration. These characteristics would indicate the lack of aesthetic appreciation, anti-intellectualism, the preference of anecdote over abstraction, the insistence upon a literal interpretation of the Bible, the entanglement of religious fundamentalism with deep superstition, the squandering which often accompanies "pay day" or a welfare check, the tendency for self-pity, and the conversion of the "sick role" into what local physicians sometimes half-seriously term a "chronic passive-dependency syndrome" (Caudill, 1962:283). Use of the term "regression" to describe these circumstances is congruent with Toynbee's conclusion that the mountaineer has "failed to hold his ground," that he has "gone downhill in a most disconcerting fashion," and that he has "relapsed" into conditions of barbarism.

Two particular manifestations of regressive behavior stand out as major problems of Appalachia. One of these may be called the *Welfare Syndrome*. The other is the occasionally neurotic dependence upon kin which is manifested in extreme *Familism*. Space limitations preclude more than a summary of the Welfare Syndrome. Many of the members of the folk subculture have regressed to a state of social dependency. Although what has been intended as a temporary assistance has been converted into a way of life, the explanation of this behavior is not to be sought in standard concepts of rational motivation. There is nothing particularly "sensible" about living on welfare payments little above subsistence when opportunities for goal-directed behavior are, if not abundant, at least in many cases available. To one who proceeds solely on assumptions of rationalism, permanent reliance upon public welfare seems to be use of means (of temporary assistance) as ends (or terminal adaptations). The frustration-instigated behavior concept supplies an explanation of such behavior, for frustration-instigated behavior is characteristically a *terminal response to frustration* and not a means to an end. Without intending a play on words, one may say that the satisfaction which occurs from frustration-instigated behavior is precisely in the form of relief rather than of goal-attainment.

Just as the Welfare Syndrome may be interpreted as a form of regression, so may exaggerated Familism. The literature on Appalachian life consistently points to an intensive *emotional dependence* on kin. Some young people simply never establish themselves as separate individuals. Nor are they encouraged to do so by their parents. Both parents and children maintain what may be termed a "clinging behavior" which may be based less upon genuine affection and shared activities than upon neurotic emotional entanglements characterized by a mutual resentment. Grown offspring who hate their parents cannot bear to be away from them. Migrants who have finally broken away suddenly and curiously return home at the slightest misfortunes. The subculture not only condones this behavior, but *it functions to institutionalize it*.

Aggression as a Subcultural Pattern

Much of the otherwise "senseless" conduct of the mountaineer is comprehensible in terms of an analgesic subculture theory. Herein may lie the explanation for the infamous mountain feuds. Feuding behavior is an excellent example of subculturally patterned aggression which, while providing the momentary satisfactions of revenge, serves no rational purpose. As some unsuccessful mediators have dimly perceived, the feud was not developed as an intelligently designed means to an end, nor even as an accidentally effective instrument. It is an end in itself. Had the McCoys been unavailable, the Hatfields would have probably "taken it out on" some other target.

Resignation as a Subcultural Pattern

In addition to fixation, regression, and aggression, the frustration-instigated behavior concept would lead one to predict considerable resignation to the hostile conditions of Southern Appalachian life. Seldom is an expectation more fully realized. Resignation, apathy, and fatalism are rarely so prominent as among the members of the mountain folk subculture. Since resignation consists in giving up, it is not representative of goal-oriented action. In fact, goals have receded from reality and motivation seems largely absent. Resignation has, in short, the attributes of the other frustration-instigated behaviors. It is not a means to anything; it is an "end of the line" behavior. Such a response may be difficult for the motivation-oriented observer to comprehend, but it is quite likely to provide relief from the tensions of extreme and prolonged frustration.

CONCLUSION

To maintain that man's conduct is frequently "unreasonable" is by no means to argue that it can never be explained or predicted. Students of socially thwarted minorities would have less difficulty understanding the normative orders they describe if they would recognize the extent to which such systems represent the institutionalization of basic frustration responses. The reactions will be expressed somewhat differently in various subcultures, depending upon the particular nature of the obstacles and the available tradition, but the underlying processes are essentially identical. The responses are perhaps most vivid with the mountaineer since his impoverished condition is coupled with a hostile environment and historical tragedy.

The Southern Appalachian folk subculture is certainly easier to understand in terms of the thesis presented. Responding to a given configuration of "insoluble problems," the mountaineer has developed a way of life emphasizing fixated behavior, dependency, belligerence and fatalistic resignation. Admittedly, these reactions are not "adequate adaptations to the situation." They do not represent "effective coping with the environment." Nevertheless, the responses are in a limited sense functional, for they provide relief from the pains of frustration.

Such subcultures are, however, complicated wholes maintained by internal linkages as well as by their capacity to deflect environmental pressure. One would expect them to survive for some time even if the circumstances which produce them were eliminated entirely. One explanation for their durability lies in the very fact that they have developed as nonrational responses to frustration rather than as rewarding solutions to environmental problems. It is entirely possible that these are among the most rigid of all subcultures. Such implications follow from certain basic data.

Animals that have previously developed stereotypes in a given situation are less likely to learn a simple reward response than animals that have previously acquired a reward response and then must learn another. Thus, it seems to be more difficult to substitute a reward response for a stereotype than to substitute one reward response for another....

... The stereotype response developed in the insoluble problem situation is more stable than a similar response acquired through systematic reward. This greater persistence of a response developed in the insoluble problem occurs despite the fact that under this condition the assumed response is one that is punished as frequently as it is rewarded (Maier, 1949:31-32).

The consequences are truly paradoxical in terms of rationalistic assumptions. The strength of the analgesic subculture is apparently in large part a product of its failures. Formed as a response to defeat, and offering no "adaptive" solutions to environmental problems, it virtually assures the persistence of the problems, and thereby becomes more deeply entrenched. Even if the problems were suddenly solved by outside intervention, Maier's data suggest that the responses built on years of stress would be extremely difficult to alter. The rigidity of any analgesic subculture seems inherent in its nature.

Each individual subculture may be expected to develop additional self-stabilizing components. Again, the Appalachian folk subculture provides convenient illustrations of the more general process. The subculture's punitive child-rearing practices are a case in point. One of the clearest distinctions between motivation-instigated behavior and frustration-instigated behavior is seen in the effects of punishment. From the rationalistic point of view, one would assume that punishment tends to force abandonment of forbidden behavior. In terms of the frustration-instigated behavior hypothesis, on the other hand, one might postulate that punishment aggravates frustration and that punishment would therefore tend to strengthen the fixated behavior. Maier's experiments support the latter conclusion. His data indicate, in fact, that punishment on all trials is even less likely to transform an animal's fixated response than is irregular punishment. He concludes that punishing a stubborn, undesirable response may not only fail to alter it but may actually increase its persistence and consequently make future corrections more difficult. The folk subculture offers evidence of this relationship, for Weller (1965:65-66) reports that discipline is "punishment-based" and that children are taught to obey through fear.

Furthermore, the subculture generally renders the mountaineer more susceptible to frustration-instigated behaviors by incorporating practices which impede the development of frustration tolerance. It is not customary to praise children judiciously or to reward effective conduct in any systematic fashion. Caudill (1962:73) notes "a quality which is almost never encountered in the highlands to this day: willingness to commend a person openly for a favor done or for some desirable skill or trait," and he points out that "the mountaineer was literally starved for compliments and for some outward show of appreciation." This is still the case, and one apparent result is a low frustration threshold. There is no history of reward to balance future frustrations, and there are few pleasant memories to assist one through periods of stress. The effect is to reinforce the subculture, for it becomes even more attractive to the vulnerable.

It is small wonder that these subcultures are so resistant to change. Exhortations against the symptoms of frustration will not eliminate the causes. Maier's experiments indicate instead that to teach people to restrain their frustration-instigated reactions without also attacking the source is to force them into a state of intolerable anxiety. Those who would modify such subcultures must realize that they may be for some the only emotional relief available. They must also realize that to stigmatize such practices may simply reinforce them.

The impoverished mountaineer finds himself in a situation not unlike that of other minority groups. Despite the fact that he has been provided with gradually increasing opportunities, he is faced with increasing frustrations based on the sense of relative deprivation and the growing demand that he solve his problems. The experience of relative deprivation is forced upon him through increased physical contact with other people and by way of the mass media. These convey to him an image of the "good life," and in contrast with this image his own existence appears more bleak and hopeless than before. His frustrations are also deepened by those who urge him to self-help and increase his expectations for improvement, for they may succeed in increasing his desire for a "better" life. Unless this goal is attained quickly, the problem often becomes even more frustrating simply because the motivation to solve it is intensified.

This analysis should not be interpreted as a rejection of planned social change. The argument is rather that social action might be more effectively undertaken after reappraisal of fundamental assumptions regarding human behavior. Since one important rationalistic misconception is the assumption that such behavior is predominantly goal-directed, admission of the psychological concept of frustration-instigated behavior and the sociological hypothesis of the analgesic subculture represents a modest but extremely significant concession to those who insist that values, norms and behaviors may be less than wholly rational. There is evidence that these concepts may, for example, be very effective tools in understanding and dealing with social problems such as "hardcore" poverty.

REFERENCES

Barker, R., T. Dembo and K. Lewin.
1941 Frustration and Regression. Iowa City: University of Iowa Press.

Barnes, H. E., ed.
1948 An Introduction to the History of Sociology. Chicago: University of Chicago Press.

Cahnman, Werner J. and Alvin Boskoff, eds.
1964 Sociology and History. New York: Free Press.

Caudill, Harry M.
1962 Night Comes to the Cumberlands. Boston: Little, Brown.

Dollard, J., N. E. Miller, L. W. Doob, O. H. Mowrer and R. R. Sears.
1944 Frustration and Aggression. London: Kegan Paul.

Ford, Thomas R., ed.
1962 The Southern Appalachian Region. Lexington: The University of Kentucky Press.

Kephart, Horace.
1913 Our Southern Highlanders. New York: Outing Publishing.

Maier, Norman R.
1949 Frustration. New York: McGraw-Hill.

Thomas, W. I.
1928 The Child in America. New York: Knopf.

Toynbee, Arnold J.
1946 A Study of History. New York: Oxford University Press.

Weller, Jack E.
1965 Yesterday's People. Lexington: The University of Kentucky Press.

Wrong, Dennis H.
1961 "The oversocialized conception of man in modern sociology." American Sociological Review 26 (April):187-193.

Yates, Aubrey J.
1962 Frustration and Conflict. New York: Wiley.

V

Minorities in the Labor Force: Gains in Equal Opportunity?

One can scarcely deny the presence, proportion, and recalcitrance of the minority employment problem in America. Since the evidence (part of which is presented in this chapter) is so clear, the more important question refers to the trends in minority employment. Signs of lessening discrimination are perhaps the most we can realistically expect. Factors impeding parity between minorities and the majority will also be explored in this chapter.

The Other America by Michael Harrington was very influential in the staging of the "war on poverty." The next selection, "If You're Black, Stay Back," is an excerpt from Harrington's book which graphically portrays the economic and social disadvantages of being black in America. In Harrington's view, racism binds Negroes to a poverty status; prejudicial responses to the color black will persist despite enactment of protective legislation.

According to Blau and Duncan ("Inequality of Opportunity"), gains in the relative advancement of the Negro have been limited to the acquisition of minimum education and decreased employment discrimination on entry into the labor market. But, with regard to higher education, a prerequisite for higher occupational advancement, the distance between whites and Negroes has continued to widen. It is, as they state, scarcely surprising to find whites in the United States with an occupational advantage over Negroes. A new dimension is added, however, in their finding that black-white occupational status and income differentials increase with education level. Except for those who are college educated, Negroes with higher education are relatively worse off compared to whites than are less educated Negroes. White ethnic minorities, in contrast, do as well occupationally as the population majority. An open occupational structure appears to characterize American society—except for those with the wrong color.

Several important facts are documented in "Toward Equal Employment Opportunity," excerpts from the 1968 and 1970 *Manpower Report of the President*. First, while Negroes have experienced occupational, economic, and educational gains in the 1960s, the gap between blacks and whites remains substantial. In fact, black-white median income differentials have increased. Compared with whites, Negro families in the lowest and highest fifths of the national income scale had greater dollar differences in median income in 1968 than in 1959. The disparity in median dollar income between middle-income Negro and white families has remained unchanged in the past decade.

Second, with the exception of persons of Puerto Rican origin, Spanish Americans,* although lagging behind "Anglos" occupationally, educationally, and economically, supercede Negroes in the same geographic area. Third, American Indians on reservations constitute the most socially and economically disadvantaged minority group in the United States.

What *are* the trends in equal opportunity among minorities?

---

*Persons of Latin American, Mexican, Puerto Rican, or Spanish origin.

MICHAEL HARRINGTON

If You're Black, Stay Back

If all the discriminatory laws in the United States were immediately repealed, race would still remain as one of the most pressing moral and political problems in the nation. Negroes and other minorities are not simply the victims of a series of iniquitous statutes. The American economy, the American society, the American unconscious are all racist. If all the laws were framed to provide equal opportunity, a majority of the Negroes would not be able to take full advantage of the change. There would still be a vast, silent, and automatic system directed against men and women of color.

To belong to a racial minority is to be poor, but poor in a special way. The fear, the lack of self-confidence, the haunting, these have been described. But they, in turn, are the expressions of the most institutionalized poverty in the United States, the most vicious of the vicious circles. In a sense, the Negro is classically the "other" American, degraded and frustrated at every turn and not just because of laws.

There are sympathetic and concerned people who do not understand how deeply America has integrated racism into its structure. Given time, they argue, the Negroes will rise in the society like the Irish, the Jews, the Italians, and all the rest. But this notion misses two decisive facts: that the Negro is colored, and no other group in the United States has ever faced such a problem, and that the Negro of today is an internal migrant who will face racism wherever he goes, who cannot

---

Reprinted by permission of The Macmillan Company from Michael Harrington, *The Other America* (Baltimore, Maryland: Penguin Books, 1963), pp. 72-82. Copyright © Michael Harrington, 1962, 1969.

leave his oppression behind as if it were a czar or a potato famine. To be equal, the Negro requires something much more profound than a way "into" the society; he needs a transformation of some of the basic institutions of the society.

The Negro is poor because he is black; that is obvious enough. But, perhaps more importantly, the Negro is black because he is poor. The laws against color can be removed, but that will leave the poverty that is the historic and institutionalized consequence of color. As long as this is the case, being born a Negro will continue to be the most profound disability that the United States imposes upon a citizen.

Perhaps the quickest way to point up the racism of the American economy is to recall a strange case of jubilation.

Late in 1960 the Department of Labor issued a study, "The Economic Situation of Negroes in the United States." It noted that in 1939, nonwhite workers earned, on the average, 41 per cent as much as whites, and that by 1958 their wages had climbed to 58 per cent of that of whites. Not a little elation greeted this announcement. Some of the editorialists cited these statistics as indicating that slow and steady progress was being made (At this rate, the Negro would reach parity with the white some time well after the year 2000.)

To begin with, the figures were somewhat more optimistic than the reality. Part of the Negro gain reflected the shift of rural Negroes to cities and Southern Negroes to the North. In both cases, the people involved increased their incomes by going into a more prosperous section of the country. But within each area their relative position remained the same: at the bottom. Then, the statistics take a depression year (1939) as a base for comparison, and contrast it to a year of recession (1958). This tended to exaggerate the advance because Negroes in 1939 were particularly victimized.

Another important aspect of the problem was obscured by the sweeping comparisons most editorialists made between the 1939 and 1958 figures. Even the Department of Labor statistics themselves indicate that the major gain was made during World War II (the increase from 1939 to 1947 was from 41.4 per cent to 54.3 of the white wage). In the postwar period the rate of advance slowed to a walk. Moreover, most of the optimism was based upon figures for Negro men. When the women are included, and when one takes a median family income from the Current Population Reports, Negroes rose from 51 per cent of white family income in 1947 to 57 per cent in 1952—and then declined back to the 1947 level by 1959.

But even without these qualifications, the fact is stark enough: the United States found cause for celebration in the announcement that

Negro workers had reached 58 per cent of the wage level of their white co-workers. This situation is deeply imbedded in the very structure of American society.

Negroes in the United States are concentrated in the worst, dirtiest, lowest-paying jobs. A third continue to live in the rural South, most of them merely subsisting within a culture of poverty and a society of open terror. A third live in Southern cities and a third in Northern cities, and these have bettered their lot compared to the sharecroppers. But they are still the last hired and the first fired, and they are particularly vulnerable to recessions.

Thus, according to the Department of Labor in 1960, 4 per cent of Negro employees were "professional, technical and kindred workers" (compared to 11.3 per cent for the whites); 2.7 per cent were "managers, officials and proprietors" (the white figure is 14.6 per cent). In short, at the top of the economic structure there were 6.7 per cent of the Negroes — and 25.9 per cent of the white. And this, in itself, represented considerable *gains* over the past two decades.

Going down the occupational scale, Negroes are primarily grouped in the bottom jobs. In 1960, 20 per cent of the whites had high-skill industrial jobs, while the Negro share of this classification was 9 per cent. Semi-skilled mass production workers and laborers constituted around 48 per cent of the Negro male population (and 25.3 per cent of the white males). Negro women are the victims of a double discrimination. According to a New York State study, Negro female income as a percentage of white actually declined between 1949 and 1954 (and, in 1960, over a third of Negro women were still employed as domestics).

In part, this miserable structure of the Negro work force is an inheritance of the past. It reflects what happens to a people who have been systematically oppressed and denied access to skill and opportunity. If this completely defined the problem, there would be a basis for optimism. One could assume that the Negro would leave behind the mess of pottage bequeathed him by white America and move into a better future. But that is not the case. For the present position of the Negro in the economy has been institutionalized. Unless something basic is done, it will reproduce itself for years to come.

Take, as an example, the problem of automation. This has caused "structural" unemployment through the American work force, that is, the permanent destruction of jobs rather than cyclical layoffs. When this happens, the blow falls disproportionately upon the Negro. As the last significant group to enter the factory, the Negroes have low seniority (if they are lucky enough to be in union occupations), and they are laid off first. As one of the least skilled groups in the work force, they will have the hardest time getting another job. The "older" Negro (over forty) may well be condemned to job instability for the rest of his life.

All of this is immediate and automatic. It is done without the intervention of a single racist, yet it is a profound part of racism in the United States.

However, more is involved than the inevitable working of an impersonal system. The Negro lives in the other America of poverty for many reasons, and one of them is conscious racism reinforcing institutional patterns of the economy. In 1960, according to the report of Herbert Hill, Labor Secretary of the National Association for the Advancement of Colored People, Negroes made up only 1.69 per cent of the total number of apprentices in the economy. The exact figure offered by Hill has been disputed; the shocking fact which he describes is agreed upon by everyone. This means that Negroes are denied access precisely to those jobs that are not low-paying and vulnerable to recession.

The main cause of this problem is the attitude of management, which fundamentally determines hiring policy. But in the case of apprenticeship programs, the labor movement and the Federal and state agencies involved also bear part of the responsibility. In the AFL-CIO, it is the politically conservative unions from the building trades who are the real stumbling block; the mass-production unions of the CIO have some bad areas, but on the whole they pioneered in bringing Negroes into the plants and integrating local organizations.

With the companies, one of the real difficulties in dealing with this structure of racism is that it is invisible. Here is a huge social fact, yet no one will accept responsibility for it. When questioned as to why there are no Negroes in sales, or in the office, the personnel man will say that he himself has nothing against Negroes. The problem, he will claim, is with subordinates who would revolt if Negroes were brought into their department, and with superiors who impose the policy. This response is standard up and down the line. The subordinates and the superiors make the same assertion.

Indeed, one of the difficulties in fighting against racist practices in the American economy is the popularity of a liberal rhetoric. Practically no one, outside of convinced white supremacists in the South, will admit to discriminatory policies. So it is that the Northern Negro has, in one sense, a more personally frustrating situation than his Southern brother. In Dixie, Jim Crow is personified, an actual living person who speaks in the accents of open racism. In the rest of the country, everybody is against discrimination for the record, and Jim Crow is a vast impersonal system that keeps the Negro down.

In the past few years, some Negro groups have been using the boycott to force companies to abandon racist hiring practices. This may well be an extraordinarily momentous development, for it is a step out of the other America, and equality will come only when the Negro is no longer poor.

But, as one goes up the occupational ladder, the resistance to hiring Negroes becomes more intense. The office, for example, is a bastion of racism in American society. To some of the people involved, white-collar work is regarded as more personal, and even social, than factory work. So the integration of work appears like the integration of the neighborhood or the home. And a wall of prejudice is erected to keep the Negroes out of advancement.

Perhaps the most shocking statistic in all this is the one that describes what happens when a Negro does acquire skill and training. North, East, South, and West the pattern is the same: the more education a Negro has, the more economic discrimination he faces. Herman Miller, one of the best known authorities on income statistics, has computed that the white Southern college graduate receives 1.85 times the compensation of his Negro counterpart, and in the North the white edge is 1.59.

What is involved in these figures is a factor that sharply distinguishes racial minorities from the old immigrant groups. When the Irish, the Jews, or the Italians produced a doctor, it was possible for him to begin to develop a practice that would bring him into the great society. There was prejudice, but he was increasingly judged on his skill. As time went on, the professionals from the immigrant groups adapted themselves to the language and dress of the rest of America. They ceased to be visible, and there was a wide scope for their talents.

This is not true of the Negro. The doctor or the lawyer will find it extremely difficult to set up practice in a white neighborhood. By far and large, they will be confined to the ghetto, and since their fellow Negroes are poor they will not receive so much money as their white colleagues. The Negro academic often finds himself trapped in a segregated educational system in which Negro colleges are short on salaries, equipment, libraries, and so on. Their very professional advancement is truncated because of it.

For the mass in the racial ghetto the situation is even more extreme. As a result of the segregation of neighborhoods, it is possible for a city like New York to have a public policy in favor of integration, and yet to maintain a system of effective segregation. In the mid-fifties, for example, the New York public-school system took a look at itself, dividing schools into Group X, with a high concentration of Negroes or

Puerto Ricans, and Group Y where Negroes and Puerto Ricans were less than 10 per cent of the student body. They found that the X schools were older and less adequate, had more probationary and substitute teachers, more classes for retarded pupils, and fewer for bright children. This situation had developed with a framework of a public, legal commitment to integrated education. (Some steps have been taken to remedy the problem, but they are only a beginning.)

In the other America each group suffers from a psychological depression as well as from simple material want. And given the long history and the tremendous institutionalized power of racism, this is particularly and terribly true of the Negro.

Some commentators have argued that Negroes have a lower level of aspiration, of ambition, than whites. In this theory, the Jim Crow economy produces a mood of resignation and acceptance. But in the study of the New York State Commission Against Discrimination an even more serious situation was described: one in which Negro children had more aspiration than whites from the same income level, but less opportunity to fulfill their ambition.

In this study, Aaron Antonovsky and Melvin Lerner described the result as a "pathological condition . . . in our society." The Negro child, coming from a family in which the father has a miserable job, is forced to reject the life of his parents, and to put forth new goals for himself. In the case of the immigrant young some generations ago, this experience of breaking with the Old Country tradition and identifying with the great society of America was a decisive moment in moving upward. But the Negro does not find society as open as the immigrant did. He has the hope and the desire, but not the possibility. The consequence is heart-breaking frustration.

Indeed, Antonovsky suggests that the image of Jackie Robinson or Ralph Bunche is a threat to the young Negro. These heroes are exceptional and talented men. Yet, in a time of ferment among Negroes, they tend to become norms and models for the young people. Once again, there is a tragic gap between the ideal and the possible. A sense of disillusion, of failure, is added to the indignity of poverty.

A more speculative description of the Negro psychology has been written by Norman Mailer. For Mailer, the concept of "coolness" is a defense reaction against a hostile world. Threatened by the Man, denied access to the society, the Negro, in Mailer's image, stays loose: he anticipates disillusion; he turns cynicism into a style.

But perhaps the final degradation the Negro must face is the image the white man has of him. White America keeps the Negro down. It forces him into a slum; it keeps him in the dirtiest and lowest-paying jobs. Having imposed this indignity, the white man theorizes about it. He does not see it as the tragic work of his own hands, as a social product. Rather, the racial ghetto reflects the "natural" character of the Negro: lazy, shiftless, irresponsible, and so on. So prejudice becomes self-justifying. It creates miserable conditions and then cites them as a rationale for inaction and complacency.

One could continue describing the psychological and spiritual consequences of discrimination almost endlessly. Yet, whatever the accurate theory may be, it is beyond dispute that one of the main components of poverty for the Negro is a maiming of personality. This is true generally for the poor; it is doubly and triply true for the race poor.

How can the Negroes escape their prison in the other America?

To begin with, this wall of prejudice will be breached only when it is understood that the problem of race is not just a matter of legal and political equality. It is important that the right to the vote be won in the South, that discriminatory legislation be struck down, and so on. But that is only the beginning. The real emancipation of the Negro waits upon a massive assault upon the entire culture of poverty in American society: upon slums, inferior education, inadequate medical care, and all the rest. These things are as much a part of being a Negro as the color of a man's skin.

Housing is perhaps the most crucial element in racial poverty. As long as Negroes and other minorities are segregated into neighborhoods, the impact of all civil-rights legislation is softened. It is possible to have a public policy for integrated schooling, but if the school districts are themselves a product of residential discrimination, the schools will continue to be Jim Crow. But, here again, America at the beginning of the sixties does not seem prepared to devote the resources to the problem that are required if it is to be solved. And because of this, the terrible indignity of the ghetto will continue.

On the job, the Negro is the prime victim of the unwillingness of the society to face the crisis brought about by automation. It is, of course, the Negro "type" of job that is being destroyed. The crisis is hitting precisely in those areas where gains in integrated work were made in the past two decades, in the semiskilled jobs of mass-production industries. The Government, as noted before, is not making adequate provisions for planning and retraining and all the rest. And given the racist character of the American economy, this is a particularly severe blow against the Negro. It amounts to rebuilding the wall of prejudice, to destroying advances which have already been made.

In a sense, this technological crisis offers America a unique opportunity. The old system is being transformed. If the nation were to attack the problem of structural unemployment, it could at the same time make great strides toward racial equality. For any serious program aimed at providing displaced workers with skill and opportunity will automatically help the Negro as a Negro, so long as it does not contain racist features. A new and integrated structure could be built; the crisis could be a starting point for enormous progress.

But in recent years Negroes were more and more asked to accept their position in society, to sacrifice their own needs to the common good. Once again, the poorest were asked to pay the way of the better off. This took the form of various sincere people calling upon the Negro movement not to "obstruct" various welfare programs by insisting that they be integrated. In other words, the Negroes were being asked to help to build a welfare state that would discriminate against them in a double sense, that would not really benefit them because they are so poor as to be beyond the reach of the new benefits, and that would continue and reinforce the racist pattern of all of American society.

It is crucial that the nation understand that there can be no progress toward destroying the other America at the price of Negro rights. This is not simply a matter of morality and ethics, important as those factors are. It is also a brute sociological fact. The poor, as I have documented in describing other parts of the culture of poverty, are generally speaking those people who are beneath the welfare state. A quarter of them are Negro. Any program aimed at really aiding the dispossessed cannot exclude the Negroes without excluding millions of others who desperately need help. A housing program with discrimination against the black man is at the same time discriminatory against the white man, for it will perpetuate the segregation of poverty and it will keep the poor generally on the margin of the society. The only kind of housing program that could break through the social isolation of the poor and that could render these millions visible and return them to our society is an integrated program. And as long as the slums remain (or even as they are replaced by "poor farm" housing projects tucked away in some corner of the city), the culture of poverty will remain.

Clearly, the Negroes cannot achieve their emancipation on their own. They are, quite literally, a minority in the society, and they do not possess the political power to win the vast and comprehensive changes in public policy that are necessary if there is to be real equality. Here, once again, the fate of the lowest, the most dispossessed, depends on what the better off, and particularly the labor movement, will do.

If, as is quite possible, America refuses to deal with the social evils that persist in the sixties, it will at the same time have turned its back on the racial minorities. There will be speeches on equality; there will be gains as the nation moves toward a constitutional definition of itself as egalitarian. The Negro will watch all this from a world of double poverty. He will continue to know himself as a member of a race-class condemned by heredity to be poor. There will be occasional celebrations — perhaps the next one will be called in twenty years or so when it is announced that Negroes have reached 70 per cent of the white wage level. But that other America which is the ghetto will still stand.

There is a bitter picket-line chant that one sometimes hears when a store is being boycotted in the North:

> If you're white, you're right,
> If you're black, stay back.

It is an accurate sociological statement of the plight of the Negro in American society.

PETER M. BLAU
OTIS DUDLEY DUNCAN

Inequality of Opportunity

... It is hardly surprising that Negroes in the United States do not have the same occupational opportunities as whites. The lower occupational status of Negroes cannot be fully accounted for by their lower educational attainment, since their chances of success are inferior on every educational level. Neither is it attributable to the fact that the majority of Negroes were born in the South and the status of Southerners is inferior to that of Northerners, since the occupational status of Negroes remains inferior when region of birth is controlled. Negroes do have less advantageous social origins than whites; their education is indeed poorer than that of whites; disproportionate numbers of them are actually from the South where opportunities are inferior; and they start their careers on lower levels. Yet even when these differences are statistically standardized and we examine how Negroes would fare if they did not differ from whites in these respects, their occupational chances are still inferior to those of whites. It is the cumulative effect of the handicaps Negroes encounter at every step in their lives that produces the serious inequalities of opportunities under which they suffer.

A finding that may be surprising is that the difference between Negroes and whites in occupational status as well as income is even greater among the better educated than among the less educated, with the partial exception of the minority who complete a college education.[1]

Reprinted by permission of the authors and publisher from Peter M. Blau and Otis Dudley Duncan, *The American Occupational Structure* (New York: John Wiley & Sons, Inc., 1967), pp. 238-241. Copyright © 1967 by John Wiley & Sons, Inc.

Inequality of Opportunity

In short, better educated Negroes fare even worse relative to whites than uneducated Negroes. To be sure, the same number of years of schooling may not provide the same degree of training and knowledge for Negroes as for whites, because the educational facilities that the white majority supplies for Negroes are usually inferior. But whether the discrimination against Negroes actually occurs in the educational system or subsequently in the occupational system—and it undoubtedly occurs to some extent in both—the fact remains that the results of this discrimination are more pronounced for the better than for the less educated Negroes. This fact has some important implications.

Since Negroes receive less return in the form of superior occupational prestige and income for their educational investments than whites, they have less incentive to make such investments, that is, to make the sacrifices that staying in school to acquire more education entails, particularly for underprivileged youngsters. Acquiring an education is simply not very profitable for Negroes, which may explain why some Negroes exhibit little motivation to pursue their schooling. Negroes must be strongly imbued with the basic value of education for them to have improved their educational attainments in recent years despite the comparatively low rewards education brings them.[2] Moreover, whereas educated persons are generally considered to be more enlightened and, specifically, to be less prejudiced against Negroes and other minorities than less educated ones,[3] the data show that in actuality there is more discrimination against Negroes in highly than in less educated groups. It can hardly be a pattern of prejudice unique to the uneducated laborers and operatives that forces enlightened employers to discriminate against hiring Negroes on these levels, as is sometimes alleged, for there is even more discrimination on higher levels. Another anomaly implicit in these findings is that although it is the uneducated Negro who is the main object of the prejudiced stereotype, the educated one being often explicitly exempt from it, it is the better educated Negro who in practice suffers most from discrimination.

Men born in the South, white as well as Negro, have inferior occupational chances, whether they remain there or migrate north. The occupational handicaps of southern whites and of southern-born Negroes living in the North are due to their inferior preparation, as indicated by the finding that the differences between them and their northern counterparts disappear when education and other background factors are statistically controlled. The persisting residual difference for Negroes who have remained in the South is in all likelihood the result of discrimination in employment. There is some evidence that the discrimination against Negroes has declined in recent decades, but progress has been very slow. The improvements in the relative position of the Negro have been largely confined to minimum education and less discrimination in hiring at the point of entry into the labor market. In respect to higher education, necessary for advancement to more responsible positions, the gap between whites and Negroes not only has failed to narrow but actually has continued to widen in the last half-century.

Members of white ethnic minorities, in contrast to Negroes, fare as well as if not better than the dominant majority. This does not mean that there is no discrimination against any white ethnic minorities; as a matter of fact, the occupational differences between the second generation of northern European or western European descent and that of other origins suggests that there is some discrimination against descendants of the less prestigeful immigrant groups, such as Italians and Poles. Whatever discrimination against selected white minorities exists, however, is not so pronounced as to suppress the strong achievement motivation characteristic of many sons of immigrants, and their drive to succeed has apparently overcome their background handicap as well as such discrimination, as manifest in their high occupational achievements and rates of mobility. The finding that these sons of immigrants are more successful in their careers than the sons of the native-born majority who have remained near their homes but not than those sons of the majority group who have left their region of birth indicates that something the second generation and migrants have in common promotes occupational achievements. This may be the varied cultural experiences to which both sons of immigrants and men who live in a different part of the country from where they were raised are exposed, or it may be the fact that migration as well as immigration is selective of men with strong achievement motives that are passed on to sons. . . .

The general conclusion to which these findings point is that the American occupational structure is largely governed by universalistic criteria of performance and achievement, with the notable exception of the influence of race. The close relationship between educational attainment and occupational achievement, with education being the most important determinant of occupational status that could be discovered, testifies to this universalism. So does the finding that there is little discrimination against white ethnic groups in occupational life, though discrimination against selected minorities unquestionably exists, concealed in our data due to the superior accomplishments of some members of the second generation. Most of the groups that are economically disadvantaged, such as those born in other countries and those born in the South, have lower educational attainments commensurate with their lower occupational positions. An important exception to this pervasive universalism is the severe discrimination the Negro suffers at every step in the process toward achieving occupational success. Although there is some indication that discrimination against Negroes has declined in this century, and hence that universalism has continued to spread, the trend is not consistent, does not encompass all areas of occupational life, and has only begun to penetrate into the South. But universalism cannot restore equality. Indeed, the data suggest that the relative position of the Negro in regard to higher levels of attainment has become worse in recent decades.

NOTES

1. It should be noted that there may be a "floor effect." Since the less-educated whites achieve only relatively low occupational status, the less-educated Negroes cannot be very far below them in status.

2. Alternatively, we could argue that, given the lower level of rewards for Negroes, less increment in rewards is needed for Negroes than for whites to produce the same marginal utility and hence the same incentive power to acquire more advanced education. In other words, the argument would be that the higher occupational returns whites obtain for the same educational investments compared to Negroes are necessary to produce the same marginal utility and incentive value, precisely because the level of rewards is higher for whites than for Negroes.

3. Samuel A. Stouffer, *Communism, Conformity, and Civil Liberties,* Garden City: Doubleday, 1955, p. 90; and Robin M. Williams, Jr., *Strangers Next Door,* Englewood Cliffs: Prentice-Hall, 1964, p. 55.

MANPOWER REPORTS OF THE PRESIDENT

Toward Equal Employment Opportunity

Equal employment opportunity is the primary goal of the Nation's manpower programs. By aiding disadvantaged workers—many of them members of minority groups—to qualify for and find productive jobs, these programs help to overcome the barriers that impede economic and employment progress for Negroes and other minorities, as well as for the even larger numbers of poor people among the white majority.

In addition, a number of programs aimed specifically at overcoming discrimination in employment have been set up. The legal framework for these programs was established by the Civil Rights Act of 1964, related legislation, and Executive orders, which forbid discrimination in employment on the basis of race, color, sex, age, religion, or national origin.

As efforts to implement equal opportunity have proceeded, the complexity and the interaction of the many forms of discrimination and segregation have become increasingly evident. In seeking a satisfactory job, a minority group member may be handicapped as much by discrimination in education and training earlier in his life as by present bias in hiring and promotion. Furthermore, people in city ghettos and poor rural areas may be unable to reach the areas of expanding employment opportunity, often located in city suburbs. There are also pervasive psychological barriers created by discrimination and segregation, which have to be overcome before minority group members can compete on an equal basis for jobs and promotion....

Reprinted from *Manpower Report of the President* (Washington, D.C.: Government Printing Office, 1970), pp. 89-95, 100-103. The section on the American Indian is from the 1968 *Manpower Report of the President*, pp. 68-69.

Toward Equal Employment Opportunity

The concern here is with the progress that has been made, and the great deficiencies that still remain, in moving toward equal employment opportunity for Negroes and other minorities. It assesses the record with respect to their employment and unemployment, occupational levels, education, and income.... Whatever the index of social and economic conditions used, the record tells of recent gains offset by continuing intolerable inequalities between the country's ethnic minorities and the white majority....

NEGROES

The employment situation of the country's largest minority group—more than 22 million Negroes—has both positive and negative aspects. According to a member of the Board of Governors of the Federal Reserve System, himself a member of this group:

So far in the decade of the 1960's, Negroes have benefited relatively more than the population as a whole from the vigorous expansion of the national economy.... Increased occupational mobility and significant strides in education have also played vital roles.... Looking ahead over the next decade, the Negro community as a whole can be expected to improve its economic position to a greater extent than the population generally.[1]

Yet "there is scarcely an aspect of ... educational and labor market experience ... in which pronounced differences between whites and blacks do not exist," and these differences are invariably to the advantage of the whites, whether they are in rates of unemployment, occupational levels, education, or rates of pay.[2]

Employment and Unemployment

Employment gains by Negroes have been more rapid than those by white workers over the past 8 years. Aided by the heavy demand for manpower during these years of economic expansion, Negroes increased their employment by 1.6 million or 23 percent between 1961 and 1969.[3] In contrast, employment of white workers rose by only 8 percent over these 8 years, although in absolute numbers the increase in their employment was, of course, much larger than that for black workers.

Negro men, women, and teenagers all experienced some gains in job opportunities. The employment rise for Negro men was much faster than that for white men between 1961 and 1969 (16 percent compared with 9 percent). However, the employment gains by Negro women merely kept pace with those of white women. And though Negro as well as white teenagers had sharp employment increases, their job gains were barely large enough to take care of the greatly increased number seeking employment and so had little impact on their extremely high unemployment rate.

The average unemployment rate for all Negro workers was reduced by nearly one-half (from 12.4 to 6.4 percent) between 1961 and 1969, reflecting the gains in Negro employment during this period. Here again, the improvement was most marked for Negro men, whose unemployment rate was cut by two-thirds. Among Negro women workers, the reduction in unemployment was smaller, and among teenage girls it was insignificant. The gap in unemployment rates between Negro and white youth actually widened over the 8 years, since unemployment among white teenagers was reduced substantially during this period. (See table 1.)

Unemployment of Negroes, as of white workers, reached its lowest point since the Korean conflict in early 1969, after that rose slightly,

TABLE 1

Unemployment Rates for Adults and Teenagers, by Color, 1961 and 1969

Color, sex, and age	1961	1969	Percent change, 1961-69
White	6.0	3.1	−48.3
Men, 20 years and over	5.1	1.9	−62.7
Women, 20 years and over	5.7	3.4	−40.4
Teenagers, 16 to 19 years	15.3	10.7	−30.1
Boys	15.7	10.1	−35.7
Girls	14.8	11.5	−22.3
Negro and other races	12.4	6.4	−48.4
Men, 20 years and over	11.7	3.7	−68.4
Women, 20 years and over	10.6	5.8	−45.3
Teenagers, 16 to 19 years	27.6	24.0	−13.0
Boys	26.8	21.3	−20.5
Girls	29.2	27.7	−5.1

and then dropped again late in the year. . . . These developments were reason for cautious satisfaction. In earlier periods, any increase in unemployment has tended to bring a disproportionate rise in joblessness among Negro workers—many of whom are unskilled and are among the "last hired" and thus, under common personnel practice, liable to be the "first fired." It has been widely feared that even a small overall increase in unemployment might once again entail a much larger rise in the rate of joblessness among Negroes, but the upcreep in unemployment rates during the summer and early autumn of 1969 applied equally to white and Negro workers.

Occupational Advances

The most encouraging aspect of the employment record for Negroes is their rapid movement into higher level occupations. More than three-fifths of the increase in Negro employment between 1961 and 1969 was in professional, other white-collar, and skilled occupations. There was also a large rise in the number of Negroes in operative jobs. By contrast, in the lowest paid occupations—private household work and farmwork—Negro employment declined substantially, while the number of nonfarm laborer jobs remained virtually unchanged. (See chart 1.)

CHART 1

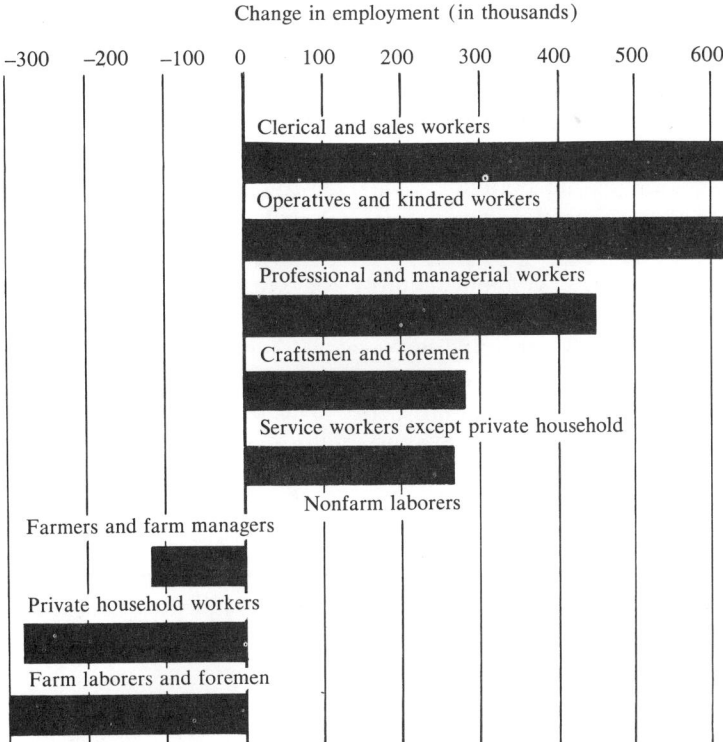

Note: Includes small numbers of members of other races.
Source: Department of Labor.

Negro workers moved into better jobs between 1961 and 1969

The breakthrough of Negroes into white-collar occupations not only continued but probably accelerated during 1969. In professional and technical occupations, the number of Negro workers increased by 8 percent from 1968 to 1969—double the rate of increase (4 percent) for white workers. In clerical occupations, the rise in Negro employment reached 12 percent, which was three times the increase for whites. Even in managerial occupations, where the proportion of Negro workers has remained very low, there was evidence of progress—a gain of 13 percent in their employment, as compared with only 2 percent in that of white workers. In sales occupations, however, Negroes made less headway (as shown in table 2). And despite the increasing numbers of Negroes employed in white-collar occupations, their proportionate share in such jobs has remained essentially unchanged.

The employment record in blue-collar occupations is moderately encouraging. The number of Negro craftsmen and foremen rose by 8 percent over the year, while employment of white craftsmen increased by only 1.3 percent. In operative positions, Negro and white employment increased at about the same rate (3 to 4 percent). And in nonfarm laboring jobs, at the bottom of the blue-collar scale, employment of Negroes showed practically no change, while the number of white laborers rose slightly. In addition, the exodus of Negroes from private household and farm jobs continued during the year, at a faster rate than among white workers.

The occupational upgrading of Negro workers indicated by these figures has already given millions of people—workers and their families—a larger share in the national prosperity. This upgrading also testifies to the greatly improved climate of opportunity for Negroes in many fields of public and private employment and so offers hope of continued rapid progress.

It must be emphasized, however, that occupational parity for Negroes has not been reached or even approached as yet. Though the gains by Negro workers have been substantial, especially in professional, clerical, and skilled occupations, they are still seriously underrepresented in these and other relatively high status, highly paid occupations and disproportionately concentrated in unskilled, low-paid laboring and service jobs.

To some extent, these differences reflect educational deficiencies and lack of skill. However, other factors such as inadequate knowledge of better job opportunities and racial discrimination also account for the disparity in employment of Negroes. For example, if at each level of education Negro men had the same opportunities for jobs as whites, the proportion of Negro craftsmen would double, and the percentage of managers and proprietors would triple. On the other hand, the percentage of Negro men in service jobs would decline by half, and the pro-

TABLE 2

Employed Persons 16 Years and Over, by Color and Occupation Group, 1968-69 (Numbers in thousands)

Color and occupation group	1968		1969		Percent change, 1968-69
	Number	Percent distribution	Number	Percent distribution	
WHITE					
Total	67,751	100.0	69,518	100.0	2.6
White-collar workers	33,561	49.5	34,647	49.8	3.2
Professional and technical workers	9,685	14.3	10,074	14.5	4.0
Managers, officials, and proprietors	7,551	11.1	7,733	11.1	2.4
Clerical workers	11,836	17.5	12,314	17.7	4.0
Sales workers	4,489	6.6	4,527	6.5	.8
Blue-collar workers	24,063	35.5	24,647	35.5	2.4
Craftsmen and foremen	9,359	13.8	9,484	13.6	1.3
Operatives	12,023	17.7	12,368	17.8	2.9
Nonfarm laborers	2,681	4.0	2,795	4.0	4.3
Private household workers	947	1.4	917	1.3	−3.2
Service workers, except private household	6,118	9.0	6,372	9.2	4.2
Farmworkers	3,062	4.5	2,935	4.2	−4.1
NEGRO AND OTHER RACES					
Total	8,169	100.0	8,384	100.0	2.6
White-collar workers	1,991	24.4	2,197	26.2	10.3
Professional and technical workers	641	7.8	695	8.3	8.4
Managers, officials, and proprietors	225	2.8	254	3.0	12.9
Clerical workers	967	11.8	1,083	12.9	12.0
Sales workers	158	1.9	166	2.0	5.2
Blue-collar workers	3,462	42.4	3,591	42.8	3.7
Craftsmen and foremen	656	8.0	709	8.5	8.1
Operatives	1,932	23.6	2,004	23.9	3.7
Nonfarm laborers	874	10.7	877	10.5	.3
Private household workers	777	9.5	714	8.5	−8.1
Service workers, except private household	1,538	18.8	1,525	18.2	−.8
Farmworkers	403	4.9	356	4.2	−11.7

Note: Detail may not add to totals due to rounding.

portion of nonfarm laborers would be cut by two-thirds. For Negro men in professional and technical jobs, the proportion would remain about the same.[4]

Educational Gains

Rising levels of education among Negroes were, nevertheless, indispensable to their recent occupational progress, and larger educational gains will be essential to enable greater numbers to enter white-collar and skilled jobs.

The higher educational attainment of young adult Negroes than of middle-aged and older ones is an index of the substantial advances in their schooling during recent decades. According to 1969 data, nearly 3 out of every 5 Negroes 25 to 29 years of age have completed high school, almost twice the proportion among those aged 45 to 54 and four times that for the 55- to 64-year-old group. (See chart 2.) College education is also much more common among younger than older Negroes, though still achieved by only a small minority. A little over 20 percent of those aged 20 and 21 have completed 1 or more years of college, but in the older age groups the proportion drops progressively (to only 6 percent in the 55- to 64-year-old group). Even these limited gains in college education of Negroes have been important in opening opportunities for them in professional and administrative positions.

CHART 2

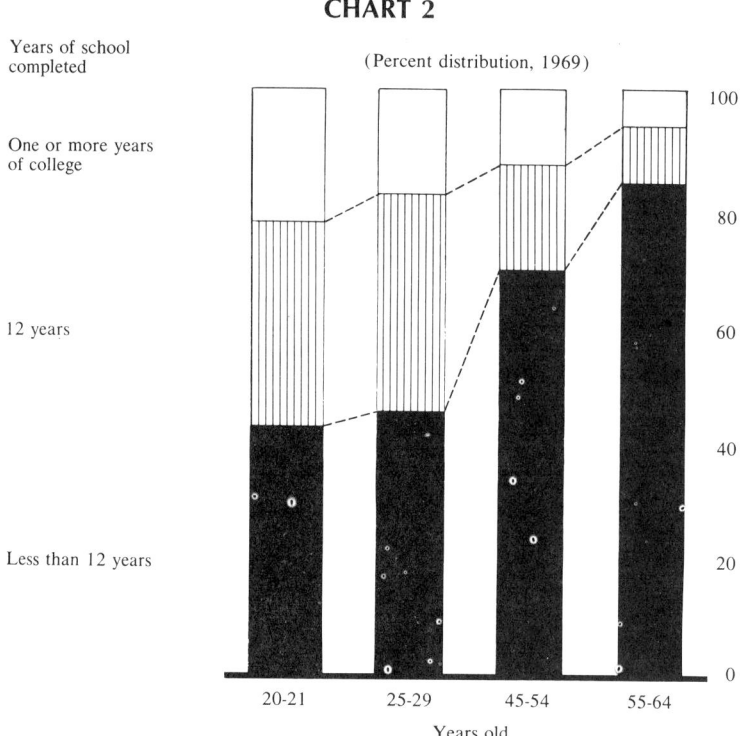

Source: Department of Labor, based on data from the Department of Commerce.

Negro young adults are better educated than older Negroes

The heavy farm-to-city migration of Negroes since World War II has been one of the main reasons for their more extended schooling. They have also been helped and encouraged to stay in school longer by federally aided programs designed to improve the schools, especially in poor school districts, and to reduce dropout rates. However, accomplishments in these directions fall far short of those needed.

The disparity in education between Negroes and whites is narrowing but remains wide even among young people. This is indicated by 1969 data on the proportions of people in different age groups who have completed 4 years of high school (including those with 1 or more years of college education):

Age group	Percent White	Percent Negro	Negro to white ratio (in percent)
20 to 21 years	82	58	71
22 to 24 years	81	56	69
25 to 29 years	77	56	73
30 to 34 years	73	50	68
35 to 44 years	66	37	56
45 to 54 years	59	29	49
55 to 64 years	45	15	33

Source: Department of Commerce, Bureau of the Census.

Furthermore, educational attainment, as measured by years of schooling, gives no indication of the great differences in the quality of schooling, as measured by achievement tests. A 1965 survey showed that, in the 12th grade, the average Negro youth scores at a ninth-grade level, 3 years behind the average white youth.[5] The gap in school achievement is apparent early and broadens between the sixth and 12th grades....

Family Income

Reflecting the generally favorable trends in their employment and occupations, the average income of Negroes has risen substantially. Their median family income was nearly $5,600 in 1968, compared with about $4,400 in 1965 (in constant 1968 dollars, adjusted for price increases). This represented a gain in real income of nearly 30 percent in only 3 years and an acceleration over the preceding period. Six years, 1959 to 1965, were previously required for an advance of similar magnitude.

The number and percent of Negroes moving into middle income groups have also increased sharply. Of the 3.3 million Negro families in metropolitan areas in 1968, nearly one-fourth (23 percent) had incomes of $10,000 or more—triple the proportion in 1959. For the 1.3 million Negro families outside these areas, however, incomes as high as this are rare indeed (reported by only 8 percent in 1968). (See chart 3.)

The Negro-white differential in the proportion of families with incomes of $10,000 or more was about twofold in metropolitan areas in

1968. This represented a substantial improvement since 1959, when the proportion of families at this income level was about four times higher for whites than for Negroes. The differential in family income would be still wider if the average number of wage earners were no larger in Negro than white families. To a far greater extent than white families, Negro households depend on the earnings of one or more workers besides the family head.

CHART 3

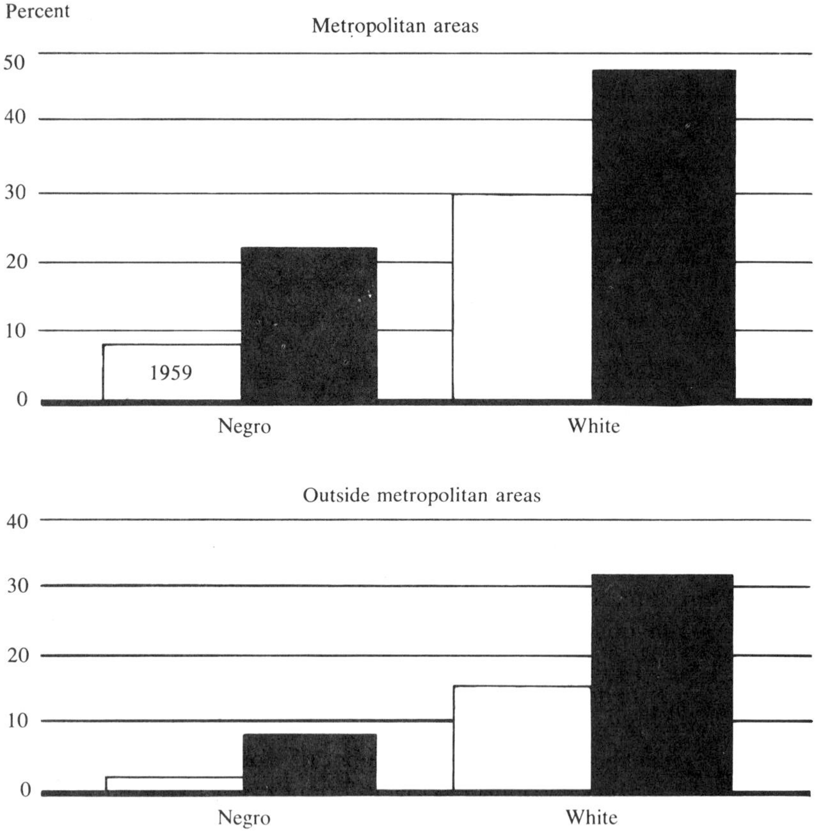

Source: Department of Labor, based on data from
the Department of Commerce.

*Proportion of Negro families
with income of over $10,000 has risen
but is still far less than for whites*

Negro families at all income levels have shared in the recent income gains. In fact, in relative terms the income rise has been most rapid for those at the bottom of the income scale. But the dollar rise in incomes has been much greater for the higher income group. This is shown in table 3, which gives the median incomes for families in each fifth of the income scale (in constant 1968 dollars).

In 1968, the median income for Negro families in the lowest fifth was only $1,723, far below the poverty threshold, though more than double the median for this group in 1959. In contrast, the 1968 median income for the highest fifth was a comfortable $13,000, up by slightly more than 50 percent above the corresponding 1959 figure of $8,483.

TABLE 3

Distribution of Family Income, by Color, 1959 and 1968 (Numbers in constant 1968 dollars)

Quintile	WHITE			NEGRO AND OTHER RACES			White-Negro income difference	
	Median income		Percent change, 1959-68	Median income		Percent change, 1959-68		
	1959	1968		1959	1968		1959	1968
Lowest fifth	$2,199	$3,196	45.3	$856	$1,723	101.3	$1,343	$1,473
Second fifth	4,806	6,447	34.1	1,999	3,564	78.3	2,807	2,883
Middle fifth (overall median)	6,742	8,937	32.6	3,482	5,591	60.6	3,260	3,346
Fourth fifth	8,801	11,789	34.0	5,263	8,283	57.4	3,538	3,506
Highest fifth	13,031	19,341	48.4	8,483	13,000	53.2	4,548	6,341

Source: Based on data from the Department of Commerce, Bureau of the Census, Current Population Reports, Series P-60.

Similarly, Negro families have had more rapid percentage gains in income than white families, but this has not been true in terms of purchasing power. The dollar difference in median incomes between white and Negro families in the bottom fifth of the income scale was nearly $1,500 in 1968, compared with about $1,350 in 1959. For families in the highest fifth in income the difference was over $6,300 in 1968, though it had been about $4,500 (in constant 1968 dollars) 9 years before. In the middle-income groups, the differential in dollar income between Negro and white families showed little change; the absolute difference in their purchasing power remains wide . . .

SPANISH AMERICANS

The 10 million Spanish Americans in the United States are the country's second largest ethnic minority group.[6] About 6.5 million reside in the southwestern States of Arizona, California, Colorado, New Mexico, and Texas. Some families have lived in the Southwest since long before that part of the country was annexed from Mexico. Others are first, second, or third generation Mexican Americans. Still others, living primarily in the eastern part of the country, have come from Puerto Rico, where they already had American citizenship, or from Cuba, other Caribbean islands, or Central or South American countries. Nearly all came in search of better employment opportunities or greater political freedom. However, many are handicapped by limited education, lack of skill, and inadequate knowledge of English, and their cultural patterns set them apart from the country's mainstream in ways that inhibit their economic progress. Their language and cultural differences are one of the causes for the prejudice and inequality of treatment which they often encounter in the labor market.

Nevertheless, when individual Spanish Americans have overcome their language and educational handicaps, they are not likely to meet the discriminatory barriers commonly faced by Negroes. Propertied and educated Spanish Americans for the most part find the doors open to them in both employment and social life (except where licensing requirements for professional practice bar immigrants who received professional training in their native countries from entering the same specialty in the United States).

Mexican Americans

Mexican Americans fare worse than "Anglos" in the occupations they are able to enter and in their earnings, but they are generally somewhat better off than Negroes in the same geographic areas, according to the fragmentary evidence available. How far Mexican Americans fall behind Anglos in access to preferred industries and occupations is shown by a survey conducted by the U.S. Commission on Civil Rights in six Texas metropolitan areas in 1966. As table 4 indicates, relatively more Mexican Americans were in the lower wage industries like apparel and textiles than in higher paid ones like oil and gas extraction, or in predominantly white-collar fields like banking. But the proportion in white-collar and skilled jobs was much higher for them than for Negroes.

Still clearer evidence of the concentration of Spanish Americans in the lower level jobs comes from the recent hearings of the Equal Employment Opportunity Commission on minority employment in Los Angeles. Though Spanish Americans represented only about 10 percent of the population of Los Angeles in 1967, they held 30 percent of the laborer jobs in the area. Patterns of underemployment of Spanish Americans were found in the motion picture and television industries and also in banking, insurance, and aerospace companies.

TABLE 4

Percent of Mexican American, Negro, and Anglo Workers Employed in Selected Industries and Occupations in Six Metropolitan Areas of Texas, 1966

Industry and occupation	Percent of employees who were—		
	Mexican American	Negro	Anglo
Oil and gas extraction, total	2.1	1.6	96.3
White-collar workers	.9	.5	98.6
Craftsmen	1.2	.2	98.6
Other blue-collar workers	7.0	6.2	86.8
Banking, total	8.3	8.7	83.0
Retail trade (general merchandise), total	22.8	7.0	70.3
White-collar workers	21.0	1.9	77.1
Craftsmen	29.9	3.4	66.7
Other blue-collar workers	28.9	30.1	41.0
Food and kindred products, total	37.2	11.4	51.4
White-collar workers	10.8	2.7	86.5
Craftsmen	28.1	7.5	64.4
Other blue-collar workers	52.8	16.7	30.5
Apparel and textiles, total	81.4	3.9	14.7
White-collar workers	42.0	1.0	57.0
Craftsmen	86.6	1.5	11.9
Other blue-collar workers	85.5	5.3	9.2

Source: *The Mexican American Population of Texas*, Staff Report, U.S. Commission on Civil Rights, 1968, pp. 21-22.

The concentration of poor Mexican Americans in some slum areas of Los Angeles and Houston is indicated by the Department of Labor's new urban employment surveys for the year ending June 30, 1969. Nearly half of the population in the Los Angeles poverty areas, and one-fifth in Houston, were Mexican Americans (or, in a few cases, people of other Spanish American backgrounds). The unemployment rates for Mexican American workers were about 6 percent in both the Los Angeles and Houston areas—far above the average rate for all workers in the country but also much below the rates for Negro workers in the same areas. . . .

Substandard wages were another prevalent problem. The proportion of Mexican American workers earning less than $65 for a full-time week —a rate roughly comparable to the Federal minimum wage standards— was as follows:

	Percent of workers earning less than $65 for a full-time week, July 1968-June 1969	
	Men	Women
Los Angeles	2.5	20.4
Houston	11.3	47.0

Furthermore, a great many Mexican Americans strive to earn their livings as migrant farmworkers. In 1968, over 95 percent of the 150,000 migrant farmworkers from Texas were Mexican American.[8] These workers are still among the most deprived in the country, despite some recent improvement in their situation. Ending the importation of Mexican braceros has helped somewhat, however, and so have strengthened regulations with respect to housing standards, minimum wages, and other living and working conditions.

The low average level of education amoung Mexican Americans is a major factor impeding their movement into better paying jobs. Adult Mexican Americans in one county of Texas, for example, had a median of only 5.9 years of schooling in 1966. In 17 other counties on or near the Mexican border, median years of schooling were even lower (from 1.4 to 5.4 years). The younger Mexican Americans have somewhat more schooling than older ones, but the low overall educational level cannot be attributed primarily to immigration: less than one-sixth of the adult population in the 18 counties were foreign born.[9] Rather, these people's lack of education reflects linguistic, cultural, and economic problems. Until recently, only English was used in the schools of the Southwest; this has been one reason for the high dropout rate for Mexican American children during the first 9 years of school. In addition, the large numbers whose parents are migrant farmworkers have had their education interrupted many times as their families followed the crops....

Puerto Ricans

Puerto Ricans in the United States suffer from the same employment disadvantages as other Spanish Americans. Chief among these are the language barrier, inadequate education and training, and discrimination. In some respects, the language problem may be even more difficult for Puerto Ricans than for Mexican Americans in the Southwest; outside of Spanish-speaking neighborhoods such as East Harlem, the Spanish language and customs are not generally understood in New York City. Also, unlike immigrants, Puerto Ricans are under no pressure to master English in order to gain American citizenship.

Migration from Puerto Rico to the mainland United States has been largely a post-World War II phenomenon, closely related to the level of prosperity and availability of jobs on the mainland. When jobs become scarce on the mainland, the net inflow of workers is reduced or even reversed.

Most of the early in-migrants from Puerto Rico settled in New York City, where they found relatively unskilled jobs, particularly in consumer industries. Today the Puerto Rican population of New York City is close to 1 million. However, the proportion of people arriving from Puerto Rico who remain in New York City has declined somewhat, as better employment opportunities have opened up for them in other sections of the country.

Unfortunately, there is as yet little information on how Puerto Ricans have fared in the United States as a whole. However, in New York City, where most of the Puerto Ricans on the mainland still live, they fare less well than any other minority group.

The poverty areas of Harlem, Bedford-Stuyvesant, and the South Bronx are among those covered by the Department of Labor's urban employment surveys during the year ending in June 1969. The unemployment rates for Puerto Ricans in these poverty areas were found to be higher than those for Mexican Americans in the poverty areas of Los Angeles or Houston. Puerto Ricans also had more unemployment and lower earnings than Negroes in the New York City slums. . . .

The fact that Puerto Ricans, as a group, had less work and lower earnings than the Negroes in these poverty areas reflects in part their lower educational level. Nearly half of those aged 18 or over had no more than 8 years of school, and many were educated in Puerto Rico—in Spanish, not English. The New York City Board of Education reported that during the 1967-68 school year, some 100,000 pupils of foreign-language background (mostly Puerto Ricans) were learning English as a second language in the city schools.

It is not surprising, therefore, that both the men and the women were concentrated in low-paid, low-skilled, low-status jobs—as operatives, laborers, or household or other service workers. Only a small percentage were in professional, technical, or managerial jobs.

The Equal Employment Opportunity Commission held hearings in January 1968 on minority employment in 100 major firms in New York City. The data presented there showed that Puerto Ricans were more under-represented in the better paying, higher status jobs than any other minority group. Although they made up 10 percent of the city's population, they held only 3 percent of the white-collar jobs in the companies studied and only 1 percent of the managerial positions. . . .

AMERICAN INDIANS

American Indians were reported in the 1960 census as numbering 552,000, including all native peoples of Alaska. Since that time the total has grown to well over 600,000. Of this number, somewhat more than 400,000 are reported by the Bureau of Indian Affairs of the U.S. Department of Interior to be residents of Indian reservations. This reservation population has never been accurately identified either by number or by characteristics.

Despite the lack of available data, it is clear that Indians living on reservations are among the most disadvantaged minorities in the country. Many suffer from serious handicaps of poor health, deficient education, unfamiliarity with English, lack of marketable skills, high unemployment, and low income.

These conclusions are based on scattered information limited, for the most part, to reservation and reservation-community Indians. Further complicating appraisal of the situation is the steady and increasingly planned departure of many of the abler members of the Indian communities. It is estimated that net out-migration from the reservations is now approaching 10,000 each year, largely offsetting the high rate of natural population growth. Among this number are hundreds of families whose working members have benefited from vocational training or direct job placement services of the Bureau of Indian Affairs.

Employment and Unemployment

The Indian labor force — defined as all Indians of employable age neither in school nor prevented from working by retirement, ill health, or child-care obligations—is estimated at 130,000, some 10 percent greater than in 1962. About 82,500 of them were at work in 1967, but how many were fully employed is not known. Fragmentary information indicates that some occupational upgrading is taking place, that fewer Indians are working at farm jobs and more at skilled and semiskilled jobs, and that year-round employment is increasing—trends evident since 1950. These advances are minimal, however, when compared with those of the labor force generally.

Since 1962 the Bureau of Indian Affairs has expanded its program to promote the location of manufacturing industries on the reservations. In 1960, nine plants providing a total of 599 jobs were built on or near reservations. By September 1967, the number of plants had risen to 113, employing 5,510 Indians. This development is accompanied by on-the-job training. For persons seeking employment away from the reservation, there is a program of institutional training and job placement that has expanded steadily in recent years.

The usual definition of unemployment is not a satisfactory measure of joblessness on the reservations, because so few job opportunities are available there. Accordingly, the Bureau of Indian Affairs reports as unemployed all members of the reservation labor force (as defined above) who are not at work. The Bureau's semiannual reservation reports show a significant favorable trend. From about 49 percent in 1962, the unemployment rate declined to 41 percent in 1966 and, by 1967, to 37 percent. This reduction of 12 percentage points, when applied to the 1967 labor force of 132,000, indicates that 15,000 more Indians were at work last year than would have had jobs if the 1962 unemployment rate had continued unchanged. This improvement appears to have resulted from recent emphasis on Indian employment opportunities near the reservations and development of reservation-based industries, both greatly strengthened by long-sustained national prosperity.

Income

Three-fourths of the reservation families had cash incomes of less than $3,000 in 1966, according to estimates by the Bureau of Indian Affairs. Yet Indian families are larger, on the average, than those of any other ethnic group. No other ethnic group approaches so high a proportion of families living in poverty. However, these comparisons make no allowance for substantial Federal services available to Indians.

Education ...

There are signs of continuing improvement in education of American Indians. School enrollment has been growing steadily. The majority of the children now attend public schools, rather than special Indian schools. Moreover, the education available is showing qualitative improvement, as teaching is improved and extracurricular activities are expanded with financial aid under the Elementary and Secondary Education Act of 1965.

The number of Indians attending college also has shown some growth. In 1966, over 4,000 Indians were enrolled in universities and colleges—1,500 more than in 1957, with half the gain taking place since 1964. In 1966, 120 Indians graduated from 4-year colleges and universities, more than twice as many as in 1961 . . . .

NOTES

1. Address by Andrew F. Brimmer at Tennessee A. and I. State University, Nashville, Tenn., June 8, 1969.

2. Herbert S. Parnes, Robert C. Miljus, Ruth S. Spitz, and others, *Career Thresholds: A Longitudinal Study of the Education and Labor Market Experience of Male Youth 14-24 Years of Age* (Columbus, Ohio: Center for Human Resource Research. The Ohio State University, February 1969), vol. I, pp. 189-190. (While this study refers only to the experiences of young men, other studies by the same authors indicate that the situation of older men is identical.)

3. Figures for Negroes and other minority races, of which Negroes represent about 92 percent, are used to indicate developments in employment, unemploy-

ment, occupations, and income cited for Negroes in this section. The data on educational gains, however, refer to Negroes only.

4. Harvey R. Hamel, "Educational Attainment of Workers," *Monthly Labor Review,* February 1968, p. 33, table 3.

5. James S. Coleman, *Equality of Educational Opportunity* (Washington: Department of Health, Education, and Welfare, Office of Education, 1966), p. 21.

6. The Equal Employment Opportunity Commission, in which rests the authority for implementation of title VII of the Civil Rights Act, has for purposes of the act defined this group as those of Latin American, Mexican, Puerto Rican, or Spanish origin. It also notes that the following States are among those having large concentrations of Spanish Americans: Arizona, California, Colorado, Florida, New Jersey, New Mexico, New York, and Texas.

7. Raul Moncarz, *A Study of the Effect of Environmental Change on Human Capital Among Selected Skilled Cubans* (Tallahassee: Florida State University, 1969). This recent study of over 500 Cuban refugees, funded by the Manpower Administration of the Department of Labor, indicates that those who had been members of the health professions (with the exception of physicians) experience difficulties in gaining entry into, and practice in, their professions. On the other hand, a great majority of civil and electrical engineers and architects covered by this small survey work in their chosen fields. The difficulties experienced by Cuban professional refugees stem not only from inadequate knowledge of English, but also from licensing practices in this country.

8. *Texas Migrant Labor; The 1968 Migration,* The 1968 Annual Report of the Texas Good Neighbor Commission, established by the Texas State Legislature on Sept. 1, 1965.

9. *Summary of Staff Background Paper on Economic Activities and Economic Development in 18 Counties of South Texas* (Washington: U.S. Commission on Civil Rights, Dec. 6, 1968), pp. 5 and 6.

VI

Working Women: Toward Occupational Parity?

Women's liberation, a movement which had been dormant in America for several decades, has become galvanized once more. Replacing the earlier dominant emphasis on women's voting rights is the pressure for equality of women vis-à-vis men in the labor market. This particular thrust is understandable in light of the sizeable increase in employment among women since the 1920's. As with ethnic minorities, the selections in this chapter deal with labor market trends and with factors obstructing equal opportunity for working women.

In every society, wrote Gunnar Myrdal in 1944, Negroes, women, and children are distinctively visible and regularly suppressed. This statement opens an appendix in *An American Dilemma*, Myrdal's famous study of the Negro problem in America, in which he paints a vivid parallel between the social and economic status of Negroes and women. In "Women: A Parallel to the Negro Problem," Myrdal links the ideology and institution of Negro slavery to the situation of women, locating the roots of this similarity in social definition. Both Negroes and women in American culture, he asserts, have been victimized by a paternalistically dominated society.

If female "slavery" no longer exists, its prior existence continues to affect the occupational lives of contemporary women. This is the implicit message contained in "Women in Labor" by Marijean Suelzle. Following a brief discussion of factors promoting the burgeoning labor force participation by women, Suelzle presents evidence of the relative occupational disadvantages of women vis-à-vis men. Labor market disparities can be traced, she believes, to false but prevailing cultural myths. She attempts to repudiate some of these popularly held ideas about women and work.

Occupational discrimination perpetrated on women is as difficult to document as it is real. However, earnings represent one reasonable measure of discrimination. Two recent governmental statements suggest a decline in the female-male pay differentials. Donald McNulty ("Differences in Pay Between Men and Women Workers") reports on some dimensions generally ignored in the analysis of data which demonstrate a considerably higher pay level for men than for women engaged in similar work. He found that differences in female-male average earnings for similar work were much smaller within single organizations than when measured for clusters of establishments. This implies that the general female-male average earnings differential is not always the result of pay differences within organizations, but may be the product of considerably dissimilar groups of establishments with widely disparate pay levels. Another finding which helps to explain this inconsistent differential is that men's earnings were constant whether in establishments employing men only or in those employing both sexes. However, average earnings were consistently greater for women in organizations employing both sexes than in those hiring women only. McNulty concludes with a brief discussion of reasons other than employer discrimination which account for existing female-male pay differentials.

Robert Moran ("Reducing Discrimination Among Working Women") explores the impact of the Equal Pay Act of 1963, federal legislation requiring equal pay for equal work regardless of sex. While recognizing the existence of pay discrepancies between men and women in similar jobs, Moran contends that progress resulting from this congressional action has been witnessed.

Even granting the favorable influence of the Equal Pay Act of 1963 on female earnings relative to men, a significant problem in this area remains—this piece of legislation fails to cover higher status occupations such as managers and professionals because they are exempted from the wage and hour law. Not only must women hurdle the obstacles barring entrance into higher status occupations, but once there, they are without legislation requiring equal pay for equal work. And as Suelzle documents, women in higher status occupations are no more immune to discriminatory pay practices than their sisters on the bottom of the occupational structure.

Is progress being made toward occupational parity for women?

GUNNAR MYRDAL

Women: A Parallel to the Negro Problem

In every society there are at least two groups of people, besides the Negroes, who are characterized by high social visibility expressed in physical appearance, dress, and patterns of behavior, and who have been "suppressed." We refer to women and children. Their present status, as well as their history and their problems in society, reveal striking similarities to those of the Negroes...

In the historical development of these problem groups in America there have been much closer relations than is now ordinarily recorded. In the earlier common law, women and children were placed under the jurisdiction of the paternal power. When a legal status had to be found for the imported Negro servants in the seventeenth century, the nearest and most natural analogy was the status of women and children. The ninth commandment — linking together women, servants, mules, and other property—could be invoked, as well as a great number of other passages of Holy Scripture. We do not intend to follow here the interesting developments of the institution of slavery in America through the centuries, but merely wish to point out the paternalistic idea which held the slave to be a sort of family member and in some way—in spite of all differences—placed him beside women and children under the power of the *pater-familias*.

There was, of course, even in the beginning, a tremendous difference both in actual status of these different groups and in the tone of sentiment in the respective relations. In the decades before the Civil War, in the

---

Reprinted by permission of the author and publisher from Gunnar Myrdal, *An American Dilemma* (New York: Harper & Row, Publishers, 1944), pp. 1073-78. Copyright © 1944, 1962 by Harper & Row, Publishers, Inc.

conservative and increasingly antiquarian ideology of the American South, woman was elevated as an ornament and looked upon with pride, while the Negro slave became increasingly a chattel and a ward. The paternalistic construction came, however, to good service when the South had to build up a moral defense for slavery, and it is found everywhere in the apologetic literature up to the beginning of the Civil War. For illustration, some passages from George Fitzhugh's *Sociology for the South,* published in 1854, may be quoted as typical:

The kind of slavery is adapted to the men enslaved. Wives and apprentices are slaves; not in theory only, but often in fact. Children are slaves to their parents, guardians and teachers. Imprisoned culprits are slaves. Lunatics and idiots are slaves also.[1]

A beautiful example and illustration of this kind of communism, is found in the instance of the Patriarch Abraham. His wives and his children, his men servants and his maid servants, his camels and his cattle, were all equally his property. He could sacrifice Isaac or a ram, just as he pleased. He loved and protected all, and all shared, if not equally, at least fairly, in the products of their light labour. Who would not desire to have been a slave of that old Patriarch, stern and despotic as he was? . . . Pride, affection, self-interest, moved Abraham to protect, love and take care of his slaves. The same motives operate on all masters, and secure comfort, competency and protection to the slave. A man's wife and children are his slaves, and do they not enjoy, in common with himself, his property?[2]

Other protagonists of slavery resort to the same argument:

In this country we believe that the general good requires us to deprive the whole female sex of the right of self-government. They have no voice in the formation of the laws which dispose of their persons and property. . . . We treat all minors much in the same way. . . . Our plea for all this is, that the good of the whole is thereby most effectually promoted. . . .[3]

Significant manifestations of the result of this disposition [on the part of the Abolitionists] to consider their own light a surer guide than the word of God, are visible in the anarchical opinions about human governments, civil and ecclesiastical, and on the rights of women, which have found appropriate advocates in the abolition publications. . . . If our women are to be emancipated from subjection to the law which God has imposed upon them, if they are to quit the retirement of domestic life, where they preside in stillness over the character and destiny of society; . . . if, in studied insult to the authority of God, we are to renounce in the marriage contract all claim to obedience, we shall soon have a country over which the genius of Mary Wolstonecraft would delight to preside, but from which all order and all virtue would speedily be banished. There is no form of human excellence before which we bow with profounder deference than that which appears in a delicate woman, . . . and there is no deformity of human character from which we turn with deeper loathing than from a woman forgetful of her nature, and clamourous for the vocation and rights of men.[4]

... Hence her [Miss Martineau's] wild chapter about the "Rights of Women," her groans and invectives because of their exclusion from the offices of the state, the right of suffrage, the exercise of political authority. In all this, the error of the declaimer consists in the very first movement of the mind. "The Rights of *Women*" may all be conceded to the sex, yet the rights of *men* withheld from them.[5]

The parallel goes, however, considerably deeper than being only a structural part in the defense ideology built up around slavery. Women at that time lacked a number of rights otherwise belonging to all free white citizens of full age.

So chivalrous, indeed, was the ante-bellum South that its women were granted scarcely any rights at all. Everywhere they were subjected to political, legal, educational, and social and economic restrictions. They took no part in governmental affairs, were without legal rights over their property or the guardianship of their children, were denied adequate educational facilities, and were excluded from business and the professions.[6] The same was very much true of the rest of the country and the rest of the world. But there was an especially close relation in the South between the subordination of women and that of Negroes. This is perhaps best expressed in a comment attributed to Dolly Madison, that the Southern wife was "the chief slave of the harem."[7]

From the very beginning, the fight in America for the liberation of the Negro slaves was, therefore, closely coordinated with the fight for women's emancipation. It is interesting to note that the Southern states, in the early beginnings of the political emancipation of women during the first decades of the nineteenth century, had led in the granting of legal rights to women. This was the time when the South was still the stronghold of liberal thinking in the period leading up to and following the Revolution. During the same period the South was also the region where Abolitionist societies flourished, while the North was uninterested in the Negro problem. Thereafter the two movements developed in close interrelation and were both gradually driven out of the South.

The women suffragists received their political education from the Abolitionist movement. Women like Angelina Grimke, Sarah Grimke, and Abby Kelly began their public careers by speaking for Negro emancipation and only gradually came to fight for women's rights. The three great suffragists of the nineteenth century — Lucretia Mott, Elizabeth Cady Stanton, and Susan B. Anthony—first attracted attention as ardent campaigners for the emancipation of the Negro and the prohibition of liquor. The women's movement got much of its public support by reason of its affiliation with the Abolitionist movement: the leading male advocates of women suffrage before the Civil War were such Abolitionists as William Lloyd Garrison, Henry Ward Beecher, Wendell Phillips, Horace Greeley and Frederick Douglass. The women had nearly achieved their aims, when the Civil War induced them to supress all tendencies distracting the federal government from the prosecution of the War. They were apparently fully convinced that victory would bring the suffrage to them as well as to the Negroes.[8]

The Union's victory, however, brought disappointment to the women suffragists. The arguments "the Negro's hour" and "a political necessity" met and swept aside all their arguments for leaving the word "male" out of the 14th Amendment and putting "sex" alongside "race" and "color" in the 15th Amendment.[9] Even their Abolitionist friends turned on them, and the Republican party shied away from them. A few Democrats, really not in favor of the extension of the suffrage to anyone, sought to make political capital out of the women's demands, and said with Senator Cowan of Pennsylvania, "If I have no reason to offer why a Negro man shall not vote, I have no reason why a white woman shall not vote." Charges of being Democrats and traitors were heaped on the women leaders. Even a few Negroes, invited to the women's convention of January, 1869, denounced the women for jeopardizing the black man's chances for the vote. The War and Reconstruction Amendments had thus sharply divided the women's problem from the Negro problem in actual politics.[10] The deeper relation between the two will, however, be recognized up till this day. Du Bois' famous ideological manifesto *The Souls of Black Folk*[11] is, to mention only one example, an ardent appeal on behalf of women's interests as well as those of the Negro.

This close relation is no accident. The ideological and economic forces behind the two movements—the emancipation of women and children and the emancipation of Negroes — have much in common and are closely interrelated. Paternalism was a preindustrial scheme of life, and was gradually becoming broken in the nineteenth century. Negroes and women, both of whom had been under the yoke of the paternalistic system, were both strongly and fatefully influenced by the Industrial Revolution. For neither group is the readjustment process yet consummated. Both are still problem groups. The women's problem is the center of the whole complex of problems of how to reorganize the institution of the family to fit the new economic and ideological basis, a problem which is not solved in any part of the Western world unless it be in the Soviet Union or Palestine. The family problem in the Negro group, as we find when analyzing the Negro family, has its special complications, centering in the tension and conflict between the external patriarchal system in which the Negro was confined as a slave and his own family structure.

As in the Negro problem, most men have accepted as self-evident, until recently, the doctrine that women had inferior endowments in most of those respects which carry prestige, power, and advantages in society, but that they were, at the same time, superior in some other respects. The arguments, when arguments were used, have been about the same: smaller brains, scarcity of geniuses and so on. The study of women's intelligence and personality has had broadly the same history as the one we record for Negroes. As in the case of the Negro, women themselves have often been brought to believe in their inferiority of endowment. As the Negro was awarded his "place" in society, so there was a "woman's place." In both cases the rationalization was strongly believed that men, in confining them to this place, did not act against the true interest of the subordinate groups. The myth of the "contented women," who did not want to have suffrage or other civil rights and equal opportunities, had the same social function as the myth of the "contented Negro." In both cases there was probably—in a static sense—often some truth behind the myth.

As to the character of the deprivations, upheld by law or by social conventions and the pressure of public opinion, no elaboration will here be made. As important and illustrative in the comparison, we shall, however, stress the conventions governing woman's education. There was a time when the most common idea was that she was better off with little education. Later the doctrine developed that she should not be denied education, but that her education should be of a special type, fitting her for her "place" in society and usually directed more on training her hands than her brains.

Political franchise was not granted to women until recently. Even now there are, in all countries, great difficulties for a woman to attain public office. The most important disabilities still affecting her status are those barring her attempt to earn a living and to attain promotion in her work. As in the Negro's case, there are certain "women's jobs," traditionally monopolized by women. They are regularly in the low salary bracket and do not offer much of a career. All over the world men have used the trade unions to keep women out of competition. Woman's competition has, like the Negro's, been particularly obnoxious and dreaded by men because of the low wages women, with their few earning outlets, are prepared to work for. Men often dislike the very idea of having women on an equal plane as co-workers and competitors, and usually they find it even more "unnatural" to work under women. White people generally hold similar attitudes toward Negroes. On the other hand, it is said about women that they prefer men as bosses and do not want to work under another woman. Negroes often feel the same way about working under other Negroes.

In personal relations with both women and Negroes, white men generally prefer a less professional and more human relation, actually a more paternalistic and protective position—somewhat in the nature of patron to client in Roman times, and like the corresponding strongly paternalistic relation of later feudalism. As in Germany it is said that every gentile has his pet Jew, so it is said in the South that every white has his "pet nigger," or—in the upper strata—several of them. We sometimes marry the pet woman, carrying out the paternalistic scheme. But even if we do not, we tend to deal kindly with her as a client and a ward, not as a competitior and an equal.

In drawing a parallel between the position of, and feeling toward, women and Negroes we are uncovering a fundamental basis of our culture. Although it is changing, atavistic elements sometimes unexpectedly break through even in the most emancipated individuals. The similarities in the women's and the Negroes' problems are not accidental. They were, as we have pointed out, originally determined in a paternalistic order of society. The problems remain, even though paternalism is gradually declining as an ideal and is losing its economic basis. In the final analysis, women are still hindered in their competition by the function of procreation; Negroes are laboring under the yoke of the doctrine of unassimilability which has remained although slavery is abolished. The second barrier is actually much stronger than the first in America today. But the first is more eternally inexorable.[12]

NOTES

1. P. 86.
2. *Ibid.*, p. 297.
3. Charles Hodge, "The Bible Argument on Slavery," in E. N. Elliott (editor), *Cotton Is King,* and *Pro-Slavery Arguments* (1860), pp. 859-860.
4. Albert T. Bledsoe, *An Essay on Liberty and Slavery* (1857), pp. 223-225.
5. W. Gilmore Simms, "The Morals of Slavery," in *The Pro-Slavery Argument* (1853), p. 248. See also Simms' "Address on the Occasion of the Inauguration of the Spartanburg Female College," August 12, 1855.
6. Virginius Dabney, *Liberalism in the South* (1932), p. 361.
7. Cited in Harriet Martineau, *Society in America* (1842, first edition 1837), Vol. II, p. 81.
8. Carrie Chapman Catt and Nettie Rogers Shuler, *Woman Suffrage and Politics* (1923), pp. 32 ff.

Women: A Parallel to the Negro Problem 187

9. The relevant sections of the 14th and 15th Amendments to the Constitution are (italics ours):
14th Amendment
Section 2. Representatives shall be apportioned among the several States according to their respective numbers, counting the whole number of persons in each State, excluding Indians not taxed. But when the right to vote at any election for the choice of Electors for President and Vice President of the United States, Representatives in Congress, the executive and judicial officers of a State, or the members of the Legislature thereof, is denied to any of the *male* inhabitants of such State, being twenty-one years of age, and citizens of the United States, or in any way abridged, except for participation in rebellion, or other crime, the basis of representation therein shall be reduced in proportion which the number of such *male* citizens shall bear to the whole number of *male* citizens twenty-one years of age in such State.

15th Amendment
Section 1. The right of citizens of the United States to vote shall not be denied or abridged by the United States or by any State on account of *race, color or previous condition of servitude.*

10. While there was a definite affinity between the Abolitionist movement and the woman suffrage movement, there was also competition and, perhaps, antipathy, between them that widened with the years. As early as 1833, when Oberlin College opened its doors to women—the first college to do so—the Negro men students joined other men students in protesting (Catt and Shuler, *op. cit.,* p. 13). The Anti-Slavery Convention held in London in 1840 refused to seat the women delegates from America, and it was on this instigation that the first women's rights convention was called (*ibid.,* p. 17). After the passage of the 13th, 14th, and 15th Amendments, which gave legal rights to Negroes but not to women, the women's movement split off completely from the Negroes' movement, except for such a thing as the support of both movements by the rare old liberal, Frederick Douglass. An expression of how far the two movements had separated by 1903 was given by one of the leaders of the women's movement at that time, Anna Howard Shaw, in answer to a question posed to her at a convention in New Orleans:

"'What is your purpose in bringing your convention to the South? Is it the desire of suffragists to force upon us the social equality of black and white women? Political equality lays the foundation for social equality. If you give the ballot to women, won't you make the black and white woman equal politically and therefore lay the foundation for a future claim of social equality?'...

"I read the question aloud. Then the audience called for the answer, and I gave it in these words, quoted as accurately as I can remember them:

"'If political equality is the basis of social equality, and if by granting political equality you lay the foundation for a claim of social equality, I can only answer that you have already laid that claim. You did not wait for woman suffrage, but disfranchised both your black and white women, thus making them politically equal. But you have done more than that. You have put the ballot into the hands of your black men, thus making them the political superiors of your white women. Never before in the history of the world have men made former slaves the political masters of their former mistresses!'" (*The Story of a Pioneer* [1915], pp. 311-312.)

11. 1903.

12. Alva Myrdal, *Nation and Family* (1941), Chapter 22, "One Sex a Social Problem," pp. 398-426.

MARIJEAN SUELZLE

Women in Labor

To read the newspapers one would think that the top jobs in public life are opening up for women and that our occupational status was rising generally: Interstate Commerce Commissioner Virginia Mae Brown became the first woman to head an independent federal administrative agency; Helen D. Bentley became chairman of the Maritime Commission; the first four female scientists explored the Antarctic; Barbara J. Rubin, a jockey, was the first woman to win a pari-mutuel race; and a 13-year-old girl, Alice De Rivera, integrated the all-male Stuyvesant High School in New York. While publicity on the "breakthroughs" does break down some psychological barriers, it exaggerates and misrepresents the real occupational changes. In order to find out what these real changes are, we must look at social trends that affect the changing profile of women in the labor force and at some myths and stereotypes that surround the working woman.

In 1920 the average woman worker in this country was 28 years old and single. Today she is 39 years old, married and living with her husband. In 1920 she was most likely to be a factory worker or other operative, but large numbers of women were also clerical workers, private household workers and farm workers. Her occupational choice was extremely limited. Today the average woman in the labor force is most likely to be a clerical worker, with other large numbers of women being service workers outside the home, factory workers or other operatives and professional or technical workers. She may be working in

---

Reprinted by permission of the publisher from Marijean Suelzle, "Women in Labor," *Transaction* 8 (November-December 1970): 50-58. Copyright © 1970 by Transaction, Inc., New Brunswick, New Jersey.

any one of 479 individual occupations, but most women are concentrated in a relatively small number of occupations.

TIMES OF LIFE AND WORK

Caroline Bird has identified five factors influencing the changing profile of the woman worker. First, the vital statistics of birth, marriage and death have changed so that women have more years of life when they are not bearing or rearing children. One of the most important factors effecting the change is greater longevity, especially for women. The baby girl born in 1900 (that is, the grandmother of many women entering the labor force today) had a life expectancy of 48 years, whereas the baby girl born today has a life expectancy of 74 years, a figure that can be expected to go higher. About half today's women marry by age 20, and more marry at age 18 than at any other age. On the average, they will have had their last child by age 30 and will be in their mid-thirties by the time their youngest child is in school. The mother will have about 40 years, or one-half, of her life ahead of her, freed from child-rearing responsibilities.

A second important factor affecting the profile of the woman worker is education. Girls have consistently outnumbered boys among high school graduates, although the difference has narrowed. In 1900, girls were approximately 60 percent of all high school graduates, whereas recently the number of girls graduating from high school is only slightly higher than the number of boys—50.4 and 49.6 percent respectively in 1968. During this period, of course, the number of both girls and boys graduating from high school has been growing steadily. Each year more women enroll in and graduate from institutions of higher education, but women still lag behind men in pursuing education beyond high school, and, according to Dean Knudsen, the lag is *increasing*. Women earned 19 percent of the bachelor's or first professional degrees awarded in 1900, as against 41 percent in 1965; 19 percent of the master's degrees awarded in 1900, as against 32 percent in 1965; and 6 percent of the doctor's degrees awarded in 1900, as against 11 percent in 1965. But if we take the period 1940 to 1964 and asked what proportion of girls were enrolled for degree credit, Dean Knudsen has shown that the proportion of girls has declined by 5.5 percent.

A third factor is the experience of employment itself. In 1900, women were only 18 percent of all workers; in 1940, about 25 percent. The proportion reached a high of 36 percent during World War II, dropped back to 28 percent with the return of male veterans to civilian jobs, before beginning to climb again to 37 percent today. The shift in production from home to factory has influenced the rise in the numbers and proportion of women in the labor force. The work ethic, self-fulfillment and the right of each individual to happiness have increasingly become associated with educational and career attainment, the paycheck and its rate of increase. Thus, the homemaker role as the

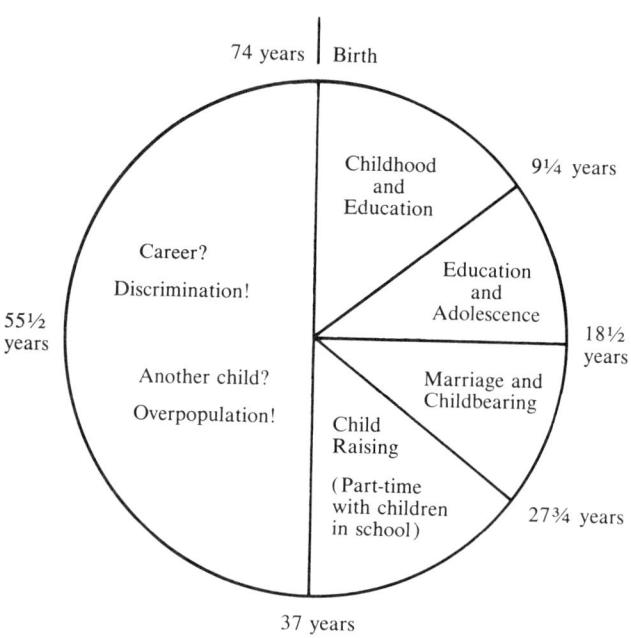

The baby girl born in 1970 has a life expectancy of 74 years. About half of today's women marry by age 20, and more marry at age 18 than at any other age. On the average, they will have had their last child by age 30 and will be in their mid-thirties by the time their youngest child is in school. The mother will have about one-half of her life ahead of her. If she decides to re-enter the job market after a period of absence for childrearing, she will face difficulty in upgrading her skills and discrimination in an occupational structure geared to continuous (male) employment. At the same time, an increased concern with the population explosion will influence her not to have more than two children.

only role capable of meeting the cultural ideals is called into question. Far from a shameful necessity reflecting the inadequacy of the husband as provider, earnings have become a point of pride for wives of men who are obviously able to "support" them adequately.

A fourth minor factor affecting the profile of the woman worker is the increasing desegregation of work: Sex-typing of jobs, however, remains the norm. The woman worker is concentrated in a relatively small number of occupations. One-third of all working women are employed in seven occupations–secretary, saleswoman, general private household worker, teacher in elementary school, bookkeeper, waitress and professional nurse. This can be contrasted to the scarcity of women in such professional positions as physician, engineer, and scientist despite the increased job openings created by the tremendous interest in research and development. Job channeling and labeling come about through custom, an unquestioning acceptance of certain assumptions about masculinity and feminity. The question asked is often "Is it fitting and proper?" rather than "Is she qualified?"

The fifth and final factor affecting the profile of the woman worker is a general desegregation of the sexes—in the professions, the church, education, recreation and public accommodation.

To the above five factors identified by Caroline Bird, a sixth can be added, that of an increasing awareness of and concern over the population explosion. Although population predictions are necessarily tentative, Dr. Richard S. Miller, a Yale University ecologist, projects the current doubling time of the world's human population as 36 years into the next century, 20 years beginning in 2000 and 16 years beginning in 2020. The total world population by his projection is 28 billion people in 2036, an obvious impossibility. Some women today are aware not only that motherhood is not enough but also that, for the first time in history, it is actually socially irresponsible to have as many children as one would like. The efforts of such social movements as Zero Population Growth, with their goal of one adult, one child, have already caused some women to report negative social reactions when they are expecting their third (or more) child. Such social criticism is leading many women to seek career alternatives rather than bearing more than two (or in some cases any) children.

CHANGING PROFILE OF WOMEN IN THE LABOR FORCE

According to the U. S. Department of Labor Women's Bureau, there have been some startling changes in the profile of women in the labor force, as there have been in the profile of the woman who actually works. However, the changes have *not* all been unidirectional and do not bear out the "onward and upward ideology" reflected in the media. While the rate of labor force participation has expanded, earnings relative to males are down, as are the rates of women employed in most higher status occupations. Factors pushing and attracting women into the labor force are increasing while, at the same time, rewards for so participating are declining.

Fifty years ago, in 1920, less than one-fourth of all women 20 to 60 years of age in the population were workers (23 percent). Today almost half of all women 18 to 64 years of age in the population are workers (49 percent). The age at which women were most apt to be working has remained the same over the last 50 years although the rate has changed. During both periods women were most apt to be working at ages 20 to 24; but only 38 percent were working in January 1920, as opposed to 56 percent in April 1969. The pattern of employment throughout the life cycle has also changed. In 1920 female participation in the labor force dropped off at age 25, decreased steadily with age, and by the time they were aged 45 to 54 only 18 percent were working. In contrast, female participation in the labor force today drops off at age 25 but rises again at age 35 to a second peak of 54 percent at ages 45 to 54. The changed pattern of employment throughout the life cycle reflects the different employment outlook of the 35-year-old woman in 1920. In 1920 less than one out of every five women 35 to 64 years of age was in the labor force. Today almost half the women at age 35 can expect to work 24 to 31 more years. More than one-half of today's young women will work full-time for 25 or more years. Today 37 percent of all workers are women.

As I mentioned earlier, women are concentrated in a relatively small number of occupations. The number of occupations in which 100,000 or more women were employed increased between 1950 and the present time by the addition of seven occupations—baby-sitter, charwoman and cleaner, counter and fountain worker, file clerk, housekeeper (apart from private household) and stewardess, musician and music teacher and receptionist—hardly impressive additions when one bears in mind the increased educational attainment of women during this period.

Another example of the clear sex-typing of (underpriced) "women's work" shows up if we examine sex ratios in the major occupational categories. In more than half of the 36 occupations in which 100,000 or more women were employed in 1960, at least three out of four workers were women; in at least one-third, nine out of ten were women.

Women have been gaining status in some sectors of the economy, but they have been losing it in others. For example, in the executive branch of the Federal Civilian Service, increasing numbers of young women are taking the Federal Service Entrance Examination and being appointed to professional positions at entrance levels. Their numbers have doubled between 1963 and 1967 (rising from 18 to 35 percent). In addition, 29 percent of those selected as management interns in 1967 were women, as compared to only 14 percent in 1965. At the same time, however, the proportion of women teachers at the college and university level has declined. Only 22 percent of the faculty and other professional staff in institutions of higher education were women in 1964, down from the proportion in 1940 (28 percent), 1930 (27 percent) or 1920 (26 percent).

When averages are computed separately for men and for women in the labor force, women are consistently shown to be the disadvantaged group. Women workers are concentrated in lower-paying jobs, they earn less than men in all kinds of jobs, and their unemployment rate is higher. Furthermore, the gap between the earnings of women and of men has been steadily widening since 1956 (see table). Thus, the status of women in the labor force relative to the status of men has been declining for at least the past 15 years. Furthermore, the areas in which women have been making positive occupational gains are more than being offset by those areas in which opportunities have been decreasing.

The increase in women's employment is a case of moving in, not up. Top positions for women are too few relative to their increased educational attainments over the past 50 years. There are many reasons for the pay and status differentials, most of them based on hoary stereotypes concerning women's work. But these attitudes and practices are fostered not only by the employer but the woman employee herself. For even though many of these myths have been shattered by serious investigation, there are few truths that make their way easily and quickly into public knowledge to become new myths. Some of the current myths are these:

Myth 1: Women naturally don't want careers, they just want jobs.

As a generalization about women entering or in the job market in 1970, the statement may or may not be accurate. It is a myth because of the "naturally." There is nothing natural about the low aspirations of women, any more than the low aspirations of ethnic minorities in public life. To assume that "ambition" is unfeminine is to admit no individual variability: it depends on the person, not the sex.

In a recent study Matina Horner administered a story completion test to female and male undergraduates. Women were asked to write a story based on the sentence "After first-term finals, Anne finds herself at the top of her medical-school class." (Men were given the same task, but with the word "John" replacing the word "Anne" in the sentence.)

"PAY GAP" BETWEEN MEN AND WOMEN GETS WIDER

Median earnings per year, full-time workers

1957	$3,008	$4,713
1958	$3,102	$4,927
1959	$3,193	$5,209
1960	$3,293	$5,417
1961	$3,351	$5,644
1962	$3,446	$5,794
1963	$3,561	$5,978
1964	$3,690	$6,195
1965	$3,823	$6,375
1967	$3,973	$6,848
1968	$4,150	$7,182
1969	$4,457	$7,664
(Latest available)		

Source: United States Department of Commerce.

UNEMPLOYMENT RATE: HIGHER FOR WOMEN THAN MEN

Rate of unemployment, average for year

1960	5.9%	5.4%
1961	7.2%	6.4%
1962	6.2%	5.2%
1963	6.5%	5.2%
1964	6.2%	4.6%
1965	5.5%	4.0%
1966	4.9%	3.2%
1967	5.2%	3.1%
1968	4.8%	2.9%
1969	4.7%	2.8%

Source: United States Department of Labor.

WOMEN EARN LESS THAN MEN IN ALL KINDS OF JOBS

Median annual earnings, full-time workers

Occupation	Women	Men
Scientists	$10,000	$13,200
Professional, technical	$ 6,691	$10,151
Proprietors, managers	$ 5,635	$10,340
Clerical workers	$ 4,789	$ 7,351
Sales workers	$ 3,461	$ 8,549
Craftsmen	$ 4,625	$ 7,978
Factory workers	$ 3,991	$ 6,738
Service workers	$ 3,332	$ 6,058

Source: United States Department of Labor, National Science Foundation Data for 1968.

MOST WOMEN WORKERS ARE IN LOWER-PAYING JOBS

People Employed as:	% of all Women Workers	% of all Male Workers
Proprietors managers	4%	14%
Professional technical	15%	14%
Craftsmen	1%	20%
Factory workers	15%	20%
Clerks sales workers	42%	13%
Service workers	16%	7%
Household workers	6%	Less than 1%

Source: United States Department of Labor

Over 65 percent of the girls told stories which reflected strong fears of social rejection, fears about definitions of womanhood or denial of the possibility that any mere woman could be so successful:

Anne is pretty darn proud of herself, but everyone hates and envies her.

Anne is pleased. She had worked extraordinarily hard, and her grades showed it. "It is not enough," Anne thinks. "I am not happy." She didn't even want to be a doctor. She is not sure what she wants. Anne says to hell with the whole business and goes into social work—not hardly as glamorous, prestigious or lucrative; but she is happy.

It was luck that Anne came out on top because she didn't want to go to medical school anyway.

In contrast, less than 10 percent of the boys showed any signs of wanting to avoid success. Rather, they were delighted at John's triumph and predicted a great career for him.

Generalized statements about women's ambivalence about ambition, based on findings such as the above, become part of a myth system when they are used to make predictions and decisions about individual women. It is always necessary to allow for individual differences no matter how true the generalization. Nearly 10 percent of the boys in Horner's study *did* show a tendency to avoid success. And nearly 35 percent of the girls *did not* as the following story indicates:

Anne is quite a lady—not only is she tops academically, but she is liked and admired by her fellow students—quite a trick in a man-dominated field. She is brilliant—but she is also a woman. She will continue to be at or near the top. And . . . always a lady.

Especially pernicious is the tendency to take a generalization beyond the level of description to make assumptions that the differences are biologically determined. This amounts to blindness to the statistical probability that most women will work for a large part of their adult lives.

WOMEN'S IMAGE

At the present time there is an elaborate educational system designed to teach women to underestimate themselves. Society's expectations enter the teaching process before girls reach school, but once they do, school textbooks continue to keep a ceiling on the aspirations of little girls. A recent study of five social studies textbooks written for grades one to three revealed that men were shown or described in over 100 different jobs and women in less than 30. Almost all the women's jobs are those traditionally associated with women. Women are shown as having so few jobs of interest available to them that they might as well stay home and have children. But even their work at home is downplayed. Women are not shown teaching or disciplining their children, baking complicated dishes or handling money in a knowledgeable way.

Because the father is making money and therefore the more important member of the family, a house is where Mr. Brown "and his family live." Even pictures show men or boys seven times as often as women or girls.

Moreover, examination of any toy catalog will show page after page of dolls and household appliances for little girls, but no little girls' outfits for engineer, chemist, lawyer or astronaut. TV commercials (bear in mind the length of time the average American child spends before the TV set) endlessly show women helpless before a pile of soiled laundry until the male voice of authority overrides hers to tell how brand X with its fast-acting enzymes will get her clothes cleaner than clean.

If a woman desires or has to work, and if her early socialization hasn't "taken," then for the mature woman there are such venerable institutions as Dr. Spock to make her feel guilty for doing so, especially if she has children.

> "Why can't a woman," asked Dr. Benjamin M. Spock, "be less like a man? . . .
>
> "The absurd thing is that men go into pediatrics and obstetrics because they find them interesting and creative, and American women shun childbearing and childrearing because they don't. . . .
>
> "Man is the fighter, the builder, the trap-maker, the one who thinks mechanically and abstractly. Woman has stayed realistic, personal, more conservative.
>
> "Everybody can disprove me by saying these are culturally determined, but I can disprove them by saying that these are emotionally determined."

This type of rhetoric, reinforcing male vanity, has been used until recently to prevent Third World people from taking themselves seriously in occupational terms also, as the following paraphrase by Karen Oppenheim illustrates:

> "Why can't a Negro," asked Dr. Benjamin M. Spock, "be less like a white? . . .
>
> "The absurd thing is that whites go into agricultural science and overseeing because they find them interesting and creative, and American Negroes shun cotton picking and plant pruning because they don't. . . .
>
> "Whites are the fighters, the builders, the leaders, the ones who think mechanically and abstractly. Negroes have stayed rhythmic, personal, more happy-go-lucky.

"Everybody can disprove me by saying these are culturally determined, but I can disprove them by saying that these are emotionally determined."

To the influence of textbooks, the media and books on child care we can add the fact that many young women have never had the experience of dealing with a woman in a responsible position of authority. School guidance counsellors assist in the cooling-out process by discouraging women from entering nontraditional fields of employment.

Myth 2: If women do pursue a career they tend to be more interested in personal development than in a career as a way of life.

Another form of this myth is "She will only get married, have children and drop out of the labor force anyway." Figures from the Women's Bureau show the fallacy in this line of reasoning. *One-tenth* of *all* women remain single, and these women work for most of their lives. In fact, those who enter the labor force by age 20 and remain unmarried will work 45 years on the average—*longer* than the 43-year average for men. In addition, *one-tenth* of all *married* women do not have children. If they enter the labor force by age 20, they will work 35 years on the average, eight years less than men. Although it is difficult to estimate the average time spent in the labor force by women with children (the tendency is to work, drop out when the children are small and then reenter), the average woman today will be in her mid-thirties by the time her youngest child is in school. If she reenters the labor force at age 35 and has no more children, she will average another 24 years of work. Women in the labor force who are widowed, separated or divorced at age 35 will work on the average another 28 years (17 percent of women in the population aged 16 or over were widowed or divorced in 1967; 15 percent of those were in the labor force).

Apart from those women who are single, widowed, divorced, married with no children or married with their youngest child in school, there are women with pre-school age children who are motivated to work either due to financial necessity or to the desire for a continuous career pattern. For all of these women it is not only (or perhaps not even primarily) their lack of motivation that prevents their career advancement so much as it is institutionalized assumptions concerning the normality of marriage, motherhood and the inevitability of withdrawal from the labor force. A striking example of this was reported by journalist Jane Harriman who wrote in a recent *Atlantic* article that she was fired from her job when she asked her boss to give her leave to have a baby. That the baby was to be illegitimate only underscores the assumptions and expectations that people have about motherhood. Why, for that matter, shouldn't there be paternity leaves, or paternity firings? . . .

A related, equally serious, result of assuming women to be a marginal and uncommitted work force is the lack of adequate day care facilities. In 1965 the Census Bureau conducted a national study of women who had worked 27 weeks or more in 1964, either full- or part-time, and who had at least one child under 14 years of age living at home. The 6.1 million mothers surveyed had 12.3 million children under 14 years of age, of whom 3.8 million were under six years. But licensed public and private day care facilities available three years later could provide for only about half a million of those children!

The California Advisory Commission on the Status of Women, for example, had to report that the actual unmet need for children's center services was an unknown quantity. Most districts reported waiting lists from 50 to 100 percent of their present capacity. A two-year delay after being placed on a waiting list was not unusual. One out of every five poverty level residents not in the labor force, but who wanted a regular job, listed inability to obtain child care as the primary reason for not looking for work. Even the available facilities were found to be inadequate. The problems encountered in existing programs and services included obsolete and unsafe facilities, lack of a state-level child care coordinating council, staff shortages, lack of continuity of funding, segregation of children by economic class, lack of adequate licensing standards, transportation and lack of facilities for children under two, for school-aged children up to the age of 12 years and for sick children.

Myth 3: There will be a higher absenteeism and turnover rate amongst women than amongst men, due to the restrictions imposed by children on working mothers.

The third myth is used to rationalize discriminatory employment practices related to women. However, in a 1969 study the Women's Bureau found labor turnover rates more influenced by the skill level of the job, the age of the worker, the worker's record of job stability and the worker's length of service with the employer than by the sex of the worker. Indeed a study of occupational mobility of individuals 18 years of age and over showed that men changed occupations more frequently than women. Between January 1965 and January 1966, 10 percent of the men, as against 7 percent of the women, were employed in different occupations. Similarly, women on the average lose more workdays due to acute conditions than do men, but men lose more workdays due to chronic conditions such as heart trouble, arthritis, rheumatism and orthopedic impairment. Considering both conditions, during a one-year period, *women lost less time* than men because of illness or injury (5.3 days for women versus 5.4 days for men 17 years of age and over).

Myth 4: Women are only working for pin money, for extras.
The fourth myth is used to justify discrimination in employment when a job is given to a less qualified man because "she didn't need the money anyway." The Women's Bureau found 1.5 million female family heads—more than one-tenth of all families were headed by a woman in 1966—were the sole breadwinners for their families. Moreover, families headed by women were the most economically deprived: in 1967 almost one-third of such families lived in poverty, and they were the most persistently poor. Their median income was only $4,010 rising to $5,614 if the woman head was a year-round full-time worker. The income is substantially lower than the $8,168 median income of male-head families in which the male head worked full-time year-round but the wife was not in the labor force. Even where both husband and wife are working, the woman's income is often not for frivolous luxuries but means the difference between economic survival or not. In March 1967, 43 percent of those wives whose husbands' incomes were between $5,000 and $7,000 were in the labor force; 41 percent where husbands' incomes were between $3,000 and $5,000; 33 percent between $2,000 and $3,000; 27 percent between $1,000 and $2,000; and 37 percent when husbands' incomes were under $1,000.

At the state level, the California Advisory Commission on the Status of Women found nearly one in ten families in California headed by a woman. Similar to the national findings, in California economic need is the most compelling reason to work for the great majority of women with young children. The two factors most responsible for the need are the amount and the regularity of the husband's earnings. Women's earnings are not supplementary but basic to the maintenance of their family. Women comprise 35.7 percent of the California labor force, and the California economy depends significantly on women workers.

Myth 5: Women control most of the power and wealth in American society.
The inference that is supposed to be drawn from this notion is that women are "the power behind the throne," the major controllers of economic wealth even though they do not earn it. A weak form of the argument, for example, is that women are the major American stockholders. The argument is false. The Women's Bureau found 18 percent of the total number of shares of stock reported by public corporations

were owned individually by women, 24 percent individually by men. The remaining 58 percent were held or owned by institutions, brokers and dealers. In estimated market value, stock registered in women's names was 18 percent of the total, in men's names 20 percent. A glance at the board of directors of public corporations will reveal an almost totally male membership, casting great doubt on how much social control women have, even over the stock they do own.

Women may spend a major portion of their husbands' earnings, but the expenditures are typically for the smaller consumer items. Major purchases such as those of a house or a car will be decided by the husband or by the husband and wife together, rarely by the wife alone. Most women do not even know the exact amount of their husbands' income, so it is he who has the ultimate power over how much of it she can spend. In any event, the amount of power over expenditure is nonexistent when the most important buying decision to be made is that between brand X and brand Y of detergent. Job discrimination, the inability to realize one's true potential, is a high price to pay for the dubious privilege of deciding what color socks he will wear.

Myth 6: It will be too disruptive to an efficient work orientation if women and men are permitted to mingle on the job.
Studies have repeatedly shown that traditional attitudes such as these are illogical, based on bias and prejudice, rather than on fact. With respect to the ego threat implied by a woman co-worker or supervisor, men are likely to report that they would feel their masculinity threatened, if they do not have a working wife or if they have never worked for a female supervisor. If they have had the experience, however, their view changes to the positive. Relevant here is the fact that it is much harder for women to get the title than to get the work. Too often, women end up in clerical dead-end jobs, keep getting assigned more and more authority and responsibility as their experience and competence increase, but with no corresponding title or salary increase. They may run the office, but it will be in the old "helpmate" pattern, in the private sense of adjunct to the boss rather than in the public sense of official recognition (social or economic) from others.

The problem of women entering male fields is similar, especially if the field is one of higher status than women are usually allowed to enter. Women and men work compatibly without disruptive sexual involvement as graduate students, laboratory technicians and bank tellers. The real problem with women entering the male-dominated trades or professions, or with men entering the clerical field, would seem to be the salaries. This would create the problem of women being paid "too much" and men "too little" for what has come to be defined as appropriate for women and men.

In brief, myths concerning sexuality on the job are mostly invoked when there is a danger of a crossing-over of female and male status and pay differentials on the job. Although the principle of "equal pay for equal work" is widely accepted and sometimes even legally enforced, great care is taken to ensure that women and men are not given the same job titles and corresponding opportunities for advancement.

Myth 7: Women are more "human-oriented," less mechanical, and they are better at tedious, boring or repetitive tasks than men are.

The myth embodies the dual notion that women's place is in the (human-oriented) home and that women are innately inferior to men in intellectual capacity. When feminists were demanding the right to an education in the last century, educators such as Dr. Edward H. Clarke in a book entitled *Sex in Education* published in 1873, expressed learned judgments that the demand for equality in education was physically impossible. A boy could study six hours a day, according to Dr. Clarke, but if a girl spent more than four the "brain or special apparatus will suffer ... leading to those grievous maladies which torture a woman's earthly existence, called leucorrhoea, amenorrhoea, dysmenorrhoea, chronic and acute ovaritis, prolapsus uteri, hysteria, neuralgia, and the like." While this quaint wording makes us smile at the ignorance of an earlier generation, it should be noted that Dr. Clarke was only painfully seeking a rationalization for making the value judgment that "what is" must inevitably, innately, biologically—and therefore logically—"continue to be so." Dr. Clarke was Professor of Materia Medica at Harvard from 1855 to 1872 and for five succeeding years an Overseer. He opposed the suggestion that women be admitted to Harvard College. Women were not educated equally with men; women could not be educated equally with men.

Yet few people today smile at the ignorance of today's generation in denying women equal access to a scientific education. The young woman who wants to be an engineer, astronaut, or scientist will be ridiculed out of her decision by her family, school counselors, textbooks, and teachers, and by her peers. The woman who wants a technical education will find many colleges and trade schools do not accept women in pre-employment apprenticeship courses in fields such as carpentry and electronics. The woman who works in a factory will find herself assigned to the tedious, repetitive, boring jobs, denied on-the-job training, placed on a separate seniority list than men (last hired, last promoted, first fired) and, of course, paid less. Women are not educated equally with men;

women cannot be educated equally with men. The scientific and technical arena is the last hold out of Dr. Clarke's earlier philosophy. The woman who is unable to become an engineer or a carpenter and the woman who is assigned to the tedious factory position are both being discriminated against by the same myth.

Employers still advertise in separate male and female help wanted columns; unions still advertise for journeywomen and journeymen. The journeywoman is given less training, her promotional ladder is shorter or non-existent, and she is paid less. The woman in the factory, i.e., the woman at the lowest level in the hierarchy of this form of discrimination, suffers the greatest economic deprivation. She is the least educated, most unskilled, and often her job is necessary for her sheer physical survival. Union leadership is often absent or unresponsive to her plight. If she has a family to support or is a single head of household, she does not have the time to attend union meetings that a man, because he also has a wife who is his caretaker, does. The lack of opportunity for on-the-job training and her social education to a more passive role than her male counterpart also militate against her organizing in her own self-interest as long as her wages remain at the survival level, i.e., as long as she has something—anything—to lose.

As Marjorie B. Turner points out, we know nothing about the comparative propensity of women and men to join unions on an industry-wide basis. The Women's Bureau reports that 1 out of 7 women in the nation's labor force, but 1 out of 4 men workers, belonged to a union in 1966. Whether this is a reflection of sex labelling in jobs, discrimination, segregated locals, or difficulty or disinterest in organizing women is unknown.

The evidence regarding innate sex differences in mechanical and verbal aptitudes is sufficiently contradictory that no generalizations are warranted. Through the preschool and early school years, girls exceed boys in both verbal performance and ability with numbers. By high school, boys fairly consistently excel at mathematics. In addition, boys more accurately assess their abilities and performance by high school, whereas girls seem to show an earlier decline in tested performance. Such differences could, of course, be genetic. However, it seems equally or more plausible to suggest that they are related to social pressures operating differently on women and men to mold them into the adult roles they are assigned by tradition to play. As children, girls are taught to be passive and submissive, and this is conducive to grade school performance. By high school, boys are taught to prepare for careers, and this is conducive to high school performance. The cultural interpretation is consistent with Matina Horner's findings regarding the stronger motive to avoid success in college women than in college men. Until a culture evolves in which both sexes are treated as *people* with equal opportunities and expectations, the question of genetic differences in intellectual functioning will have to remain moot.

Even granting that sex differences may have a genetic base, the statistical picture that emerges is still one of highly overlapping curves for women and men, rather than separate ones. We would be led to predict perhaps a 60:40 or smaller split in the sexes among certain occupations, but not one that is 100:0. Clearly, whether or not sex differences in mechanical aptitude are genetically determined, the current labor market certainly assumes that they are. But evidence to support the opposite conclusion was provided by the demonstrated competence of women in a wide range of occupations during World Wars I and II. Even today, the Women's Bureau reports that by mid-1968 women were being or had been trained as apprentices in 47 skilled occupations. Many of the apprenticeships, such as that of cosmetologist or dressmaker, reflected traditional roles. But some women were being trained as clock and watch repairman, electronic technician, engraver, optical mechanic, precision lens grinder, machinist, plumber, draftsman, electrical equipment repairer, electronic subassembly repairer and compositor.

Women's entry into traditionally male apprenticeship fields illustrates the fallacy of the myth that women are better than men at tedious, boring or repetitive tasks. It is doubtful whether the boredom, repetitiveness or tediousness differs greatly between a clock and watch repairman (male) and a typist (female) or between a precision lens grinder (male) and a dental technician (female). As Caroline Bird has documented, women's work in one part of the world or at one historical period may be man's work in another part of the world or at another time. What doesn't change is that whatever men do is regarded as more important, and gets more rewards, than what women do. The boundaries are defined by status, not aptitude, for even in traditionally female fields the persons in the highest positions of authority are most likely to be male.

Myth 8: Women need to be "protected" because of their smaller size.

There is no question but that women are physically smaller on the average than are men, but the inferences drawn from, and the restrictions imposed by, the biological fact are socially determined. In other cultures and at other times it has been women who have pulled the plows or carried burdens on their heads because of their presumed superior physical strength. Today it is men who suffer from hernias, back troubles and a shorter life expectancy because of the heavier physical tasks they are expected to assume. The industrial revolution made most, if not all, heavy physical work unnecessary, providing employers are willing to invest in the necessary laborsaving equipment. As long as there is a marginal, exploitable, male labor force (as has been the case with Third World peoples in America), it is often cheaper for the employer to use manual labor than to provide the requisite equipment.

Protective laws with respect to lifting should be extended to cover all *people* not restricted to one sex. Where lifting is required, a person's physical ability to hold the job should be medically, not sexually, determined. There may be some jobs involving lifting which only a few women—or men—would be able to perform. At the present time there seems little inclination for women to enter such fields as professional football. (There is one exception, and she may truly prove the rule: she was squashed by an opposing guard.) There has, however, been much resistance to women jockeys, whose smaller size is a decided asset.

As long as there are protective laws governing women only, and not protective laws for workers in general, such laws can be used to perpetuate discrimination. A job requiring heavy lifting can be placed in the lower rung of a promotional hierarchy, even if experience at that job bears no relation to subsequent positions in the hierarchy. It has the effect of preventing women from entering *any* of the positions in the hierarchy because they are not allowed to enter the one with the weight-lifting restriction at the bottom.

With respect to restrictions on night work ostensibly concerning the safety of women going to and from their jobs, the rationalization only seems to occur when the overtime or shift work involved would place her in a higher status occupational category as well. As baby-sitter, as charwoman, as librarian, as telephone operator, as nurse, as keypuncher, the woman working at night is considered perfectly capable of looking after her own safety. It is well worth remembering that men often place women on pedestals only so they do not have to look us in the eye!

VICIOUS CIRCLE

The myth systems that perpetuate sexual discrimination bring us round full circle. Women are stereotyped as lacking in aggressive and managerial qualities; if they do have the qualities or the opportunity to learn them, laws and customs are invoked to prevent their being used. Women and men are not judged as individuals based on demonstrated competence, but on the basis of sexual stereotypes. Moreover, women's underestimation of their own abilities combines with others' underestimation of their abilities to produce the declining status of women in today's labor force.

As Cynthia Fuchs Epstein points out, success is difficult for women because of the nature of informal channels of support and communication. Breaking a color, ethnic or sex occupational barrier means that the newcomers have not shared the same worlds as their colleagues. Casual chats, informal rituals, jokes, shared experiences—all become strained and serve to keep the newcomer in the psychological position of "the stranger."

It is true that women are becoming more emancipated, but it is an emancipation from the home and not towards higher status in the labor force. Although the mass media provide great fanfare for women as they become "firsts" in traditionally male fields, the publicity obscures the overall decline in women's status in the labor force. The Horatio Alger myth of American society was always a cruel hoax. Perpetuated with respect to women, it is simply laughable, when the average woman with five years of college can expect to earn the equivalent of a man with a high school education.

DONALD J. McNULTY

Differences in Pay Between Men and Women Workers

Occupational earnings surveys conducted by the Bureau of Labor Statistics almost invariably report substantially higher average rates of pay for men than for women performing the same general type of work. Users of BLS surveys often assume that these relationships are largely the result of pay differences within individual establishments. They fail to take into account that the reported averages for the two groups of workers may in many instances relate to substantially different groups of establishments with widely different pay levels. As this article shows, variations in occupational pay for the sexes are considerably larger when the comparisons are based on published averages relating to a large number of establishments than when the comparisons are made within individual establishments.

The study is based on information obtained from surveys of occupational earnings and related practices conducted in 84 metropolitan areas by BLS from July 1965 to June 1966.[1] Eight office and three plant occupations, with substantial numbers of both men and women, were selected for comparison purposes. Differences in the averages for men and women were examined by region and major industry division, by establishments grouped according to whether they employed both or only one sex in the occupation, and, finally, by individual establishments.

DIFFERENCES AMONG ESTABLISHMENTS

At the all-establishment level, men's earnings averaged more than women's in each of the 11 occupations by amounts ranging from 35 per-

---

Reprinted by permission from Donald J. McNulty, "Differences in Pay Between Men and Women Workers," *Monthly Labor Review*, 90 (December 1967), 40-43.

cent for order clerks to 5 percent for office boys and girls. (See table 1.) There was no consistency between the level of earnings for an occupation and the difference in the averages between men and women. For example, earnings of class A accounting clerks and class A tabulating machine operators averaged about the same, but the amounts by which men's earnings exceeded those for women were 19 and 8 percent respectively.

Although the level of earnings in specific occupations varied considerably by region,[2] regional differences in the averages for men and women were frequently as large as those reported for the entire country. As indicated below, the West was the only region in which the differences were usually smaller than those recorded for the Nation:

Percent by which men's earnings in selected occupations exceeded the average for women in the same job and region

Occupation	Northeast	South	North Central	West
Office				
Clerks, accounting:				
Class A	20	23	21	14
Class B	22	26	26	18
Clerks, order	35	29	43	27
Clerks, payroll	29	30	26	18
Office boys and girls	3	6	7	6
Tabulating machine operators:				
Class A	7	13	6	5
Class B	10	12	8	12
Class C	2	6	9	17
Plant				
Elevator operators	26	3	53	6
Janitors	12	20	25	14
Packers, shipping	26	14	21	24

The largest difference recorded was for elevator operators in the North Central region, where the average for men exceeded the average for women by 53 percent. This large difference was due partly to the disproportionate distribution of the sexes among industries with widely varying pay levels. Nearly two-fifths of the women elevator operators in the region were employed in retail establishments and nearly one-third in hotels, both of which reported relatively low wages for this occupation. One-half of the men, on the other hand, were employed in office buildings; fewer than 5 percent were employed in retail establishments and less than 20 percent in hotels. In the North Central region's largest city, Chicago, labor-management agreements covering elevator operators had rate ranges of $2.52 to $2.66 an hour for operators in office buildings, and $1.32 to $2.16 an hour for operators in retail establishments.

TABLE 1.

Average Earnings[1] of Men and Women in Eleven Occupational Classifications in all Metropolitan Areas[2] and Six Major Industry Divisions Combined,[3] February 1966[4]

Occupation	All establishments			Establishments employing both men and women			Establishments employing only men or women		
	Average weekly or hourly earnings		Percent by which men's earnings exceeded women's	Average weekly or hourly earnings		Percent by which men's earnings exceeded women's	Average weekly or hourly earnings		Percent by which men's earnings exceeded women's
	Men	Women		Men	Women		Men	Women	
OFFICE									
Clerks, accounting class A	$120.00	$100.50	19	$120.50	$107.50	12	$120.00	$ 97.50	23
Clerks, accounting class B	97.00	79.00	23	97.00	85.00	14	97.50	77.00	27
Clerks, order	108.50	80.00	36	110.50	88.00	26	108.00	78.00	38
Clerks, payroll	113.00	89.50	26	116.00	107.50	8	111.00	88.00	26
Office boys or girls	68.50	65.50	5	70.50	67.50	4	68.00	64.00	6
Tabulating machine operators:									
Class A	121.50	112.50	8	121.00	114.50	6	121.50	110.00	10
Class B	103.00	93.50	10	103.00	99.00	4	103.00	91.00	13
Class C	83.00	78.00	6	84.50	81.50	4	83.00	76.50	8
PLANT									
Elevator operators, passenger	1.93	1.34	44	1.66	1.46	14	2.00	1.30	54
Janitors, porters, and cleaners	2.04	1.74	17	2.06	1.75	18	2.03	1.48	37
Packers, shipping	2.36	1.94	22	2.38	2.01	18	2.36	1.89	25

[1] Earnings of office workers relate to regular straight-time salaries that are paid for standard workweeks. Earnings of plant workers relate to hourly earnings, excluding premium pay for overtime and work on weekends, holidays, and late shifts.
[2] 221 Standard Metropolitan Statistical Areas in the United States as established by the Bureau of the Budget through March 1965.
[3] The 1957 revised edition of the *Standard Industrial Classification Manual* and the 1963 Supplement were used in classifying establishments by industry divisions. The industry divisions combined are manufacturing; transportation, communication, and other public utilities; wholesale trade; retail trade; finance, insurance and real estate; and selected services. The scope of the study includes all establishments with total employment at or above the minimum limitation (50 employees). In 12 of the largest areas the minimum size was 100 employees or more in manufacturing, public utilities and retail trade firms.
[4] Average month of reference. Data were collected during the period July 1965 through June 1966.

Differences in Pay

The difference in the earnings of men and women elevator operators in the South, on the other hand, amounted to only 3 percent. Men averaged $1.04 an hour and women, $1.01. In the southern region, the employment pattern of women elevator operators was almost the same as in the North Central region. However, only about a fourth of the men were employed in office buildings with more than 18 percent employed in retail establishments and more than 35 percent in hotels.

Differences in the occupational averages for men and women were often as great in the individual industry groups as for all industries combined. The percents by which men's earnings exceeded those of women in four occupational classifications are provided below for each of the six major industry divisions covered by the study:

Industry divisions	Percent by which men's earnings exceeded women's in four occupations			
	Order Clerks	Accounting Clerks, Class A	Office boys and girls	Janitors
All industries	36	19	5	17
Manufacturing	39	19	−1	12
Transportation, communication, and other public utilities	11	16	8	18
Wholesale trade	27	16	4	20
Retail trade	37	18	3	17
Finance, insurance, and real estate	23	16	6	16
Services	35	14	1	2

Note: Minus sign indicates men's average lower than women's.

The six industry divisions are each comprised of many diverse industries which have widely different pay levels. The unequal manner in which these industries contribute to the employment of men and women in the selected occupations does, of course, affect the averages for men and women in the major industry division.

The occupational wage advantages for men were usually much smaller among establishments employing both sexes in the same job than among all establishments, including those employing men or women only in an occupation (see table 1). For example, in establishments employing both sexes in an occupation, men class A accounting clerks earned 12 percent more than women, compared with 19 percent in all establishments. The corresponding figures for elevator operators were 14 percent in establishments employing both sexes in an occupation and 44 percent in all establishments. These relationships usually prevailed in each region and industry division.

In nearly all instances, occupational earnings for men were about the same among establishments employing both sexes as among those employing men only. In contrast, occupational averages for women were consistently higher among establishments employing both men and women in the same job than in establishments employing women only. Establishments employing women only in an occupation were frequently found to be in the lower paying industry segments of nonmanufacturing. Thus, wage differences were also affected by variation in the proportions of workers in an occupation who were in establishments employing both sexes or only one sex in the job. The tabulation below shows the percent of all men (or women) in given occupations who were working in establishments employing both sexes in that occupation.

	Percent of all men (or women) in given occupations working in establishments employing both sexes in that occupation	
Occupation	Men	Women
Office		
Clerks, accounting:		
Class A	53	31
Class B	70	24
Clerks, order	29	22
Clerks, payroll	43	9
Office boys and girls	26	44
Tabulating machine operators:		
Class A	25	59
Class B	26	34
Class C	24	33
Plant		
Elevator operators	21	25
Janitors	48	96
Packers, shipping	20	42

For example, 9 percent of all women who were employed as payroll clerks worked in establishments which hired both sexes in the same occupation. The rest of the female payroll clerks worked in establishments that employed women only.

INDIVIDUAL ESTABLISHMENT DIFFERENCES

The differences in average earnings of men and women performing similar tasks were much smaller within individual establishments than the differences recorded for groups of establishments. As indicated in table 2, the median establishment difference in the average earnings of men and women was 5 percent or less for all but 1 of the 11 occupations studied. The median establishments for 3 of the occupations reported identical averages for men and women. For the two lower classes (B and C) of tabulating machine operators, women averaged slightly more than men in the median establishment. The largest difference was recorded for order clerks. In this job men averaged 15 percent more than women; in the middle one-half of the comparisons the wage advantage of men ranged from 3 to 26 percent. Although there were some variations, these relationships were generally similar in each region and in the

TABLE 2.

Median and Middle Ranges of Individual Establishment Percent Differences[1] Between the Average Earnings of Men and Women, All Metropolitan Areas by Region[2] and Industry Group, February 1966

Occupation	United States Median	United States Middle range	Northeast Median	Northeast Middle range	South Median	South Middle range	North Central Median	North Central Middle range	West Median	West Middle range
OFFICE										
Clerks, accounting class A	3	−2 to 10	4	0 to 11	3	−3 to 10	4	−1 to 11	—	−2 to 7
Clerks, accounting class B	3	−3 to 11	3	−3 to 10	3	−3 to 14	3	−1 to 12	−1	−5 to 5
Clerks, order	15	−3 to 26	16	6 to 26	13	1 to 25	15	5 to 32	9	0 to 19
Clerks, payroll	3	−1 to 11	3	3 to 13	1	−1 to 17	5	0 to 11	—	—
Office boys	—	−4 to 6	—	5 to 6	—	−2 to 3	1	−4 to 7	1	−1 to 6
Tabulating machine operators: Class A	−2	−3 to 3	1	4 to 3	3	−1 to 4	−1	−4 to 5	−1	−2 to 1
Class B	−2	−7 to 3	—	9 to 3	−2	−11 to 4	−2	−7 to 3	−2	−3 to 0
Class C	−4	−8 to 2	−7	11 to 0	—	—	−3	−7 to 3	—	—
PLANT										
Elevator operators	—	0 to 0	—	0 to 0	—	—	—	0 to 5	—	—
Janitors, porters, cleaners	5	0 to 15	12	2 to 12	3	0 to 8	7	0 to 16	1	0 to 8
Packers, shipping	1	0 to 8	4	0 to 11	1	0 to 3	—	0 to 8	—	—

Occupation	Manufacturing Median	Manufacturing Middle range	Public Utilities Median	Public Utilities Middle range	Wholesale trade Median	Wholesale trade Middle range	Retail trade Median	Retail trade Middle range	Finance Median	Finance Middle range	Services Median	Services Middle range
OFFICE												
Clerks, accounting class A	3	−2 to 8	2	−1 to 8	6	−2 to 12	11	3 to 18	7	−1 to 12	1	−4 to 2
Clerks, accounting, class B	4	−1 to 11	1	−2 to 9	2	−4 to 14	6	−1 to 10	2	−5 to 11	−1	−7 to 7
Clerks, order	19	6 to 26	—	—	15	1 to 21	—	—	—	—	—	—
Clerks, payroll	4	0 to 12	1	−2 to 10	—	—	—	—	—	—	—	—
Office boys	—	−6 to 3	1	−1 to 3	—	—	—	—	3	−2 to 9	−4	−20 to 1
Tabulating machine operators: Class A	−1	−3 to 1	—	—	—	—	—	—	2	−4 to 7	—	—
Class B	−2	−7 to 2	—	−3 to 0	—	—	—	—	−3	−9 to 3	—	—
Class C	−3	−8 to 1	—	—	—	—	—	—	−6	−7 to 3	—	—
PLANT												
Elevator operators	—	0 to 8	11	4 to 17	—	—	—	—	19	4 to 29	—	0 to 0
Janitors, porters, cleaners	2	0 to 6	—	—	6	0 to 18	9	1 to 17	6	—	6	1 to 15
Packers, shipping	—	—	—	—	6	2 to 14	4	1 to 11	—	—	—	—

[1] Figures shown are the percent by which men's earnings exceed women's. A minus sign indicates that men's earnings were lower than women's.
[2] The regions are defined as follows: *Northeast*—Connecticut, Maine, Massachusetts, New Hampshire, New Jersey, New York, Pennsylvania, Rhode Island, and Vermont; *South*—Alabama, Arkansas, Delaware, District of Columbia, Florida, Georgia, Kentucky, Louisiana, Maryland, Mississippi, North Carolina, Oklahoma, South Carolina, Tennessee, Texas, Virginia, and West Virginia; *North Central*—Illinois, Indiana, Iowa, Kansas, Michigan, Minnesota, Missouri, Nebraska, North Dakota, Ohio, South Dakota, and Wisconsin; *West*—Arizona, California, Colorado, Idaho, Montana, Nevada, New Mexico, Oregon, Utah, Washington, and Wyoming.

Note: Dashes indicate no date reported or data insufficient to warrant publication.

different industry divisions covered by the study. As indicated by the middle range of differences, women frequently averaged more than men performing similar tasks in the same establishments.

The question arises as to why in individual establishments there are differences in the average earnings of men and women performing similar tasks, particularly, since the enactment of the Equal Pay Act of 1963.[3] Differences in average earnings of men and women performing similar tasks in the same establishment may be due to factors other than discriminatory pay practices of the employer. One such factor is the practice of paying office workers according to established rate ranges determined by the employee's length of service in the job. In such situations, longer average service results in higher average earnings. Most frequently, the average length of service for men is greater than for women. A recent study[4] points out that average job tenure of men clerical workers was nearly twice as long as for women. This, however, varies somewhat by occupation. Another factor influencing the differences in average earnings is the descriptions used to classify workers in the BLS occupational classifications. These classifications are usually more general than those used in individual establishments because their definitions must be broad enough to allow for minor differences among establishments in specific duties performed. Consequently, the occupational classifications may include workers with different duties. In janitorial work, for example, individual establishments may have men performing the heavier tasks and working in unpleasant surroundings, at one rate of pay, and women doing the lighter, less difficult work, at a lower rate.

Although the study did not develop information specifically relating to discriminatory practices in the payment of wages to the sexes, the available evidence suggests that this is not a major factor contributing to the wage differences noted.

NOTES

1. The 84 areas were selected as a sample designed to provide detailed data for each of the individual areas and to permit projection of these data to all 221 Standard Metropolitan Statistical Areas in the United States as established by the Bureau of the Budget through March 1965. Area survey data were obtained from representative establishments within six broad industry divisions: (1) Manufacturing; (2) transportation, communication, and other public utilities; (3) wholesale trade; (4) retail trade; (5) finance, insurance, and real estate; and (6) selected services. Within each industry division, the surveys covered establishments employing 50 workers or more, except in 12 of the largest areas where the minimum establishment size was 100 employees in manufacturing, public utilities, and retail trade.

2. For definition of regions, see footnote 2, table 2.

3. Briefly stated, the act requires that employers must pay employees of one sex the same rates as those paid the employees of the opposite sex for equal work on jobs requiring equal skill, effort, and responsibility. Exception from paying identical wages is provided, when it can be shown that wage differentials are the result of rate policies reflecting seniority, merit, or quality and quantity of work performed. See *Equal Pay for Equal Work Under the Fair Labor Standards Act: Interpretative Bulletin of the Code of Federal Regulations, Title 29, Part 800* (U.S. Department of Labor, Wage and Hour and Public Contracts Divisions, 1966), WHPC Publication 1157.

4. "Job Tenure of Workers, January 1966," *Monthly Labor Review*, January 1967, pp. 31-37.

ROBERT D. MORAN

Reducing Discrimination Among Working Women

Significant steps have been taken in recent years in an attempt to end discrimination against women in employment. Laws and regulations have been placed on the books requiring that women be paid at the same rate as men for equal work and that equality of job opportunity be available to all, regardless of race, color, religion, sex, national origin, and age.

Although much has been accomplished in this field at the State level, this article is limited to actions taken by the Federal Government and concentrates on the activity under the Equal Pay Act of 1963.

Federal measures to bar discrimination in employment, which are of particular interest to women, include the following: (1) The Equal Pay Act of 1963, which requires equal pay for equal work, regardless of sex;[1] (2) Title VII of the Civil Rights Act of 1964, which states that discrimination on the basis of race, color, religion, sex or national origin is an unlawful employment practice;[2] (3) Executive Order 11246, as amended by Executive Order 11375 of October 13, 1967, which bars discrimination on the basis of race, color, religion, sex, or national origin by Federal contractors;[3] and (4) The Age Discrimination in Employment Act of 1967, which protects most individuals over age 40 until they reach the 65th birthday, regardless of sex.[4] . . .

THE ACT OF 1963

. . . In making the equal pay bill a part of the Fair Labor Standards Act, the congressional action . . . had the effect of making equal-pay coverage

---

Reprinted by permission from Robert D. Moran, "Reducing Discrimination: Role of the Equal Pay Act," *Monthly Labor Review* 93 (June 1970): 30-34.

generally coextensive with the minimum wage coverage. As a result, today equal pay is required for only about half of the jobs in the United States. The major exclusions from the equal pay coverage include numerous jobs in State and local governments, domestic employment, outside salespersons, and all of the higher paying jobs that are exempted from the wage and hour law as bona fide executive, administrative, and professional positions. Recently bills have been proposed to close the gap for the high paying jobs and make it possible to equate them for equal pay purposes. At least three such bills are currently pending in Congress.[5]

In brief, the Equal Pay Act provides that where men and women are doing "equal" work on jobs which require equal skill, effort, and responsibility, and which are performed under similar working conditions in the same establishment, they must receive equal pay. The jobs under comparison must be of a closely related character, but the Congress made it clear that they do not have to be identical; as Senator McNamara, one of the bill's sponsors, put it, "such a conclusion would be obviously ridiculous." Certain exceptions are permitted where differences in pay are found to be based on any "factor other than sex," such as bona fide seniority or merit system or payment of wages under a piecework plan.

In enacting the 1963 equal pay amendment, Congress also took the precaution of preventing pay reductions by employers in order to effect compliance with the equal pay requirements. It specifically prohibited the reduction of the wages of any employee for the purpose of eliminating an improper wage differential. The law also prohibits a labor organization from causing or attempting to cause an employer to discriminate against an employee in violation of the statute. . . .

ENFORCEMENT

. . . The Wage and Hour Division of the Department of Labor, which administers the law, has uncovered substantial violations of the Equal Pay Act to date. By the end of April 1970, over $17 million in underpayments had been found owed to more than 50,000 employees, nearly all of them women. During the same period, the Department of Labor's legal staff filed over 140 equal pay cases in court; about one-third of these have been decided. Even a cursory glance at the decisions so far rendered reveals that legal actions under the act are rapidly developing a body of principles that may have far-reaching effect on job structuring and pay practices throughout the country.

Jobs that never before were thought to be equal within the meaning of the Equal Pay Act are now being closely scrutinized. A Federal district court in Dallas, for example, has held[6] that the traditionally all-male job of orderly in a hospital was equal to the all-female job of nurse's aide. Courts elsewhere have followed this principle, causing hospitals in many parts of the United States to begin paying their nurse's aide's at a rate equal to that of their orderlies.

As the body of equal pay laws continues to grow, it is probable that many other jobs will be found to be equal under the act. Investigations have been conducted to determine whether the work of tellers and clerks in banks, insurance companies, and similar institutions is equal. Similar questions arise in manufacturing regarding inspectors, assemblers, and other types of production line jobs; in retail trade, concerning sales clerks and cashiers, tailors and fitters; in food service establishments, regarding cooks, chefs, and a number of other jobs; and in various other types of establishments, as regards custodians, janitors, and security agents. The list could be extended much further.

VIOLATIONS TOO COSTLY

Employers cannot afford to take these equal pay developments lightly, for the cost of inequality in compensation practices for jobs held to be equal under the act can be high. It is estimated that as the result of a single court decision,[7] a glass container manufacturer in New Jersey may have to pay more than a quarter million dollars in back wages to 230 women selector-packers in the bottle inspection department for the period during which they were paid less per hour than were male employees doing work which, the court found, was equal. In addition, each of these women will have to be paid a 21.5-cent-an-hour increase in wages, to bring them to their male counterparts' level of compensation.

In this particular case, Chief Judge Abraham Freedman, speaking on behalf of the appellate court, observed that the Equal Pay Act was intended "as a broad charter of women's rights in the economic field" and "sought to overcome the age-old belief in women's inferiority and to eliminate the depressing effects on living standards of reduced wages for female workers and the economic and social consequences which flow from it."

Among the principles established by *Wheaton Glass* are these: Jobs must be only "substantially equal," not "identical," to permit job comparisons under the act; there must be a rational explanation for the amount of a wage differential, and it is the employer's burden to provide it; and the employer's past history, if any, of unequal pay practices is an important factor in determining whether there is a violation of the act.

Another important principle, established by an earlier court ruling,[8] is that job comparisons under the Equal Pay Act may not be made on a group sex basis, that is, that wage differentials based on alleged differences between the average cost of employing women as a group and that of employing men as a group do not qualify as a "factor other than sex" within the meaning of the statute. In that situation, the employer had paid all his women employees 10 cents an hour less than he paid the men, claiming higher costs for women on the basis of certain selected fringe benefits.

A particularly difficult question to resolve under the Equal Pay Act has been the extent to which lifting of heavy objects ("heavy-lifting") on the job might be used to justify a wage differential. An early court decision[9] established a rule that occasional or sporadic performance of a function requiring such lifting would not render unequal the jobs that were otherwise equal. In that situation, men and women employees were doing essentially the same work but the men, from time to time, had to lift much heavier glass plates than any of their women coworkers were able to lift. Of course, where male employees are actually engaged in heavy-lifting for a considerable portion of their worktime, and such lifting is not done by their women coworkers, the jobs cannot be equated for equal pay purposes.

The heavy-lifting claim has been used more frequently than any other reason, by unions and employers alike, for the perpetuation of a lower wage rate for women workers who are otherwise doing substantially the same work as men. Investigations have revealed, however, that although some male employees in an establishment seldom, if ever, do any heavy-lifting, they still are paid at the same wage rate as those who actually do a good deal of it. Situations of this kind indicate that the heavy-lifting is not the reason for the higher rate.

Another pretext often used to justify sex-based wage discrimination are alleged training programs. A number of banks and department stores maintain a so-called trainee-system which is invariably restricted to men as a basis for paying a higher rate to the male employees. The employer will claim, for example, that he is paying women bank tellers less money because the male tellers are being primed for eventual promotion to positions of bank officers. But a closer investigation often reveals that, in fact, there is no training being given to the men. This phenomenon can probably be traced to the employer's stereotyped view that bank officers are traditionally men, hence, male tellers have promotional potential and should be paid more in order to keep them from going elsewhere.

In the absence of any visible ongoing training program which is open to both sexes, this practice cannot be justified and is considered a violation of the Equal Pay Act. This position of the Wage and Hour Division has recently been upheld by a Federal court of appeals, which ruled [10] that the exclusion of women from a training program was based on "subjective assumptions and stereotyped misconceptions regarding the value of women's work."

There are a number of other methods employed in covered establishments to frustrate the purposes of the Equal Pay Act. They are rapidly being examined and exposed. Of course, it isn't always easy to arrive at a determination as to whether certain jobs are "equal" within the meaning of the statute, particularly in large plants or firms employing hundreds or thousands of workers.

THE COST OF ENFORCEMENT

The cost in man-hours of investigating and determining equal pay questions can be exceedingly high. Litigation is equally—if not even more—expensive. Since this type of court action is becoming increasingly necessary to penetrate the long-standing discriminatory pay systems, larger appropriations for the equal pay program will most certainly be necessary in the future. The results to date, however, have been well worth the expense. Discernible progress is being achieved. The mandate of a pay rate for the job regardless of sex is beginning to be fulfilled.

While Government enforcement activities have played an important role in securing equal pay for women over the past several years, many employers have voluntarily adjusted their practices to comply with the Equal Pay Act. Many labor unions also have contributed to that result. Nevertheless, in a wide variety of establishments, women continue to be paid less than men, even while working on jobs that are "equal" within the meaning of the statute. One may only hope the situation will change soon.

NOTES

1. 77 Stat. 56, 29 U.S.C. section 206 (1963). This statute is an amendment to the Fair Labor Standards Act and is administered and enforced by the Wage and Hour Division, U.S. Department of Labor.

2. 78 Stat. 253, 42 U.S.C. section 2000(e) (1964). Title VII is administered by the Equal Employment Opportunity Commission.

3. Executive Order 11375 (32 Fed. Reg., 14303, October 13, 1967), amending Executive Order 11246 (3 C.F.R., 1964-65 Comp., p. 339, 1965). Action under the

Executive Order is the responsibility of the Office of Federal Contract Compliance, U.S. Department of Labor.

4. 81 Stat. 602, 29 U.S.C. section 620 (1967). The law is administered and enforced by the Wage and Hour Division, U.S. Department of Labor.

5. H.R. 15971 and H.R. 16098, introduced by Representative Edith Green on February 17 and 19, respectively, 1970; and S. 3612, introduced by Senator Philip A. Hart on March 19, 1970.

6. *Shultz* v. *Brookhaven General Hospital* (D.C., N.D.-Tex., October 8, 1969), 305 F. Supp. 424.

7. *Shultz* v. *Wheaton Glass Co.* (C.A. 3, January 13, 1970), 421 F. 2d 259; see *Monthly Labor Review*, April 1970, pp. 74-75.

8. *Wirtz* v. *Midwest Manufacturing Corp.* (D.C., S.D.-Ill., 1968), 18 WH Cases 556, 58 Labor Cases, para. 32070.

9. *Wirtz* v. *Meade Manufacturing, Inc.* (D.C., Kans., 1967), 285 F. Supp. 812.

10. *Shultz* v. *First Victoria National Bank* (C.A. 5, November 28, 1969), 420 F. 2d 648.

SOCIAL CHANGE AND MAN

VII

Technology, Leisure, and Work: Alienation or Freedom?

The alleged psychologically debilitating effects of mass production technology have been underscored by social critics since the Industrial Revolution. These critics share the belief that work-related alienation is a necessary concomitant of mass production techniques. Meaning in work, some contend, can come only when man is liberated from "forced labor" to pursue activity of his choice; such activity is presumed to be nonalienating. Others do not believe in a "work-leisure" dichotomy. Work and leisure, in this view, must both be nonalienating if either is to be self-fulfilling. These positions are developed in this chapter, with one author placing his argument in the context of automation, the latest development in production technology. Closing the chapter is a selection assessing the amount of leisure we can expect in the future. The projections are surprising.

Frank Lindenfeld ("Work, Automation, and Alienation") contends that alienation from work necessarily accompanies industrialization because of its requirements for rationalization, bureaucratization, and specialization. Lindenfeld locates an antidote for stultifying work and subsequent alienation within the capitalistic industrial system itself. Socialism, he believes, is not a likely curative, but increased productivity and advanced technology such as automation may be. How? Higher levels of productivity and man-replacing machines can free the mass of humanity to *choose* nonalienating activities.

While Lindenfeld envisions the psychological restoration of man to reside in the proper utilization of increased leisure time permitted by advanced technology, Ben Seligman ("The Work-Leisure Bond") attempts to document the *corruption* of leisure by that same technology. At base, Seligman believes meaning is derived from either work or leisure separately only when both work and leisure activities are self-fulfilling in themselves. If, as Seligman thinks is the case, modern man engages in alienating work, he will use leisure time merely as a first aid station for psychological repair. And, he argues, when leisure is utilized as an escape from meaningless work, it is stripped of its regenerative faculty. As a result leisure is rendered as empty as work. Seligman uses the commercialization of leisure activities, as in sports, boats, tours, and entertainment, as evidence to support his position.

Most discussions of work and leisure which analyze the potential of leisure for man's fulfillment assume an increase in the amount of nonwork time. Reginald Carter's article entitled "The Myth of Increasing Leisure Time" challenges this assumption. In this selection Carter assesses the impact of three factors (trends toward job enrichment, increased female labor force participation, and increased employment in low productivity service industries) on the amount of leisure time. Their net effect, Carter predicts, will be a decrease in available leisure time.

What *is* the relationship between technology, leisure, and work?

FRANK LINDENFELD

Work, Automation and Alienation

What constitutes the alienation of labor? First, that the work is *external* to the worker, that he does not fulfill himself in his work but denies himself, has a feeling of misery rather than well being, does not develop freely his mental and physical energies but is physically exhausted and mentally debased. The worker therefore feels himself at home only during his leisure time, whereas at work he feels homeless. His work is not voluntary but imposed, *forced labor*. It is not the satisfaction of a need, but only a *means* for satisfying other needs. Its alien character is clearly shown by the fact that as soon as there is no physical or other compulsion it is avoided like the plague.

Karl Marx,
Economical and Philosophical Manuscripts

Up to the present, man has been constrained by economic conditions to a life of toil and alienated labor. In the advanced industrial societies, it is now possible to change the economic system to eliminate alienation in work. This can be done by establishing a dual economy, where the basic means of subsistence are produced so cheaply and in such quantities by automated machinery that they can be given away freely to all. This would free men from the necessity of working for a living. It would free them to do the kind of work they wanted to do. Improve-

---

This is a revision of "Work, Automation, and Alienation," which first appeared in Frank Lindenfeld, *Radical Perspectives on Social Problems* (New York: Macmillan, 1968), pp. 207-18. Reprinted by permission of the author and publisher. Copyright © Frank Lindenfeld, 1968. The author wishes to thank Robert Blauner, Annabelle Motz, John R. Seeley, Peter Reinhard and Paul Thaxter for comments on earlier drafts of this essay.

ments in technology have provided the *means* to eliminate both poverty and alienating labor. It remains for us to find the political *will*.

This essay is about conditions in the highly industrialized countries. The questions raised are more relevant to "affluent" economies like the United States than to underdeveloped economies. Where the level of technology is rudimentary, it is difficult to raise the social issue of alienating working conditions because the anterior problem of subsistence has not even been adequately dealt with.

I wish to make several points here:

(1) The alienation of men from their work results from job specialization and bureaucratization characteristic of modern industry. The alienating organization of the work process occurs under state socialist as well as capitalist forms of industrialism.

(2) Alienation may not necessarily be consciously experienced. If it is, employees may tolerate it because they get high pay, pleasant working conditions and fringe benefits.

(3) Work can be more satisfying if large factories are decentralized into smaller units and if the employees replace control from the top by democratic self-management.

(4) The further development of technology in the form of cybernation facilitates a transition to an economics and a psychology of abundance instead of scarcity. Automated, decentralized production and free distribution of the basic necessities of life to all can liberate men from the need to work for income. When work is voluntary, people can engage in freely chosen activities which allow them to express their creative capacities and talents to the fullest.

WORK AND INDUSTRIALISM

Contemporary industrial societies drift increasingly towards specialization, rationalization and managerial control of work. In the offices and factories, major policies are determined by a few at the top; decisions made by those lower in the hierarchies concern only the means to achieve predetermined ends, and often even the means are rigidly prescribed. Employees are confined to a strictly limited sphere of competence, where they merely carry out orders to make some part of a larger product they may never see in completed form. Men accept these alienating working conditions because of economic compulsion — they need jobs in order to live.

These trends are associated with industrialism *per se* and do not necessarily disappear with the substitution of socialism for capitalism. Powerlessness, economic compulsion and subordination are just as likely to be the lot of the average employee under socialism as under capitalism.[1] Indeed these conditions may be even more pronounced in state socialist economies. In a socialist society, the feeling of alienation might be mitigated by the feeling that one is working for the good of all, rather than somebody's private profit. But I doubt whether the knowledge that industry is owned by the nation has given workers in the Soviet Union a sense of meaning and joy in their work. That feeling can come about only when work is freely chosen, and when workers have a direct say in the organization.

The modern division of labor is aptly described by Daniel Bell:

The logic of hierarchy ... is thus not merely the sociological fact of increased supervision which every complex enterprise demands, but a peculiarly technological imperative. In simple division of labor, for example, the worker had a large measure of control over his own working conditions, that is, the set-up and make-ready, the cleaning and repairing of machines, obtaining his own materials, and so on. Under a complex division of labor these tasks pass out of his control, and he must rely on management to see that they are properly done. This dependence extends along the entire process of production. As a result, modern industry has had to devise an entirely new managerial superstructure which organizes and directs production. This superstructure draws all possible brain-work away from the shop; everything is centered in the planning and schedule and design departments. And in this new hierarchy there stands a figure known neither to the handicrafts nor to the industry in its infancy — the technical employee. With him, the separation of functions becomes complete. The worker at the bottom, attending only to a detail, is divorced from any decision or modification about the product he is working on.[2]

The logic of the division of labor is that of efficiency. The cooperation of many, each engaged in producing a small part, is thought to provide a greater output than the same number separately producing the whole item. The skilled worker who assembles a whole radio is replaced by semi-skilled workers who put together various sub-assemblies, and eventually these are replaced by automatic machines that make human labor superfluous. The skilled carpenter who makes and fits doors, windows and floors is replaced by a crew with less complex skills: those who specialize in laying prefabricated sections of floor, for example. In medicine, the general practitioner gives way to specialists in particular diseases or parts of the body. In academia, the broad ranging intellect is replaced by more narrowly trained experts who explore subsections of arbitrarily defined areas of knowledge.

The technically most efficient methods are not always the most satisfying to those engaged in the work. Often one has to choose between technical efficiency (concentration on *production*) and employee happiness (concentration on the *producers*). It would be a lovely world if efficiency and happiness could always be reconciled, but this is not the case. When efficiency and happiness conflict, we have to choose one over the other. Until modern times, the choices have generally been in the direction of efficiency.[3]

What makes the age of automation unique is the possibility of consistently resolving the conflict between efficiency and happiness in favor of the latter. There is no need to dream of the efficiency of a full and rational "utilization" of human and technological resources when muscle-power becomes superfluous and machines become available in abundance. We may consciously opt for *inefficiency*, for less "production" than theoretically attainable, because we place other values first.[4] Actually, decentralized organizations are often more efficient and less costly than centralized ones. But the important thing is that decentralization is a more desirable form of human association.[5]

ALIENATION

The thread of interest in alienation extends from such classical authors as Marx, Weber and Mannheim to such contemporaries as Nisbet, Fromm and Mills. In recent discussions, both Seeman and Blauner identify five separate dimensions of alienation.[6] The most important of these are powerlessness, meaninglessness and self-estrangement.

Powerlessness refers to the employee's feeling that his voice doesn't count for much, that he is pushed around, that he cannot say what should be produced, how, at what pace and for whom. The growth of labor unions in the United States has provided many employees with the power to resist being pushed around and treated in a way that violates their dignity. Through collective bargaining, unions hase resisted management pressures for speed-ups in production and arbitrary firing of employees. (In a number of non-unionized fields and in the smaller and marginal enterprises, however, many employees are still vulnerable to being pushed around.) But although unions can coerce employers into treating workers with more dignity, employees still accept the prerogative of management to decide what gets produced and what doesn't, what prices are set, and so on.

Meaninglessness refers to the fact that the employee in a bureaucratic organization is engaged in one small, standardized task, and rarely gets to see or understand the whole process or product. Only a few at the top know how all the highly subdivided jobs are interrelated. Self-estrangement occurs when work is undertaken for its extrinsic rather than its intrinsic value, when work is not done for its own sake, or for the sake of what the work itself accomplishes, but primarily for the money. Self-estrangement means that men do not express themselves fully or utilize their talents in their work.

The opposite of alienated labor is work pursued for its intrinsic worth and meaning. This, according to Mills, is the Renaissance view of work as craftsmanship:

There is no ulterior motive in work other than the product being made and the processes of its creation. The details of daily work are meaningful because they are not detached in the worker's mind from the product of the work. The worker is free to control his own working action. The craftsman is thus able to learn from his work; and to use and develop his capacities and skills in its prosecution. There is no split of work and play, or work and culture. The craftsman's way of livelihood determines and infuses his entire mode of living.[7]

It is helpful at this point to distinguish between objective social conditions and the subjective perceptions and feelings that arise in response to them. Alienation can mean either the relationship of the employee to his work, or his awareness of that relationship.[8] The condition of alienation may not necessarily be perceived or understood as such by the alienated.[9] Thus, I doubt whether any great number of American employees *feel* alienated from their work. They accept doing something they may not entirely like in return for their paycheck. As Blauner points out, the progress of automation may help to diminish certain aspects of alienation from work. For example, those employed in continuous process industries may be much freer in their movement and may have more leeway in varying their schedules than those who tend machines or work on the assembly line. This freedom makes work in automated plants more satisfying. Blauner dismisses the question of workers' control by saying (correctly) that most employees are generally not interested in taking on managerial responsibilities: they are being used, but since they are well paid it's a good bargain, and at least on the surface they don't seem to mind.[10]

I will focus here on three dimensions of objective conditions of work: high vs. low pay, pleasant vs. unpleasant atmosphere, and using vs. non-using relationships.

Pay is self-explanatory. Pleasantness includes friendly relations with co-workers and supervisors, fewer hours and longer coffee breaks, background music and air conditioning, looseness of supervision, and so forth. (The pleasantness of working conditions is of course relative; what would have been pleasant for most people two hundred years ago would not be acceptable today.)

By "using" I mean simply conditions under which the ends of work are not determined by the worker but by others to whom he is subordinate.[11] This is the typical condition of *employees*. Modern industrialism *uses* employees as means to the ends of those in control of industrial or governmental hierarchies.[12] The employer-employee relationship is *essentially* one of servitude for the employee. A certain amount of "using the other" is inherent in almost all social relationships, including the work situations, but the question is not whether employees also "use" employers as a source of money, status, and so on. It is rather a question of which party has the decided advantage in the exchange.

Working Conditions

	Using		Non-using
	Unpleasant	Pleasant	Self-employed artist, craftsman or professional; independent farmer
Low Pay	1. sweat shop operative; bracero	3. "girl friday"	
High Pay	2. assembly line worker	4. repairman in automated plant	

In the typology, "Working Conditions," the occupational category on the right is less alienating, those on the left more alienating. The subjective awareness of alienation, however, may differ within the four categories on the left. Some of those who are being used may be aware of the fact and resent it; in which case we say they feel alienated. But many who are used are not particularly aware of this; or if they are they are not resentful, because they receive high pay or have pleasant working conditions. We would expect that consciousness of alienation would be highest among the sweat shop operatives, and lowest among repairmen in automated plants; it would be intermediate among assembly line workers and secretaries. (The categories have been ranked from 1 to 4 to indicate expected degree of awareness of alienation.)

Herein lies the paradox of the relative contentment of American employees. If the work is dull, or even stupid and meaningless, at least the pay is high, the hours are short, and there are fringe benefits such as longer vacations, medical insurance and pension systems. For meaning in their lives, people do not look so much to production as to consumption (of clothes, cars, television, homes) and they turn increasingly to do-it-yourself projects, gardening, travel, and so on.

American trade unions have not helped to develop the workers' consciousness of alienation. The role of the unions in the U. S. has been to raise wages and improve working conditions and fringe benefits through collective bargaining. The unions have never offered any serious challenge to management's prerogative to set basic goals and policies. With the exception of groups such as the Industrial Workers of the World, unions have tended to accept the worker's powerlessness over broad policies in return for sharing with the managers a little bigger slice of the bread.

Unions have acquired a vested interest in the smooth running of business enterprises and often perform the very important function for management of "stabilizing" the labor situation. Moreover, the unions themselves have become large, bureaucratic structures over which the average worker has as little power as he has over management.

Progressive employers have attempted to cope with the negative attitudes of employees towards their work through such schemes as stock distribution, profit sharing and "job enlargement." The first two are only a form of higher compensation. In enlarged jobs, workers participate in different phases of making a complex product, instead of engaging in only one repetitive task. This situation does make work more pleasant and less alienating; furthermore, the employees often turn out better quality products.[13] However, integrated work patterns do not alter the powerless and subordinate position of the employee.

WORKERS' CONTROL

One of my assumptions, implicit in the term "using," is that people should participate in deciding what they shall produce and how, and that the average man is a morally responsible and autonomous agent. But it is not certain that the results of democratic participation would necessarily be superior to those of a system in which the ends of work are decided on by a few people in powerful positions. For the average man has become conditioned to consider various alien needs as his own.[14] Factory workers might upon due reflection decide that three-quarters of all their production should go into 1,000 horsepower automobiles, color television or guided missiles. I would simply argue for the ethical superiority of a process that makes it *possible* for people to feel more responsible for their work, correct their own mistakes and be the rulers of their own activity. Beyond this, perhaps we can find some way of turning the fiction that "the consumer is boss" into the reality of democratic control of the means of production and distribution by producers and consumers alike.

Alienated labor can be diminished when the workers themselves determine what products or services they will supply, how they will organize the work and what they will do with the profits. Under workers' control, all those who work in an organization vote on production goals, wages, prices and investments. All major decisions are shared: in small organizations problems are resolved by the group meeting as a whole. In large organizations, the group may elect a rotating executive committee.

Workers' control must be distinguished from mere participation in management, which is not the same thing at all. The difference is a question of power. Co-management means that workers are consulted, but that the final decision still rests with the boss. *Control* means that the final decision rests with the workers.

There have been attempts to implement workers' control, during the Spanish revolution of 1936-1937 and more recently in Yugoslavia and Algeria.[15] In Spain agricultural workers organized their own collective farms, and industrial workers took over and ran factories with the aid of sympathetic technicians. In all of these three countries, however, workers' management was hampered by government monopoly of banking and credit and by central government directives which set general policies within which local industries had to operate.

Workers' control has its difficulties. One is that in larger enterprises, elected management committees can become undemocratic and self-perpetuating. This might be avoided by rotating managers and by having periodic meetings of all who participate in the organization, but in the long run the best method is to keep the organization small enough that most problems can be resolved in general meetings.

A second difficulty is the parochialism encouraged by local autonomy, where rich enterprises keep their "profits" and do not share with poorer ones. The remedy for this would be some kind of coordination; but instead of achieving this by government intervention, it should be done through federation. Producers' organizations could elect representatives that would meet to determine how to share equipment, money and resources and how they can cooperate in other ways. This method may not always be as efficient as central control, but in the long run will be more effective in encouraging free initiative and responsibility.

Still another difficulty is apparent when we try to extend workers' control to automated factories capable of producing large quantities of goods with only a handful of workers. It does not seem fair that the few persons needed to tend a continuous process factory should determine its goals. The wealth embodied in the capital — the machinery — is a social product that belongs to the community. One solution would be for the community to elect a factory board of directors on which the workers would have representation. The entire community, or the board, would decide what was to be produced. Those who wanted to would commit themselves to carrying out this decision. These would be engineers to draw up designs, machinists and technicians to make the production machinery, and operator-repairmen to operate and maintain the machines. The workers would decide *how* the work was to be accomplished and at what pace. Together with the board of directors they would decide what to do with any surplus, and how expansion should take place.

Workers' control is good because the people become active participants instead of passive servants. Workers' control will doubtless be accompanied by many mistakes and a certain inefficiency resulting from inadequate coordination of different enterprises, but it is a desirable system because it enables people to take initiative, to be directly responsible for their work, to correct their own mistakes and to govern their own activity.

AUTOMATION AND FREEDOM

Technology up to now has increased the alienation of man from his work. But this very technology applied in a different way can provide everyone with adequate food, shelter, clothing and basic tools and services, so that all can be free to do the kind of work they want to, or not do any at all if they so desire. Production of necessities would require so few people that it could be done only by those who wanted to.

One way to translate automation into freedom from work is to introduce a dual economy with mass production of necessities on the one hand and luxury market system on the other. (Another way is through the guaranteed income.[16]) What makes the dual economy possible is that food, clothing, shelter and basic tools can be produced cheaply, well and in such quantity as to be given away freely. Mass produced items do not have to be of inferior quality; if designed for human use instead of profit they can be functional and beautiful. In fact, automation can supply more variation in the end products than older assembly line techniques at no extra cost. The free distribution of necessities would allow more people to be artists or craftsmen, because they would not have to depend on selling their works. On the luxury side of the economy, those who did not want standardized goods could join with others to produce their own variants, or they could exchange their own products for those of others.[17]

The luxury economy would operate just as our economy now operates except that nobody would be forced to work, since all would receive necessities free. Those who participated in the luxury side of the economy would be paid.

A mere fraction of the present labor force would suffice to produce all the necessities within a dual economy. Today, it appears that only a few million persons in the U. S. are engaged in producing subsistence goods. Many of the rest are employed in packaging, selling, advertising, insuring, inspecting and transporting the commodities produced by these few. Others work for the government, the army or in war plants, or are unemployed.[18]

A dual economy would not of course obviate the need to make certain political decisions. In fact it would clarify the political nature of economic decisions. When practically anything can be produced in large quantities and provided free it becomes a political question as to whether a particular item — automobiles for instance — should be made for general distribution.

I assume that the subsistence portions of a dual economy would be decentralized, even where it would be technically possible to concentrate all production in one large plant. I assume further that the subsistence economy would have a system of workers' control, which would operate in conjunction with community-elected boards of directors. Decisions about general production goals would be discussed and debated by the entire community. Workers' control would probably also gradually overtake the luxury side of the economy, because economic security provided by the subsistence sector would allow people to leave immediately any organizations where they felt they did not have enough say.[19]

In an economy where people didn't have to work for a living, it would be necessary for some to volunteer for people-oriented services like medicine, and for others to volunteer to build, maintain and operate such mass production machinery as might be needed. If a community found itself short of volunteers for essential occupations, it might resort to a sales or production tax on the luxury economy to provide wages for workers in scarce supply in the subsistence sector. This would probably be a rare occurrence. People would work voluntarily for much the same reasons that many have joined the Peace Corps. They would do the work because they wanted to help their fellow men, because the work was interesting to them, and because they felt they expressed and fulfilled themselves thereby.[20]

What would the average person do if the free availability of all basic necessities made working for pay unnecessary? Many would take jobs in the luxury economy to get money to buy fancy consumer goods as they do now. Some would spend much of their time looking for entertainment, or traveling from one community to another. Some would volunteer for jobs in the subsistence economy because they felt willing and able to do what was needed and because they knew that working in those jobs directly contributed to the welfare of the community. If economic compulsion were removed, many persons might redirect their energies into artistic work or handicraft production.

Given the opportunity to choose, many would leave large-scale organizations and form smaller voluntary associations of workers, while some would work alone. Large bureaucratic organizations such as General Motors could exist only if enough persons were persuaded to band together of their own free will. It is possible that the lure of money or power would interest some people in devoting their lives to such "old fashioned" organizations. Nevertheless, I do not believe that their appeal would be great if the basic necessities of life were freely available and nobody had to work for money. There would be many candidates for corporation presidents, but probably few would want to be junior executives or secretaries.

NOTES

1. As Bertrand Russell put it, "When an industry is transferred to the state by nationalization it may happen that there is still just as much inequality of power as there was in the days of private capitalism, the only change being that the holders of power are now officials, not owners." Bertrand Russell, *Authority and the Individual* (Boston: Beacon Press, 1963). For a solution to this problem, Russell comes close to advocating the establishment of local "soviets": "What is needed is local small-scale democracy in all internal affairs; foremen and managers should be elected by those over whom they are to have authority." *Ibid.*, p. 50.

2. Daniel Bell, "Work and its Discontents," *The End of Ideology* (New York: Collier, 1962), pp. 234-235.

3. Thus the Israeli *kibbutzim*, committed to a communist ideology of non-specialization in work, have nevertheless found that economic pressures make the attainment of this ideal difficult in practice. Non-specialization was found to be less efficient from the strict short-run technical point of view. When production values are given highest priority, as they are in contemporary Israel, changing jobs is likely to remain an unrealized ideal. See Ivan Vallier, "Structural Differentiation, Production Imperatives, and Communal Norms: The Kibbutz in Crisis," *Social Forces* (1962), pp. 233-241.

4. See Daniel Bell, *op. cit.*

5. See some of the stimulating suggestions made by Paul Goodman in *People or Personnel* (New York: Random House, 1965).

6. For some of the literature which has appeared on the subject of alienation in recent years, see: Robert Blauner, *Alienation and Freedom* (Chicago: University of Chicago Press, 1964); Marvin B. Scott, "The Social Sources of Alienation," in

The New Sociology, Irving L. Horowitz, ed. (New York: Oxford University Press, 1964); Eric and Mary Josephson, eds., *Man Alone* (New York: Dell, 1962); Melvin Seeman, "The Meaning of Alienation," *American Sociological Review* (1959), pp. 783-791; Robert Nisbet, *Community and Power* (New York: Oxford University Press, 1962); C. Wright Mills, *White Collar* (New York: Oxford University Press, 1951); Erich Fromm, *Marx's Concept of Man* (New York: Ungar, 1961).

7. C. Wright Mills, *op. cit.*, p. 220.

8. Blauner speaks of *estrangement* as the subjective aspect of alienation. See Robert Blauner, "Work Satisfaction and Industrial Trends in Modern Society," in Reinhard Bendix and Seymour Lipset, eds., *Class Status and Power* (New York: Free Press, 1966), p. 473.

9. There may be a connection between the repressed, unconscious frustration of modern employees and their being a willing part of a destructive system. Some employees, of course, do not take their work seriously and they good-humoredly trade their labor for pay. In many others, however, a basic aggressiveness may lurk just below their level of awareness. This aggressiveness, stemming from a feeling of frustration at being powerless to control the course of their work or their lives, may lead to a secret glory in the possibility of the big bang of destruction. The alienated may indeed derive vicarious pleasure from their government's miiitary aggression against the Vietnamese, the Chinese, or whoever the current "enemy" may be.

Benefiting as we do from life in the affluent society, we are less likely to worry about the conditions of people in other countries. As Marcuse puts it, "Loss of conscience due to the satisfactory liberties granted by an unfree society makes for a *happy consciousness* which facilitates acceptance of the misdeeds of this society." Herbert Marcuse, *One Dimensional Man* (Boston: Beacon Press, 1964), p. 76.

10. See Robert Blauner, *op. cit.*

11. At first I was tempted to use the term "exploitative" instead of "using." But exploitative is perhaps too strong. The larger American business firms do not generally have a policy of conscious exploitation of the domestic labor force. Such a term would be more appropriate in Latin America. For on the contrary, many managers of modern industrial bureaucracies pride themselves on their sense of public responsibility and believe in looking after the welfare of employees as "good business." Nor do most American employees feel exploited. Exploitation is a more appropriate term for those with the lowest-paying jobs, such as auto-wash attendants or farm laborers.

12. The hierarchical principle need not be intrinsically bad. Voluntary deference to a co-worker on the basis of his greater knowledge and skill is quite different from deference based on the authoritative *position* of the co-worker.

13. See Abraham Maslow, *Eupsychian Management* (Homewood, Illinois: Dorsey Press, 1965).

14. See Herbert Marcuse, *op. cit.*, p. 6: "The question of what are true and false needs must be answered by the individuals themselves, but only in the last analysis; that is, if and when they are free to give their own answer. As long as they are kept incapable of being autonomous, as long as they are indoctrinated and manipulated (down to their very instinct) their answer to this question cannot be taken as their own.... How can the people who have been the object of effective and productive domination by themselves create the conditions of freedom?"

15. For a general account of workers' control and attempts to apply it in various countries, see Daniel Guerin, *Anarchism* (New York: Monthly Review Press, 1970); portions of Guerin's discussion on Spain are reprinted in the last section of *Radical Perspectives on Social Problems* (New York: Macmillan, 1968). See also Ernest Mandel, "The Debate on Workers' Control," reprinted by *Our Generation;*

David Riddell, "Social Self Government: Theory and Practice in Yugoslavia," *British Journal of Sociology*, 1968; Albert Meister, *Socialisme et Autogestion, L'Experience Jougoslave* (Paris: Editions de Seuil, 1964); Anton Pannekoek, *Workers' Councils*.

16. On the guaranteed annual income, see Robert Theobald, *Free Men and Free Markets* (New York: Doubleday, 1965); also, Ad Hoc Committee, "The Triple Revolution," *Liberation* (April 1964). Portions reprinted in section 7 of *Radical Perspectives on Social Problems, op. cit.* On the dual economy, see the revised edition, Percival and Paul Goodman, *Communitas* (New York: Vintage, 1960). The dual economy idea is also found in the writing of earlier generations. See Bertrand Russell, *Roads to Freedom* (London: Unwin, 1966, originally published in 1918). This concept goes back as far as William Godwin's *Inquiry Concerning the Principles of Political Justice* published in 1793.

17. Another paradigm, described in *Communitas*, consists of a decentralized system of independent communities, each relatively self-sufficient, where most persons are engaged in some form of craft or subsistence production. Isolated communities of this kind are beginning to form, but they are not likely to exist on a large scale in the foreseeable future.

18. Documentation of this point is open to dispute because the question of which occupations are necessary and which are superfluous is a value judgment. In 1961, Piel estimated there were close to 12 million persons either unemployed or working in the armed forces, the Defense Department or industries supplying defense contracts. This means that all goods and services for the domestic civilian and export market were produced by 80 percent of the labor force. See Gerald Piel, *Consumers of Abundance* (Santa Barbara: Center for the Study of Democratic Institutions, 1961). Recent Census and Labor Department data show that the number of workers in certain essential occupations has been decreasing over the last two decades, while the number in non-productive and non-essential occupations has increased enormously. The number of farm workers has decreased from over 6 million to barely 2½ million. During the same period, the number of those engaged in sales and clerical work jumped from 11½ to 18½ million (over one-fourth the total labor force!). The single fastest growing sector seems to be the government. Government employment more than doubled in the last 20 years.

19. I would favor minimum government control over the luxury half of the economy. *Cooperatively* structured organizations in the luxury economy might be allowed to grow naturally to include hundreds, possibly thousands of persons. It might be socially desirable, however, to limit the size of *hierarchical* "private enterprise" organizations in the luxury sector. Here we might follow the example of Yugoslavia. In that country, there is both a public and a private sector, but private enterprises cannot employ more than six workers without being so heavily taxed that they lose money.

20. Men work for more than just money, even in contemporary "materialist" America. This is indicated in a national sample survey of attitudes of persons in different occupations. Some four-fifths of the employed men interviewed said they would continue to work even if they didn't have to, although many would change the type of work they were doing if they could. See Nancy G. Morse and Robert S. Weiss, "The Function and Meaning of Work and the Job," *American Sociological Review*, XX, No. 2 (April, 1955), pp. 191-198.

BEN S. SELIGMAN

The Work-Leisure Bond

It is sometimes said that leisure will enable man to regain his sense of self. Leisure is presumed to be one of the good things in life. It is enjoyment and respite from work, and perhaps, as with the ancient Greeks, it will allow us to achieve understanding. We no longer disdain to use free time, for there is so much of it now. Such an attitude contrasts sharply with the Puritan ethic which specified work itself as the highest good; since leisure was reserved to those who could afford not to work, it was for a long time the object of marked disapproval. Yet today our technological society has engendered a cult of leisure, not, to be sure, as an aristocrat might enjoy it, but rather as a period of time in which masses of people are to draw pleasure from continuous rounds of frenetic activity. Sebastian de Grazia, who conceives of leisure as time for contemplation, argues that it is nonexistent. The average work week, he says, still approximates forty-seven hours. Add eight and a half hours for travel to and from the job, five hours for work around the house, painting and repairing faucets and furnaces, two hours a week for shopping and other chores, and there is little time left to sit under a tree and simply think.[1]

Such a problem could arise only because work and leisure had been split from each other. In primitive societies they were closely related and intertwined with significant ritual, so that work, leisure, and play were virtually indistinguishable. When primitive man had obtained all the food he needed and had satisfied other material needs, he turned

Reprinted by permission of the publisher from Ben S. Seligman, "On Work, Alienation, and Leisure," *The American Journal of Economics and Sociology* 24 (October 1965): 353-60.

naturally to leisure and play. In fact, the availability of leisure time made possible a collection of artifacts that were functionally related to his existence, and these always grew out of a variety of rituals and social gatherings. Only with the rise of a priestly class was leisure time arrogated to a single group, together with a fair proportion of the goods not absolutely essential for subsistence and survival.[2]

Leisure becomes a social problem when its purpose, the regeneration of the human being, is denied or debased. Regeneration can be realized only when leisure confronts work which is meaningful. Then the human spirit recoups its energies for another bout with nature. In a sense leisure is earned through such a confrontation. But under modern technology free time can be used only as an escape from the oppressiveness of the industrial system. However, as we shall see, free time is itself "industrialized"; hence, there is no genuine escape. Moreover, under automation, leisure's task is to fill empty time, something that modern man does poorly anyway. The irony is that work is employed to supply leisure with objects to make the latter ostensibly enjoyable, while leisure is frequently used to advance one's status in work, as on the golf course, or in the upper reaches of the corporate milieu. But there is no organic relationship here: all that is visible is a mechanistic exploration of one realm by the other. Besides, the use of leisure as leverage in work is reserved to the upper classes in our society.

Meaningful leisure shares with work the function of transmitting the values of a culture, making them fruitful and in the process educating the individuals involved. Clearly wealth is not essential for fulfilling these purposes: during medieval times city inhabitants were able to create leisure activity around holidays and the dramatic spectacles stemming from ritual.[3] Thus the values of a community were made meaningful for all. Obviously, leisure today might perform a similar function if it substituted for the satisfactions and challenges for which work no longer suffices. But all leisure can supply is the consumption of goods and an escape from industrial routine. Where work has no substance, leisure cannot realize its regenerative potential: it is essentially a utilitarian diversion, not a confrontation of work. The monotony of work penetrates time allocated to leisure, making the latter equally monotonous. Or one may attempt to use leisure as a realm from which to borrow prestige, since work is no longer capable of doing that. That is, leisure becomes a way out of work; but if work is nonexistent, empty, giving leisure the same characteristics, devoid of sense, what is it that we depart from and what is it that we enter?[4]

No doubt one must attend to a variety of cultural compulsions, even in leisure activity. No time, as Wilbert Moore says, is free from social constraints.[5] In this sense leisure, like work, operates in a context of necessity. But what is necessary today severely limits the capacity of man to employ leisure as regeneration or to develop personality, as David Riesman hopes it may. This would be an extraordinary contingency in an age when leisure is organized, administered, institutionalized, and commercialized. The various elements of leisure that have a spontaneous character, such as play, are eroded as the result of the imposition of an external form, often making it absurd. Further, the individual is frequently thrust into leisure, such as it is, utterly unprepared. Psychiatrists are not unfamiliar with the new suburban phenomenon known as weekend neurosis, when a man literally goes to pieces each Friday at 5 P.M. What then would extensive free time mean for the untutored and the unimaginative, who are equally unprepared, and who, under automation, will have time endless visited upon them? The painful discovery of their own self-limitations is apt to make them easy victims of leisure racketeers, those ready to peddle gadgets and nostrums suited to the emptiness of time. A more troublesome prospect, as disillusion sets in, will be the avoidance of both work and leisure.

The loss may very well be immeasurable, since leisure, particularly in its play elements, performs a cultural function by inculcating a sense of rules, surely an important device for associating the individual to the group. Where leisure involves games, one creates conditions of equality not found in ordinary work pursuits. This provides an important regenerative element, for in leisure play the individual "avenges himself upon reality, but in a positive and creative way."[6] When leisure attains this active mode the relationships between individuals may be enhanced in a manner that modern work fails to provide. Leisure can thus express an educative function in that it gives incentives to perfection. Unfortunately, such motives all too often are corrupted by professionalism in which the quality of pure play is leached out in order to convert leisure and play into a form of business. Once this is done, the confrontation of work and leisure is eliminated and what was once leisure is enveloped by the same work attitudes that exist elsewhere in society. The activities —sports, movies, TV—are not leisure even for the spectators, who fill the stadiums simply to engage in an expenditure of time. Hero worship replaces the admiration of skill, while violence dominates the activity itself.

Leisure ought to be a serious activity; instead, it has been corrupted by the technology of industrialism and thereby converted into unfree engagements of time. Were it genuinely free activity, it would then generate seriousness, just as the play of children is serious.[7] Of course, a temporary illusion of freedom may exist, in which case the individual believes that he has achieved the sort of regeneration characteristic of true leisure. Actually, the general experience today is no more than a momentary relaxation to be followed quickly by a resurgence of that unidentifiable tension so common to our age. The leisure we possess is essentially passive, attempting to utilize recreational facilities in a manner in which sheer waiting becomes a growing proportion of the time available.[8]

The increase in non-working time, often asserted to be leisure time, has been attributed to increased income, suburbia, and an overweening concern with consumption. Yet, as Harold Wilensky has demonstrated, such time is unevenly distributed. "A growing minority," says he, "works very long hours while increasing millions are reluctant victims of too much leisure."[9] It is patent, from the available data, that time not spent at the job has increased; this, at least, has been the case in the United States where traditionally there have been fewer holidays and shorter breaks in the waking day. Still, professionals, government officials, and corporate executives have not shared in the increased hours of free time. Their year-round tasks have required them to work on the average 400 hours more per year than do manual workers.[10] Moreover, the professional tends to work an entire lifetime, while the executive leaves his post at a later retirement age than does the ordinary worker. The latter now works fewer hours per week than he did a century ago, and when he retires he joins the unemployed as a reluctant beneficiary of the new leisure. The sort of occupations that older men once filled—ticket takers, doormen, watchmen — are virtually extinct. The irony is that those whose productivity is the highest work to support the leisure of those who are compelled to enjoy it.

Moreover, says Wilensky, whenever free time is increased, it tends to be bunched rather than evenly distributed over the work cycle. It is not uncommon, for example, to close a plant in the needle trades to give all the workers a simultaneous vacation. Long sabbaticals in the steel industry represent another form of bunching. No one asks whether a shorter work day might not be psychologically superior to the compression of free time. As it is, everyone descends on the parks, hotels, and beaches at the same moment, desperately searching for a place to park or a spot of sand on which to place a luncheon basket. We may think we are in possession of leisure, but the harrowing experiences accompanying its pursuit make it frighteningly illusory.[11] Sustaining the illusion is the *business* of leisure which aims to supply a consumer-oriented society with sport, autos, boats, liquor, dress, cosmetics, tours, and entertainment, all justified by a morality of fun. In fact, work is made completely subservient to leisure for "leisure is the way to spend money, [while] work is the way to make it. When the two compete, leisure wins hands down."[12] But it is a leisure that has been forced into a commercial mold: the important thing is to sell leisure and even make it look like work. One doesn't just go bowling: one joins a league. One doesn't waltz for pleasure, but to improve physical fitness. Or one becomes involved in spectatorship, busyness and boredom.[13]

And so we Americans travel — 105 million of us each year undertake 377 million pleasure jaunts a hundred miles or more from home. We spend $22 billion for plane fares, gasoline, hotels, and restaurants. Of course, not everyone partakes of this activity alike. While half of those with family incomes of $4,000 or less per annum take one such hundred-mile trip a year, over 83 per cent of those earning $10,000 or over are able to do so. Slum dwellers do little traveling. In 1963 some 65 per cent of America's 68 million autos were driven for a minimum of one hundred-mile trip away from home. Everything Madison Avenue can think of to get America on the road is done: Texas is the "Fun-tier" State; New York had its Fair, and California its Disneyland. The leisure market extracts $23 billion for amusements, sports, travel, and reading for relaxation, and some $17 billion for alcohol, TV, phonograph records, and dining out. Included in the 16 per cent of family incomes spent on leisure needs are souvenirs, travel guides, night clubs, cameras, sunglasses, and fishing rods for vacation time. But few go on a vacation where the car won't go.

About five times as much is spent on leisure in the United States as on medical care. The official $40 billion total — merely that which is counted in the gross national product — does not include that part of transportation which goes for leisure, about $15 billion worth. Model kits cost us $60 million a year; cameras and photographic supplies $400 million; gardening requires an outlay of $800 million. Even in the Great Depression of the 1930's, when some 15 million persons were unemployed, Americans spent $1.5 billion on sports, hobbies, and pets. To the government, leisure is an important source of revenue; to more than half the states it provides tax income. For an appropriate fee, the tourist visiting state parks is supplied with all the comforts of home; plumbing, hot and cold water taps and cocktail lounges. Imposts on playing cards, admissions, cameras, and phonograph records add to the public coffers. A large slice of the advertising business depends on convincing everyone to have fun. As Harvey Swados says, leisure is intertwined with the content and control of mass media, pointing to a central issue in our commercially oriented society.[14] Industry knows that it needs the consumption of the worker; its determination to make life comfortable has become big business.

If leisure is to have more meaning than it now exhibits, we should need public libraries that really function, museums and centers for the arts. We do fairly well with museums, but what of symphonies and the plastic arts? Leisure to be fruitful requires a better urban environment than is now available and a countryside uncluttered by billboards. Leisure ought not to be subjected to the demands of increasing productivity. Can we learn to use what we have; does the "enhancement of life" necessitate even more gadgetry? Such are some of the questions asked by leisure experts; their objectives are the training of intellect and the improvement of human skills and aesthetic sense. Unfortunately most men, when asked what they would do with more free time, have answered: "Work around the house," "Spend some time with the family," "Go to the ball game." We do not know whether they can really accept such a regimen for long. Rubber workers on a short work week in Akron simply took a second job; if they did not "moonlight," they played pool. But in that city the "living theatre is practically non-existent, there is no professional symphony, and although the public library is good, one can reach . . . in vain for a bookshop devoted to selling new books."[15] In all the communities of America only about 30,000 persons are involved in symphony orchestras, and this includes professionals, while amateur theatricals provide leisure activity for about 40,000 to 50,000 people. In contrast, 18 million Americans prefer to fish or watch prize fights. This seems to be the reality of leisure.

The aims of the high priests of leisure seem unlikely to be met: the continued high-pressure consumption of goods that provide no regeneration for man is the more probable contingency. The technological society leads the worker to bouts of drink, gambling, stockcar races, and horror movies. All this is an escape from modern work, intended to help one forget the factory or the frustration that comes from no work at all. Time must be "killed," thus revealing, as few events can, man's final separation from a world he did not make. In fact, time, both in and out of the workplace, is completely mechanical. Dragooned into leisure, man must conform to the dictates of a culture which is thoroughly pervaded by the technicist ethos. Everything is utterly rational; it is the protest, rather, that is irrational. In this there can be no freedom.[16]

We have said that work was once a means for transmitting the values of a culture. With work emptied of meaning, debased, turned into drudgery, it cannot perform this function: the worker merely seeks to escape from the factory into something called "leisure." But, as we have argued, this too has been converted into a mirror image of modern work; it is equally meaningless and equally incapable of carrying the burden of culture. To paraphrase Harry Levin, man has become less a culture bearer and more a codifier of programs and manipulator of electronics.[17]

Modern man then faces a dilemma, one that was no doubt a long time reaching a condition of complete fission, and it has been hardened now by the technology of the time.

NOTES

1. de Grazia, *op. cit.*, pp. 63 ff.; *cf.* also S. Pieper, *Leisure, the Basis of Culture* (New York, 1952).

2. *Cf.* P. Radin, *Primitive Religion* (New York, 1937); M. Herskovitz, *Man and His Works* (New York, 1948), pp. 286 ff.; *Encyclopaedia of the Social Sciences*, II, pp. 89, 100; IX, p. 402.

3. *Cf.* L. Mumford, *The City in History* (New York, 1961), pp. 269 ff.; J. Gassner, *Masters of the Drama* (New York, 1940), pp. 144 ff.

4. *Cf.* D. Riesman, *Abundance For What?* (New York, 1964), pp. 147-8; N. Anderson, *Work and Leisure* (New York, 1961), p. 2.

5. W. E. Moore, *Man, Time, and Society* (New York, 1963), p. 35.

6. R. Callois, *Man, Play and Games* (New York, 1961), p. 32.

7. *Cf.* J. Huizinga, *Homo Ludens*, paperback edition (Boston, 1955).

8. D. N. Michael, "Free Time—The New Imperative in Our Society," *Vital Speeches*, August 1, 1963, p. 616.

9. H. L. Wilensky, "The Uneven Distribution of Leisure," *Social Problems*, Summer, 1961, p. 33.

10. *Ibid.*, p. 36.

11. *Ibid.*, pp. 51-2; *cf.* also G. A. Lundberg, M. Komarovsky, and M. A. McInerny, *Leisure: A Suburban Study* (New York, 1934); M. W. Clawson, "How Much Leisure, Now and in the Future," in J. C. Charlesworth (ed.), *Leisure in America: Blessing or Curse?* (Philadelphia, 1964).

12. Mills, *op. cit.*, p. 238.

13. *Cf.* K. C. Brightbill, *The Challenge of Leisure* (Englewood Cliffs, 1960), p. 16 ff.

14. Swados, *op. cit.*, p. 129.

15. *Ibid.*, p. 102.

16. *Cf.* Charlesworth, *op. cit.*, pp. 30 ff; W. A. Faunce, "Automation and Leisure," in H. B. Jacobson and J. S. Roucek (eds.), *Automation and Society* (New York, 1959), p. 304; G. Friedmann, *The Anatomy of Work* (New York, 1961), pp. 104 ff.; R. Hoggart, *The Uses of Literacy* (London, 1957); Ellul, *op. cit.*, pp. 400 ff.; H. Marcuse, cited by H. Collins, "The Sedentary Society," in E. Larrabee and R. Meyersohn (eds.), *Mass Leisure* (New York, 1958), p. 23; H. Levin, "The Semantics of Culture," *Daedalus*, Winter, 1965.

17. Levin, *op. cit.*, p. 13.

REGINALD CARTER

The Myth of Increasing Leisure Time

... The workweek for the entire U.S. work force has declined from an average of 70 hours in 1850 to approximately 40 hours in 1969. The rate of decline has been uneven, with several specific historical events accounting for major deductions. Initially, the widespread public concern for health and welfare of women and children during the early stages of urban industrial growth from the 1880's to the 1920's stimulated a partial reduction. Secondly, the constant rise in productivity per worker in the manufacturing industries due to automation and technology permitted a shorter workweek without necessarily lowering wages. One estimate of the distribution of such improvements suggests that "60 percent of the increase in productivity has gone into higher real wages and about 40 percent into more leisure" (Zeisel, 1958, p. 149). Thirdly, durin the post-depression era several industries introduced a share-the-wealth or share-the-work philosophy through a reduced workweek. The National Recovery Administration and the Fair Labor Standards Act of 1938 encouraged this approach to relieve the unemployment conditions of that time.

Consequently, the American work force, in the last 120 years, has experienced a rapidly decreasing workweek. The union movement has continually bargained for a reduced workweek without a decrease in real wages. Moreover, since 1940 the average full-time employee has gained six more days paid vacation and four more days of paid holidays. In

---

Reprinted by permission of the author and The Society for the Study of Social Problems from Reginald Carter, "The Myth of Increasing Non-Work vs. Work Activities," *Social Problems* 18 (Summer 1970): 54-67.

short, the number of hours of work per week per full-time worker has been gradually reduced to the present average of 40 hours.

The recognition of this trend toward a shorter workyear and workweek has encouraged a number of writers to predict a further decrease in the workweek, with the consequent problems of adjusting to an increasing amount of non-work activity (DeGrazia, 1962; Theobald, 1966; Dumazadier, 1967). Only a few dissenting authors have suggested that the promise of increased non-work activity has been exaggerated (Wilensky, 1961; Galbraith, 1967; Burck, 1970). Galbraith's position will be the one most extensively reviewed in this paper.

Galbraith maintains that the average workweek in industry has actually increased moderately over the last 25 years. He cited the *Economic Report of the President* (1966) as supporting his position, noting that the workweek in 1941 was 40.6 hours, whereas in 1965 it rose to 41.1 average hours. Thus, he predicts a future rise in the average workweek hours.

However, Galbraith's statistical reference is misleading. The general trend is definitely toward a stable average workweek in manufacturing industries of approximately 39 to 40 hours. This is according to most reliable Department of Labor statistics including the *Economic Report of the President*. For example, the *Manpower Report of the President* (1968) reports this long term trend and also notes a deviation of one or two hours between various random years. For Galbraith to cite such data as supportive of his position is to seriously misrepresent labor force reality for the sake of building an argument.

Moreover, Galbraith falls into the same work-leisure dichotomy that has characterized so many writers noted earlier in this paper. Although he uses this dichotomy theoretically, he analyzes his data according to a choice between work and non-work activities.

Galbraith contends that the worker will continue to choose more work over more leisure as he finds his job more pleasant (?) and his consumption needs constantly being renewed through "modern demand management" via advertisement. This economist concisely summarizes his position in the following fashion:

On the evidence, one must conclude that as their incomes rise, men will work longer hours and seek less leisure. The notion of a new era of greatly expanded leisure is, in fact, a conventional conversation piece. Nor will it serve much longer to convey an impression of social vision. The tendency of the industrial system is not in this direction (Galbraith, 1967: 364).

Let us assume that Galbraith's analysis is accurate, although perhaps based on extremely weak and even misleading data. What are the logical conclusions of his position? How are we to assess his argument through the empirical data available? It is to these two questions that I will now shift my analysis.

If Galbraith is correct regarding the choice of work over non-work, I would expect to find an increase in the amount of overtime worked in the last two decades. I should also expect to observe an increase in the multiple jobholders. Moreover, I should also find that as an income increases so does the average number of hours worked per week. These predictions can, in part, be evaluated through a review of the relevant literature in each of these areas. Such an evaluation of the first two hypotheses shall be my main interest in the following treatment. Before I begin, however, it is necessary to make three general qualifying statements.

CHANGES IN THE PHILOSOPHY OF MANAGEMENT

Many of the large corporations have recently attempted to make the time spent at work more intrinsically meaningful to the employee through job enrichment, job rotation, and the human relations approach to decision making. Imperial Chemical Industries, American Telephone and Telegraph (Herzberg, 1968; Paul, Robertson and Herzberg, 1969) and Texas Instruments (Myers, 1968) are three firms that have initiated this trend toward increased meaningful work experiences for all employees. In short, I think that Galbraith's analysis and prediction regarding the "pleasantness" of work gains some support from these recent changes in management philosophy. How representative these firms are is difficult to assess. Wherever introduced, however, such changes will probably enhance the likelihood that the worker will choose more work over more leisure, since his work will increasingly have many of the characteristics that have traditionally been reserved for leisure (e.g., intrinsic value). Such a shift in management philosophy and practice has also been instrumental in rendering obsolete the work-leisure dichotomy, especially in terms of the professional employees.

CHANGES IN THE FEMALE LABOR FORCE

The second qualifying statement refers to the increasing role of part-time and full-time females in the labor force. Clawson (1964) concisely summarizes the trends in female labor force participation in the following fashion:

Women typically enter the labor force if at all, relatively young— at 18 to 20 years—and, in an earlier day in this country and yet in many other countries, after a few years, marry, bear children, and mostly cease to work. In recent decades, older married women, at 40 to 50 years, have increasingly returned to the labor force. With their children in the upper grades of school, or even through school, the attractions of added income and more purposeful activity have drawn these women away from housework to a job. Their better education and better health have made them more employable than their mothers at the same age. While this development has reduced the total leisure in the nation, it gives many families added income with which to undertake more activities in such leisure time as they have (p. 6).

By re-entering the labor force such women are decreasing the opportunity for overtime or the necessity of dual-jobholding for full-time male married members of the work force. I think that the effect of such a trend must be considered in assessing the questions raised by Galbraith regarding the myth of increasing non-work activities. In short, increasing female labor decreases the potential overtime assignments and necessity of multiple jobholding. The very fact that a larger portion of women are returning to, or remaining within, the labor force, however, tends to support Galbraith's basic premise that they prefer work to non-work.

CHANGES TOWARD A LOW PRODUCTIVITY SERVICE INDUSTRY ECONOMY

The third general qualifying statement is taken up by Gilbert Burck in a recent article in *Fortune* (March, 1970) entitled "There'll Be Less Leisure Than You Think." The author presents an interesting and relevant discussion of the increasing growth of inefficient service industries. Burck believes that the predictions of increased time "off-the-job" were a result of the high productivity per man hour that characterized the manufacturing industries. Several writers have assumed that with increasing technology, automation and worker education the benefits of such productivity would enable more workers to experience a shorter workweek. This, as we have seen, has been true in the case of the workweek in manufacturing firms until the midddle 1950's. However, since then, a growing percentage of the labor force has been engaged in the service industries (e.g., education, government, etc.) which have been characterized by a lower productivity per man hour, rising comparative costs, lack of market discipline, limited consumer sovereignty, and a pervasive compulsion to expand. Future labor force projections can be found in Table 1 on the following page.

Burck's basic argument can be summarized by the following quote:

TABLE 1

Distribution & Prediction of Labor Force by Industrial Group 1948, 1958, 1968, 1980 (in thousands)*

Industrial Group	1948 N=61,058	1958 N=65,532	1968 N=81,216	1980 N=101,900
Service				
Government (state & federal) Services:	5,650	7,839	12,202	18,000-20,000
Finance, insurance, and real estate	2,054	2,827	3,716	4,600
Business, personal, and professional	8,519	11,086	15,058	21,000
Trade	11,813	13,589	16,659	20,500
Transportation, Utilities & Communications	4,392	4,189	4,563	4,900
Goods				
Construction	3,164	3,522	4,065	5,500
Agriculture	8,392	5,352	4,164	3,200
Manufacturing & mining	17,074	17,128	20,789	22,200

*The leisure society is a myth because more and more man-hours will be needed to provide ever-expanding services. The chart breaks down U.S. employment by industries. Between 1948 and 1980, total employment will have increased by about 40 million, from 61 million to more than 101 million. But the number of people employed in goods production will probably have increased by no more than two million, and the number in transportation, utilities, and communications by little more than 500,000. All the additional people in the labor force, nearly 37,500,000, will have in effect found jobs in government, trade, and other services. In 1980 the services alone will provide jobs for nearly as many people as the entire economy did in 1958. The employment figures for 1948-68 come from the Bureau of Labor Statistics; they included self-employed, household and unpaid family workers (as in stores). The 1980 figures are *Fortune* estimates. Not included in the chart are the armed forces, which numbered 1,400,000 in 1948, 2,600,000 in 1958, 3,400,000 in 1968 (cf. Burck, 1970).

The basic reason why carefree abundance and leisure are not likely to fall into our laps like ripe fruit may be put very simply. The more time we save in making goods, the more time we spend providing services. The nation's total output can be conveniently divided into the production of goods (manufacturing, mining, farming, and construction), the provision of services (government, trade, finance, and personal services), and "TUC" (transportation, utilities, and communications). During the past twenty years, output of goods has more than doubled, but productivity of the goods industries rose so much that the number of people producing the goods increased only from 28 to 29 million. In the same years the output of TUC much more than doubled, but the number of people rose only a few hundred thousand, to 4,500,000. But behold the services. The number of people providing them increased by no less than 70 percent from 28 million to nearly 48 million. Thus, the services have accounted for nearly all the increase in total employment since 1950 (p. 87).

In short, with a shift in labor force participation into low productivity per man hour service industries it seems that a reduction in the workweek seems relatively unrealistic. If inefficiency is further increased by the size of the labor force involved in service occupations within the manufacturing and TUC sectors of the economy there is even some serious speculation that the present four percent increase in yearly productivity will, in turn, also be reduced. This undoubtedly will decrease the probability of a future decline in the average workweek.

With these three qualifying statements clearly in mind I shall now proceed to investigate the trends in the extended workweek.

THE EXTENDED WORKWEEK

Although the average workweek is 40 hours there are many workers who spend more than this amount of time at their place of employment. If Galbraith's prediction is correct, an increase should be observed in the amount of overtime accepted. Ideally this hypothesis could be tested through a longitudinal research design involving a questionnaire or interview schedule administered to each employee who was offered the opportunity to work overtime. The consequent answer to motivational questions (e.g., why did you accept or reject overtime?) would enable assessment of the Galbraithian prediction. Unfortunately, such data are not available to this researcher; and consequently, it is necessary to turn to the Department of Labor's Bureau of Labor Statistics for some insights.

A recent report gives some leads: "a significant portion of the nation's work force consistently works more than 48 hours per week and from all indications, this portion has been increasing rather than declining" (Henle, 1962:721). The significant portion is approximately 15 million people or over 20 percent of the total work force as of May 1965. This portion is not evenly distributed across industries or occupations but is concentrated among non-farm wage and salary employees. This sector has almost doubled since 1948. The incidence of 48 or more hours of work per week is more prevalent in trade, service, and finance industries as well as among professionals, technicians, managers, and officials (see Table 2).

TABLE 2

Persons Working 49 or More Hours in Non-Agricultural Wage & Salary Jobs, by Industry & Occupation, May 1965 (adopted from Henle, 1966, Table C, Appendix A-4)

	Percentage of employees working 49 hrs. or more*		
	Full-time Wkrs. (35 hrs. or more) as % across industries N=70 million	at a single job across industries N=11.4 million	at two or more jobs across industries N=3.6 million (est. Hamel, 1967, p. 17)
Industry			
Forestry, Fisheries, Mining	1.0	1.7	1.3
Construction	6.6	6.1	6.3
Manufacturing	34.6	27.6	35.1
Transportation and Public Utilities	8.0	7.3	9.4
Trade	16.7	25.1	12.1
Service and Finance	26.3	28.6	23.2
Public Administration	6.8	3.6	12.5
(Total=100%)			
Occupation			
White Collar:			
Professional & Technical	14.0	16.5	17.7
Managers & Officials	8.6	18.2	7.4
Clerical Workers	17.8	5.2	13.4
Sales Workers	5.5	9.1	4.9
Blue Collar:			
Craftsmen & Foremen	15.5	16.0	19.1
Operatives	22.8	20.6	19.5
Non-farm laborers	5.4	4.6	5.6
Service Workers:			
Private Household	1.6	2.3	.7
Other Service Workers	8.9	7.5	11.5
(Total=100%)			

* These data on 49 or more hours per week represent an understatement of those working 41 or more hours per week. Forty-nine hours per week is a natural breaking point in this population distribution.

Henle identified three types of individuals working extended workweeks. The first group includes those who genuinely (?) enjoy their work and therefore want to work long hours. Attitude studies have consistently reported high job satisfaction for intrinsic reasons for professional and technical employees. If we assume that such expenditure of time is personally valuable and preferable to other alternatives for these employees, then the choice of longer hours is not clearly between a desirable and an undesirable expenditure of time. In short, leisure for such individuals is often less preferable than work itself.

The second group are persons who hold responsible positions and are either required or expected to work longer hours. This second cluster is primarily comprised of managerial and official occupations.

These first two groups are basically white collar occupations, which have recently been increasing faster than the blue collar occupations. They also have a high proportion of members who work 49 or more hours. In short, there are relatively more white collar workers; and there are more of them working longer than 49 hours per week than any other occupational class. If this trend continues, it can be expected that the proportion of those working an extended workweek to increase beyond the present 19.7 percent of the total full-time labor force.

The third group is very different from the preceding two types. It is comprised of individuals who work long hours primarily because of their financial need for additional income. This is, in part, a function of their career life-span. They are most often young, white, married males in low paying occupations, especially in trades and service industries.

In order to adequately analyze the 40 plus workweek it may also be helpful to distinguish between the single and multiple jobholders. The former (11.4 million) are much more frequent than the latter (3.6 million). Moreover, different occupations and industries tend to present varying opportunities for employees either to work overtime on a single job or take on a second part-time or full-time job. The next two sections of this paper will concentrate on the characteristics of single and multiple jobholders working an extended workweek.

Before engaging in that discussion, I would like to note a restriction in this treatment. I have limited my investigation to full-time members of the work force and have deliberately omitted the many potential members of the labor force who are experiencing "forced leisure"—the unemployed, sub-employed, under-employed, and retired individuals who want to continue or start working. Due to limitations in time and space, I have chosen not to include these individuals in this paper. However, a thorough discussion of the meaning of work and non-work activities would benefit from their inclusion (Wilensky, 1961).

SINGLE JOBHOLDERS WORKING OVERTIME

The Department of Labor's Bureau of Labor Statistics is the key source of information again. A recent study (Wetzel, 1967) compares the increase in overtime hours from 1963 to 1966. Although this information only covers a relatively short period of time, it does have some interesting, and hopefully not misleading, implications for our hypothesis. The study is summarized in Table 3. The findings indicate a slow but persistent recent increase in the percentage of the labor force working overtime. The amount of workers experiencing overtime among wage and salary jobholders has increased almost two million in the three year period of 1963-1966. Moreover, this increase in the number of workers enjoying overtime benefits should be considered an underestimate of the amount *desired* by the workers. George Brooks (1956) presently a professor at Cornell University and past representative of the Brotherhood of Pulp, Sulphite and Paper Mill Workers, reinforces this position by his comment that

Hundreds of local and international officials have testified that the most numerous and persistent grievances are disputes over the sharing of overtime work. The issue is usually not that someone has been made to work, but that he has been deprived of the chance to make overtime pay. Workers are eager to increase their income, not to work for fewer hours (p. 1273).

TABLE 3

Selected Data on Persons at Work and Persons Working Overtime* (in thousands)

	1966	1965	1964	1963
Total at Work	71,349	70,005	68,706	66,888
Working full-time (35 hours or more)	57,195	56,482	54,956	53,872
Working overtime (41 hours or more)	23,619	24,152	23,226	22,688
Wage or Salary Single Jobholders				
Working Overtime	17,056	16,538	15,730	15,244
Percent of total at work	23.9%	23.6%	22.9%	22.8%
Percent of full-time workers	29.8%	29.3%	28.6%	28.3%

* (See Wetzel, 1967). There is an obvious discrepancy between Wetzel's estimate of 16,538,000 wage and salary single job-holders working overtime and Henle's estimate of 11,400,000 non-agricultural wage and salary workers employed over 49 hours per week in 1965 (see Table 2). The fact that Henle omitted the agricultural wage and salary workers plus the non-agricultural wage and salary workers employed between 41 and 48 hours per week may help, in part, to explain this discrepancy.

Wetzel (1967) characterized such overtime workers into four groups: (1) professionals, managers, officials; (2) craftsmen and blue collar workers who are highly trained and are situated in borderline labor shortage industries; (3) employees in industries experiencing seasonal demands or production problems necessitating additional hours; (4) employees in marginally paying jobs. Of these, the highest percentage of persons working overtime within an occupational group are managers, officials, and salesmen.

In summary, a slight but constant growth of an extended workweek for a large portion of the wage and salary single jobholders has been observed in recent years. Although the proportion of the labor force employed in such fashion is increasing, it does not appear to be increasing among those occupational sectors that are growing the fastest (e.g., clerical and service occupations). The occupational sectors that are experiencing some of the greatest growth are also heavily staffed by the recent increase in female labor, especially older employees returning to the labor force after child-rearing years. Such employees have traditionally not experienced much demand for overtime. Assuming that Galbraith was correct, I expected to find an increase in overtime worked, as employees chose more work over more leisure. The number of employees experiencing overtime has increased recently as predicted. However, the overtime is found in occupational groups experiencing some growth (e.g., managers, technicians, etc.) but not necessarily the greatest amount of growth (e.g., clerical and service, etc.). Consequently, as the latter group increases as a portion of the total work force we should also expect a decrease in total overtime, which prediction would be opposite that earlier hypothesized. The only occupational groups that have been both growing in percent of the work force and also in percent experiencing overtime are managers, officials, and sales personnel.

MULTIPLE JOBHOLDERS ("MOONLIGHTERS")

An overview of multiple jobholding is provided by Zeisel (1958), who has analyzed the workweek in American industry from 1850 to 1956. After 1956 the Bureau of the Census is the main source of our data. These two key sources, plus some insights from Wilensky (1961), will supply information necessary to understand the multiple jobholders and their growth, decline, or stability.

Zeisel (1958) briefly summarized his position on multiple jobholders and predicted future growth in this labor market phenomena with the following statement:

.... it is not at all clear that, for all individuals, rising incomes and the ability to afford more leisure will necessarily be translated into demand for more leisure. The recent rapid increase in dual jobholding has occurred during a

The Myth of Increasing Leisure Time 255

period of new full employment and a rapid rise in real wages. Moreover, dual jobholding is by no means concentrated among lower income persons alone. For example, a recent Census survey shows that the percentage of professionals and technical workers who held two jobs at the same time in mid-1957 was about the same as for non-farm laborers. The percentage of dual jobholders among craftsmen was higher than among operatives and service workers. Because a rising proportion of workers are employed in professional and technical occupations further increases in dual jobholding may be in prospect (p. 252).

Since 1956, the Department of Labor has been closely following the activities of dual jobholders through an extension of the May Current Populations Survey conducted by the Bureau of the Census. As a result, relatively complete recent longitudinal data are available to help assess the hypothesis regarding the expected increase.

The survey defined such workers as those employed persons who, during the survey week: (1) had jobs as wage or salary workers with two or more employers, (2) were self-employed and also held a wage or salary job, (3) worked as an unpaid family worker, but also had a second wage or salary job. The rate of multiple jobholding obtained is probably under-reported, since in many cities it is "illegal" for many of the civil servants (e.g., firemen, policemen, etc.) to hold a second job. Such protective service occupations are twice as likely to hold two jobs as the average worker.

The results of this study ran counter to the Galbraith expectations. The findings indicated that the rate of multiple jobholding has remained relatively stable since 1956. A brief analysis of the labor force behavior, however, may give some clues as to future trends.

The highest "moonlighting" rates are found among industries that either have restrictions on the number of hours worked per week (e.g., public administration, service, or clerical workers) or are low paying and flexible enough to permit a second job (e.g., professionals, teachers, farmers, entertainers).

Most second jobs are found in industries different from the primary source of income. The service and clerical industries not only supplied second jobs for those in the industry but also supported many from outside. Although the proportion of this sector of the labor force has been increasing in recent years "there has been no similar rise, so far, in the percent of dual jobholders in this industry group" (Bogan, 1966:149). A large portion of the entrants into this group of occupations is comprised of female labor. Since females have never shown a preference for either overtime or second jobs, a continuation of the past stable trend, or even a decrease in the proportion of dual jobholders, can be expected.

TABLE 4
The Opportunity to Moonlight in the United States Will Not Change Much in the Next Ten Years or So*

Indicator or Evidence of Opportunity		Trend in % of Labor Force, 1960-1970
A. Secondary jobs of moonlighters are concentrated in occupations which are visible, easily entered, require little formal training (except for teaching), and provide flexible schedules. Census categories providing more than their share of secondary jobs:		
Occupational category:	% of secondary jobs provided, Dec. 1959	
1. Farmers: owners, managers, foremen, laborers	24	down
2. Professional, technical, and kindred (especially teachers)	15	up
3. Sales	10	up**
4. Service (especially waiters, firemen, policemen, guards), excl. private household	9	up
The net effect on moonlighting rate: down slightly		
B. Primary jobs of moonlighters are concentrated in occupations with flexible schedules or seasonal slumps:		
Occupational category of primary job:	% who moonlight	
1. Professional, technical, kindred	7	up
2. Farmers and farm managers	7	down
3. Farm, laborers and foremen	6	down
4. Laborers, except farm and mine	5	down
5. Craftsmen, foremen, kindred	5	up
Net effect on moonlighting rate: down slightly		
C. Primary jobs of moonlighters are concentrated in industries with deviant schedules (shift work or night work), irregular hours, or seasonal variations:		
Industry of primary job:	% who moonlight	
1. Wage and salary workers in agriculture	11	down
2. Postal service	10	up**
3. Entertainment and recreation	10	up
4. Self-employed workers in agriculture	9	down
5. Public administration other than postal (especially custodial and professional workers)	8	up
6. Forestry, fisheries, and mining	7	down
7. Unpaid family workers in agriculture	7	down
8. Educational services	6	up
9. Construction	6	up**
The net effect on moonlighting rate: up slightly		
The over-all net effect, considering size and rate of change of occupations and industries: little change.		

* (See Wilensky, 1963:116). Sources: unless otherwise stated the figures are averages from the three Census Surveys of July 1957, July 1958, and December 1959, based on Bancroft, 1960:1049.
** Quick reversals of trend possible with adoption of new technology already available.

The findings of Wilensky (1963) generally support the position being taken here that "moonlighting" has not changed much in the past decade. He cautiously predicts, however, a slight rise in forthcoming years. His findings were drawn from a sample of 1156 employees, which included six professional groups and a cross-section of "middle mass" occupations in 1960 in Detroit and involved interviews with 119 "moonlighters." Table 4 summarizes the trend Wilensky found.

He contends that "moonlighting" is not a class phenomenon, since the differences within an occupational group (e.g., lawyers, professors, doctors) are far greater than the differences between broad economic strata. He explains such behavior by analysis of personal social discontinuity and life-cycle squeezes and drew the following portrait of the "moonlighter."

In sum, although each biography is unique, the general picture is one of social discontinuity—chaotic work histories, blocked upward moves (often including comparisons with the father in which the moonlighter comes off second best), and sometimes unusual patterns of change in religion or residence. These are combined with modest aspirations for money, goods and occupational status, an unhappy imbalance between family needs and family resources, and the chance to alleviate the problem by filling in with an extra job (1963, p. 114).

In short, the investigation of "moonlighting" rates does not lend much support to an expectation that it should be increasing. One reason this prediction was not met may be due to my choice of unit of analysis — the individual worker. Possibly the family as primary unit should have been used, which may have indicated an increase in dual jobholding families, as more women return to or stay at work. One source, *The Manpower Report of the President* (1968, p. 251), does note an increase in the percent of families with both husband and wife working from 23.9 percent in April of 1955 to 30.7 percent in March 1967. A more detailed analysis of dual jobholding families may prove to be a fruitful area of research regarding the redistribution of the use of human time both on and off the job.

CONCLUSIONS

... I think that the two basic factors that are tending to increase the amount of work activity are: (1) the change in management philosophy toward increased job enrichment, which will make time spent with the corporation more rewarding for all employees, and (2) the low productivity per man hour in the growing service occupations, which will increase the opportunity for extended workweeks. Such overtime will be primarily concentrated among managers, professionals, technicians and sales personnel. Males with flexible work schedules will continue to opt for a second job.

I think that the basic factor that is tending to decrease the amount of work activity is the increase in female participation in the labor force, especially in the service occupations.

In conclusion, the studies that I examined suggest that there has been an increase recently in the overtime and a relatively stable dual jobholding rate. In the future, I suspect that there will be an increase in overtime that will be primarily concentrated among managers, professionals, sales personnel, officials, and young married men caught in a life-cycle squeeze. Moreover, in the future, I expect to observe an increase in dual jobholding families. Consequently, I agree with Galbraith, that we should expect an overall increase in the amount of work activities rather than a decrease (unless, of course, there is a general long term recession in the economy).

The myth of a future increase in non-work activities may only be a realistic expectation for those experiencing "forced leisure" (e.g., unemployed) or for those who have decided to opt for an alternative life style which does not center around work activities (e.g., young ghetto counter-work culture, hippies, etc.). For those who choose work as an integrating force in their lives they will probably choose more of it. The next major historical era that will substantially alter the distribution of work and non-work activities will probably consist of "counter-work" cultures that will legitimate a new series of alternative evaluation systems for the use of human time. Research on the meaning of time within these "pockets" of non-labor force participants would be extremely valuable for those interested in predicting future long term trends in the legitimate usage of human time and effort. It may also be insightful for those presently attempting to predict future manpower trends.

REFERENCES

Bancroft, Gertrude
    1960   "Multiple jobholders in December, 1959." Monthly Labor Review 83 (October): 1045-1051.
Bogan, F. A. and T. Swanstrom
    1966   "Multiple jobholders in May 1965." Monthly Labor Review 89 (February): 147-154.
Brooks, George
    1956   "History of union efforts to reduce working hours." Monthly Labor Review 79 (November): 1271-1273.

Burck, Gilbert
 1970 "There'll be less leisure than you think." Fortune (March): 87-89, 162, 165-166.
Clawson, M.
 1964 "How much leisure, now and in the future?" Pp. 1-20 in James C. Charlesworth (ed.), Leisure in America: Blessing or Curse?, Monograph 4, The American Academy of Political and Social Science.
DeGrazia, Sebatian
 1962 Of Time, Work, and Leisure. New York: Twentieth Century Fund.
Dumazedier, Joffre
 1967 Toward A Society of Leisure. New York: The Free Press.
Finegan, T. A.
 1962 "Hours of work in the U.S.: A cross-sectional analysis." Journal of Political Economy 70 (October): 452-470.
Friedman, E. and R. Havinghurst
 1954 The Meaning of Work and Retirement. Chicago, Ill.: University of Chicago Press.
Galbraith, J. K.
 1967 The New Industrial State. New York: Houghton Mifflin Co.
Hamel, Harvey
 1967 "Moonlighting—An economic phenomena." Monthly Labor Review 90 (October): 17-22.
Hamel, Harvey and Forrest Bogan
 1965 "II. Multiple jobholders in May 1964." Monthly Labor Review 88 (March): 266-274.
Harwood, Edwin
 1969 "Youth unemployment—A tale of two ghettos," The Public Interest 17 (Fall): 78-87.
Henle, Peter
 1962 "Recent growth of paid leisure for U.S. workers." Monthly Labor Review 85 (March): 248-257.
 1966 "Leisure and the long workweek." Monthly Labor Review 89 (July): 721-727.
Heron, A.
 1948 Why Men Work? Stanford, California: Stanford University Press.
Herzberg, Frederick
 1968 "One more time: How do you motivate employees?" Harvard Business Review (January-February): 53-62.
Larrabee, Eric and R. Myerson (eds.)
 1958 Mass Leisure. Glencoe, Illinois: The Free Press.
Lenski, G.
 1963 The Religious Factor. New York: Anchor Books.
Lyman, E.
 1955 "Occupational differences in the value attached to work." American Journal of Sociology 61 (September): 138-144.
Manpower Report of the President
 1968 Washington, D.C.: U.S. Government Printing Office.

Morse, N. and R. Weiss
   1955   "The function and meaning of work and the job." American Sociological Review 20 (April): 191-200.
Myers, Scott
   1968   "Every employee a manager." California Management Review (Spring): 9-20.
Paul, William J., K. B. Robertson, and F. Herzberg
   1969   "Job enrichment pays off." Harvard Business Review (March-April): 61-78.
Samuelson, Paul.
   1967   Economics. New York: McGraw-Hill Co.
Tausky, Curt
   1968   "Meaning of work among blue collar men." A paper presented to the annual meeting of the American Sociological Association in San Francisco.
Theobald, Robert (ed.)
   1966   The Guaranteed Income. New York: Doubleday and Co.
Tilgher, A.
   1930   Homo Faber. Chicago: Henry Regnery Co.
Weber, Max
   1958   The Protestant Ethic and the Spirit of Capitalism. Translated by Talcott Parsons. New York: Charles Scribners Sons.
Wetzel, James
   1967   "Overtime hours and premium pay." Monthly Labor Review 90 (May): 41-45.
Wilensky, H. L.
   1961   "The uneven distribution of leisure: The impact of economic growth on free time." Social Problems 9 (Summer): 32-56.
   1963   "The moonlighter: A product of relative deprivation." Industrial Relations 3 (October): 105-124.
Zeisel, Joseph
   1958   "The workweek in American industry 1850-1956." Pp. 145-153 in Eric Larrabee and R. Myerson (eds.), Mass Leisure. Glencoe, Illinois: The Fress Press.